Critical
Pedagogy
PRIMER

PETER LANG
New York • Washington, D.C./Baltimore • Bern
Frankfurt am Main • Berlin • Brussels • Vienna • Oxford

Joe L. Kincheloe

Critical
Pedagogy
PRIMER

Second Edition

PETER LANG
New York • Washington, D.C./Baltimore • Bern
Frankfurt am Main • Berlin • Brussels • Vienna • Oxford

The Library of Congress has catalogued the first edition as follows:

Kincheloe, Joe L.
Critical pedagogy primer / Joe L. Kincheloe.
p. cm.
Includes bibliographical references.
1. Critical pedagogy. I. Title.
LC196.K55 2004   370.11'5—dc22   2003027176
ISBN 978-0-8204-7262-1 (first edition)
ISBN 978-1-4331-0182-3 (second edition)

Bibliographic information published by **Die Deutsche Bibliothek**.
Die Deutsche Bibliothek lists this publication in the "Deutsche
Nationalbibliografie"; detailed bibliographic data is available
on the Internet at http://dnb.ddb.de/.

Cover design by Lisa Barfield

The paper in this book meets the guidelines for permanence and durability
of the Committee on Production Guidelines for Book Longevity
of the Council of Library Resources.

© 2008 Peter Lang Publishing, Inc., New York
29 Broadway, 18th Floor, New York, NY 10006
www.peterlang.com

Printed in the United States of America

Table of Contents

Preface to the Second Edition

Over the past few years I have written too many second editions to books that begin with words such as "When I first wrote this book in _____ I had no idea that it would be more germane to the political and educational world of _____ than it did when I wrote the first edition of the book." Yet, here I am again, writing the preface to the second edition of the Critical Pedagogy Primer that could easily begin with exactly the preceding words. Indeed, I wrote most of the first edition of the book during 2003—the book was published in 2004—in the process of watching the horror of George W. Bush's absurd invasion of Iraq play out in front of me. It seemed so obvious to me—and literally millions of other people around the world—that the war was so unnecessary, so misguided, so fueled by the greedy neo-conservative attempt to enhance the geopolitical and economic position of the United States in the world no matter what the human cost. In the ensuing years, I have watched all my fears about the war materialize. I was wrong on a few counts: I didn't believe that the situation would be quite as horrendous as it has turned out to be; and I thought the preinvasion antiwar movement would not fade away as it has.

With these pessimistic thoughts in mind I entered into the writing of the second edition. Is it the burden of all critical theorists/pedagogues to confront the dialectic of their critical hope with the pessimism that comes from what generations of criticalists before me ironically called "progress?" I felt that it was important to rewrite the book with more emphasis on the need for a worldwide critical community to counter the empire building of imperialists in the United States and their political, corporate, and educational allies in the Western world and increasingly around the planet. Consider the last years of the first decade of the twenty-first century where we now are ideologically:

- Preemptive wars by the United States against imagined enemies have now been established as precedent.
- Teachers who support these wars in their classrooms are viewed as moderates; those of us who criticize them are viewed as dangerous subversives who should be and often are fired.
- Transnational corporations and their political allies in Western governments are relatively free to engage in the transfer of wealth from the poorest nations to the richest people in the richest nations of the world.
- Traditional constitutional rights, long regarded as sacred, are being undermined by fear mongers who use the perpetual "War on Terror" as a justification to institute a more authoritarian state (and corporate government) with the highly regulated politics of knowledge that operates to uphold the dominant power.
- School curriculum in the standardization movements of contemporary school reform is controlled by the dictates of educational leaders who know their funding and survival is in jeopardy if they don't ensure that their teachers teach to the tests. Brave school principals and teachers still resist such control of knowledge, but now they do it at their own risk.
- The move toward teacher deprofessionalization is well underway and is supported by numerous interest groups. Teachers who are not aware of critical pedagogy and are less familiar with world and local events are more unlikely to protest the standardized curriculum designed to uphold the status quo. Thus, many policy makers and educators prefer less-educated teachers to well-educated teachers.

- Teacher scripts—manuals that teachers read to students taking away any professional input on the part of the professional educator to the curriculum—are more common than ever before.

- Right-wing fundamentalist Christian influence on school boards has continued to increase. Such school boards push not only policies and curricula that mandate the teaching of fundamentalist creation stories but also a xenophobia that censors even the inclusion of literature and perspectives from "non-Christian" groups—for example, indigenous peoples, Buddhists, homosexuals, and individuals who have challenged the status quo, and so on.

- The move toward the corporate privatization of education—for-profit schools—is alive and thriving. Such schools will not be especially friendly to critical pedagogy.

- While there are many brave journalists in traditional and new media, corporate ownership and government pressure on news organizations to stay away from criticism of the status quo increases.

- Those who are ethically concerned with issues of oppression and violence toward poor people, people of color, women, non-Christians, and gays and lesbians are demeaned as proponents of an oppressive "political correctness" that makes the real victims of oppression "regular people"—white, economically prosperous, male, Christian, heterosexuals. In this configuration those of us who join the struggle for critical emancipation are the true oppressors in the contemporary world.

- Social justice is being removed from the mission statements and policies of many educational and other social institutions because of its "oppressive tendencies."

I could go on with these descriptions of the current ideological-cum-educational situation that confronts us. Such a morose delineation is not meant to depress us, but to alert those of us with a passion for fairness, justice, freedom, and human dignity to make our presence felt, to pick up the torch for a new generation dedicated to the struggle for the social good and the sanctity of a rigorous and social justice based education. In this dark hour of the human condition, my beloved wife and partner, Shirley Steinberg, and I have been blessed with the opportunity to initiate

the Paulo and Nita Freire International Project for Critical Pedagogy in the Faculty of Education at McGill University. In this endeavor we have created the basis for bringing together a worldwide community of critical educators concerned with the issues referenced in this Preface. We want people from diverse backgrounds to join the community we are putting together via this project.

We invite people working both inside and outside of traditional educational structures to share with us the socially, politically, cognitively, of course, educational transformative work they are doing in the world. In the short time we have been involved with the project, we have been overwhelmed and humbled by the large number of people who are doing good works in all corners of the world. Please let us know about your critical work by contacting our Web site. In this way, we can use contemporary technologies to bring together committed and creative people to collaborate in ways that can devise unique and pragmatic approaches of resisting the oppressive dimensions of the political and educational status quo, while developing our social and educational imagination. Such an imagination—that exists in the individual and collective intelligence of dedicated peoples and groups around the world—despite the darkness around us can change the world in general and education in particular. This is the ambitious goal to which The Paulo and Nita Freire International Project for Critical Pedagogy and this primer are dedicated.

Hope is alive, but it must be a practical and not a naïve hope. A practical hope doesn't simply celebrate rainbows, unicorns, nutbread, and niceness, but rigorously understands "what is" in relation to "what could be"—a traditional critical notion. No one will let us have our sociopolitical and educational dreams without a protracted struggle. The work is hard, and we will often be vilified for taking part in critical activity. Sometimes we will wonder whether we are the crazy ones as we sit in a crowded room as the only persons making the critical arguments discussed here. We will have to stay sane as we are attacked, and we will have to know more about history, philosophy, social theory, cognition, and pedagogy—from mainstream Western and subjugated perspectives from North America and Europe and especially from Africa, Latin American, Asia, and indigenous peoples from around the world. Hell yes, critical pedagogy involves a lifetime of rigorous

and too often unappreciated work. Nevertheless, I believe with every fiber of my being, it is worth the effort. What else are you going to do with your life? Be a cog in the engine of the mechanisms of dominant power that harm people in all of our communities and around the world. I hope not. Please visit the website for the Paulo and Nita Freire International Project for Critical Pedagogy (http://criticalpedagogyproject.mcgill.ca/drupal-5.1/). Here you will find updates on events in the world of critical pedagogy, new research in the domain, videos on the topic, archived materials, essays, blogs, and a variety of other forms of information. Everything on the site is free to anyone who logs in. The project is working to produce innovative research in the domain of critical pedagogy, while creating a worldwide community of critical pedagogues who can work together on a variety of projects. Project Director Shirley Steinberg and I invite you to become involved in our effort to connect individuals engaging in critical pedagogy in diverse and creative ways and in different settings.

CHAPTER ONE

Introduction

Educators walk minefields of educational contradictions in the contemporary pedagogical landscape. On some levels teachers and students discover that schools pursue democratic goals and education for a democratic society; on other levels they find that schools are authoritarian and pursue antidemocratic goals of social control for particular groups and individuals. Sometimes participants learn that schools are grounded on cooperative values; in high-stakes test-driven curricula they find that a competitive ethic is dominant. At other junctures students and teachers are told that the knowledge of schools is based on a diversity of cultural and global sources; when the curriculum is delineated, however, they often find that school knowledge comes primarily from dominant cultural, class, and gender groups (Apple, 1999; Schubert, 1998).

Advocates of critical pedagogy are aware that every minute of every hour that teachers teach, they are faced with complex decisions concerning justice, democracy, and competing ethical claims. Although they have to make individual determinations of what to do in these particular circumstances, they

agency

persons' ability to shape and control their own lives, freeing self from the oppression of power.

---

ideologies

traditional definition involves systems of beliefs. In a critical theoretical context idealogy involves meaning making that supports form of dominant power.

must concurrently deal with what John Goodlad (1994) calls the surrounding institutional morality. A central tenet of pedagogy maintains that the classroom, curricular, and school structures teachers enter are not neutral sites waiting to be shaped by educational professionals. Although such professionals do possess **agency**, this prerogative is not completely free and independent of decisions made previously by people operating with different values and shaped by the **ideologies** (see Chapter 3 for definition) and cultural assumptions of their historical contexts. These contexts are shaped in the same ways language and knowledge are constructed, as historical power makes particular practices seem natural—as if they could have been constructed in no other way (Bartolomé, 1998; Berry, 2000; Cochran-Smith, 2000; Ferreira and Alexandre, 2000).

Thus, proponents of critical pedagogy understand that every dimension of schooling and every form of educational practice are politically contested spaces. Shaped by history and challenged by a wide range of interest groups, educational practice is a fuzzy concept as it takes place in numerous settings, is shaped by a plethora of often invisible forces, and can operate even in the name of democracy and justice to be totalitarian and oppressive. Many teacher education students have trouble with this political dimension and the basic notion that schooling can be hurtful to particular students. They embrace the institution of education as "good" because in their own experience it has been good to them. Thus, the recognition of these political complications of schooling is a first step for critical pedagogy-influenced educators in developing a social activist teacher persona. As teachers gain these insights, they understand that cultural, race, class, and gender forces have shaped all elements of the pedagogical act. They also discover that a central aspect of democratic education involves addressing these dynamics as they systematically manifest themselves (Crebbin, 2001; Gergen and Gergen, 2000; Knobel, 1999; Noone and Cartwright, 1996).

Critical pedagogy is a complex notion that asks much of the practitioners who embrace it. Teaching a critical pedagogy involves more than learning a few pedagogical techniques and the knowledge required by the curriculum, the standards, or the textbook. Critical teachers must understand not only a wide body of subject matter but also the political structure of the school.

They must also possess a wide range of education in the culture: TV, radio, popular music, movies, the Internet, youth subcultures, and so on; alternative bodies of knowledge produced by marginalized or low-status groups; the ways power operates to construct identities and oppress particular groups; the modus operandi (MO) of the ways social regulation operates; the complex processes of racism, gender bias, class bias, cultural bias, heterosexism, religious intolerance, and so on; the cultural experiences of students; diverse teaching styles; the forces that shape the curriculum; the often conflicting purposes of education; and much more. This introduction to critical pedagogy issues a challenge to teachers, to educational leaders, and to students to dive into this complex domain of critical pedagogy. Many of us believe that the rewards for both yourself and your students will far outweigh the liabilities.

Nothing is impossible when we work in solidarity with love, respect, and justice as our guiding lights. Indeed, the great Brazilian critical educator Paulo Freire always maintained that education had as much to do with the teachable heart as it did with the mind. Love is the basis of an education that seeks justice, equality, and genius. If critical pedagogy is not injected with a healthy dose of what Freire called "radical love," then it will operate only as a shadow of what it could be. Such a love is compassionate, erotic, creative, sensual, and informed. Critical pedagogy uses it to increase our capacity to love, to bring the power of love to our everyday lives and social institutions, and to rethink reason in a humane and interconnected manner. Knowledge in this context takes on a form quite different from its more accepted and mainstream versions. A critical knowledge seeks to connect with the corporeal and the emotional in a way that understands at multiple levels and seeks to assuage human suffering.

The version of critical pedagogy offered here is infused with the impassioned spirit of Freire. I experience this spirit in my life when watching and listening to

- an A.M.E. church choir from New Orleans singing gospel songs
- Native American women making tremolo at a Sioux college graduation
- a rock band in a groove that shakes an audience to its core

- a Spanish calypso singer squeezing out every last note as the audience fills the air with heart-felt "olés"
- a dedicated and well-informed teacher bringing a group of students to life with her knowledge, passion for learning, and her ability to engage them in the process of teaching themselves and others.

I'm sure you sense this impassioned spirit in your own spaces. Critical pedagogy wants to connect education to that feeling, to embolden teachers and students to act in ways that make a difference, and to push humans to new levels of social and cognitive achievement previously deemed impossible. Critical pedagogy is an ambitious entity that seeks nothing less than a form of educational adventurism that takes us where nobody's gone before.

This impassioned spirit moves critical teachers to study power inscriptions and their often pernicious effects. The actions such teachers take to address them constitute one dimension of putting a critical pedagogy into action. Critical teacher educators must model this complex behavior for their education students in every dimension of professional education. This approach becomes extremely important when we understand the fear of the impassioned spirit and the hostility of many teacher education programs toward ideas that consider the effects of power on shaping and misshaping the pedagogical act. There are still too many teacher education programs that assume schooling is unequivocally a good thing serving the best interests of individual students, marginalized groups of students, and the culture in general. Such programs assume that the curriculum, institutional organizations, hiring practices, and field placements of the educational world are just and equitable and do not need examination on these levels. Critical teacher educators possess the difficult task of inducing students to challenge the very practices and ways of seeing they have been taught in their professional programs. Do "best practices," critical students ask, "help create a democratic consciousness and modes of making meaning that detect indoctrination and social regulation?"

Such critical pedagogical ways of seeing help teacher educators and teachers reconstruct their work so that it facilitates the empowerment of all students. In this context, critical educators understand that such an effort takes place in an increasingly power-inscribed world in which dominant modes of exclusion are continuously "naturalized" by power wielders' control of information. "What does this have to do with teacher education?" Critics may ask. "We live in a democracy," they assert. Why do we have to spend all this time with such political issues? Isn't our focus teaching and learning? However, democracy is fragile, critical educators maintain, and embedded in education are the very issues that make or break it. Are teachers merely managers of the predetermined knowledge of dominant cultural power? Is teacher education merely the process of developing the most efficient ways for educators to perform this task? Do teachers operate as functionaries who simply do what they are told? Contrary to the views of many, these questions of democracy and justice cannot be separated from the most fundamental features of teaching and learning (Cochran-Smith, 2000; Grimmett, 1999; Horton and Freire, 1990; McLaren, 2000; Powell, 2001; Rodriguez and Villaverde, 2000; Vavrus and Archibald, 1998).

The chapters of this book analyze and expand upon these themes of critical pedagogy. Throughout the book, I focus on questions of democracy, justice, and quality in the pedagogical context. There is no doubt that these issues are complex and passionate feelings surround them. In this context, I attempt to provide a fair picture of critical pedagogy but not a neutral one. As a political animal, I hold particular perspectives about the purpose of schooling and the nature of a just society. These viewpoints shape what follows. The best I can do is to reflect on where such perspectives come from and decide whether or not I want to maintain my dedication to them. Be aware of these biases and make sure you read what I have to say critically and suspiciously. Furthermore, be certain to read all texts in this same way, especially the ones that claim an objective and neutral truth. As I tell my students, whenever individuals tell me they are providing me with the objective truth I guard my wallet. As critical pedagogy maintains, little in the world and certainly little in the world of education is neutral. Indeed, the impassioned spirit is never neutral.

The Central Characteristics of Critical Pedagogy

All descriptions of critical pedagogy—like knowledge in general—are shaped by those who devise them and the values

they hold. The description offered here is no different. Many will agree with it and sing its praises, while others will be disappointed—and even offended—by what was included and what was left out. As with any other description I would offer about any social or cultural phenomenon, my delineation of the central characteristics of critical pedagogy is merely my "take" and reflects my biases and perspectives.

Critical Pedagogy Is Grounded on a Social and Educational Vision of Justice and Equality

Educational reformers can discuss collaborative school cultures and reflective practices all they want, but such concepts mean very little outside a rigorous, informed vision of the purpose of education. Many educational leaders and school boards are crippled by the absence of informed discussion about educational purpose. Without this grounding their conversations about what to do in schooling go around in circles with little direction and less imagination. Clichés abound as wheels are perpetually reinvented and old wine seeks new packaging. In the contemporary era there are endless attempts at school reform with little improvement to show for the efforts. Without an educational vision, most educational reforms create little more benefit than applying Aspercream to ease the pain of a massive head wound. The educational vision, the purpose of schooling promoted here, demands a fundamental rethinking, a deep reconceptualization of

- what human beings are capable of achieving
- the role of the social, cultural, and political in shaping human identity
- the relationship between community and schooling
- the ways that power operates to create purposes for schooling that are not necessarily in the best interests of the children that attend them
- how teachers and students might relate to knowledge
- the ways schooling affects the lives of students from marginalized groups
- the organization of schooling and the relationship between teachers and learners.

A critical pedagogical vision grounded as it is in social, cultural, cognitive, economic, and political contexts understands schooling

as part of a larger set of human services and community development. Any viable vision of critical education has to be based on larger social and cognitive visions. In this context, educators deal not only with questions of schooling, curriculum, and educational policy but also with social justice and human possibility. Understanding these dynamics, critical educators devise new modes of making connections between school and its context as well as catalyzing community resources to help facilitate quality education with an impassioned spirit. With this larger vision in mind and knowledge of these different contexts, educators are empowered to identify the insidious forces that subvert the success of particular students. This ability is not generally found in typical educational practice. Without it, educators and school leaders experience great difficulty in determining what is important knowledge in their particular school or school district. Without it, such individuals cannot determine why some policies and pedagogies work to accomplish some goals and not others (Bamburg, 1994; MDRC, 2002; Wang and Kovach, 1996).

This stunting of potential takes place in the pedagogy of low expectations where concern with disciplining the incompetent poor to create a more ordered and efficient society takes the place of a democratic critical social vision. Historical accounts of schools designed for these regulatory purposes alert us to the dangers of such educational structures (see Kincheloe, Slattery, and Steinberg, Chapter 5 for a discussion of this theme). Throughout history, such schools have served to categorize, punish, restrict, and restrain those students who failed to fit the proper demographic. Our critical vision of education enables us to see education in a systemic context. In this context, we gain an appreciation of the importance of the relationship between education and other social dynamics (FAUSSR, 1998). These interactions are complex, as all social, political, economic, cultural, and educational decisions are interrelated. With such an understanding, we can begin to reshape these relationships and the educational decisions we make in relation to them in new and previously unexplored ways.

In concrete terms, the implementation of this vision means that teachers can begin to develop distinct practices to help particular students flourish in schools located in specific

communities. In this context, critical teachers draw on their larger vision to help them determine what types of human beings they want to graduate from their schools. Do we want socially regulated workers with the *proper* attitudes for their respective rung on the workplace ladder? Or do we want empowered, learned, highly skilled democratic citizens who have the confidence and the savvy to improve their own lives and to make their communities more vibrant places in which to live, work, and play? If we are unable to articulate this transformative, just, and egalitarian critical pedagogical vision, then the job of schooling will continue to involve taming, controlling, and/or rescuing the least empowered of our students. Such students do not need to be tamed, controlled, and/or rescued; they need to be respected, viewed as experts in their interest areas, and inspired with the impassioned spirit to use education to do good things in the world.

Critical Pedagogy Is Constructed on the Belief That Education Is Inherently Political

Whether one is teaching in Bangladesh or Bensonhurst, Senegal or Shreveport, East Timor or West New York, education is a political activity. Who is hired for the third-grade position at Scarsdale Elementary, the decision to adopt the Success for All curriculum in District Nine in Brooklyn, the textbook chosen for the eighth-grade science class at Cedar Bluff Middle School, the language used to teach math at Coconut Grove Elementary School in Miami—these decisions all hold profound political implications. They refer to power and how it is distributed and engaged in the world of education and life in schools. For example, the decisions made in the previous examples will often privilege students from dominant cultural backgrounds—upper middle class, white, heterosexual, first language English, and Christian—while at the same time undermining the interests of those who fall outside these domains.

By utilizing IQ tests and developmental theories derived from research on students from dominant cultural backgrounds, schools not only reflect social stratification but also extend it. This is an example of school as an institution designed for social benefit actually exerting hurtful influences. Teachers involved in the harmful processes most often do not intentionally hurt students; they are merely following the dictates of their superiors

and the rules of the system. Countless good teachers work every day to subvert the negative effects of the system but need help from like-minded colleagues and organizations. Critical pedagogy works to provide such assistance to teachers who want to mitigate the effects of power on their students. Here schools as political institutions merge with critical pedagogy's concern with creating a social and educational vision to help teachers direct their own professional practice. Any time teachers develop a pedagogy, they are concurrently constructing a political vision. The two acts are inseparable.

Many times, unfortunately, those who develop pedagogies are unconscious of the political inscriptions embedded within them. A district supervisor who writes a curriculum in social studies, for example, that demands the simple transference of a body of established facts about the great *men* and great events of American history is also teaching a political lesson that upholds the status quo (Degener, 2002; Keesing-Styles, 2003; 21st Century Schools, 2003). There is no room for students or teachers in such a curriculum to explore alternate sources, to compare diverse historical interpretations, to do research of their own and produce knowledge that may conflict with prevailing interpretations. Such acts of democratic citizenship may be viewed as subversive and anti-American by the supervisor and the district education office. Indeed, such personnel may be under pressure from the state department of education to construct a history curriculum that is inflexible, based on the status quo, unquestioning in its approach, "fact-based," and teacher-centered. Dominant power operates in numerous and often hidden ways.

Peter McLaren (2000) writes that this power dimension of critical pedagogy is central and that practitioners must be aware of efforts to dilute this power literacy. Today, critical pedagogy has been associated with everything from simply the rearrangement of classroom furniture to "feel-good" teaching directed at improving students' self-esteem. Simply caring about students, while necessary, does not constitute a critical pedagogy. The power dimension must be brought to bear in a way that discerns and acts on correcting the ways particular students get hurt in the everyday life of schools. When critical pedagogy embraces multiculturalism, it focuses on the subtle workings of racism, sexism, class bias, cultural oppression, and homophobia. It is not

sufficient for a critical multiculturalism (Kincheloe and Steinberg, 1997; Kincheloe, Steinberg, Rodriguez, and Chennault, 1998) to build a program around supposedly depoliticized taco days, falafels, and Martin Luther King's birthday.

The ability to act on these political concerns is one of the most difficult tasks of critical pedagogy. Over the decades many conservative educators have participated in a Great Denial of the political dimension of education. In this denial, curricula and syllabi that fail to challenge the status quo are viewed as neutral documents presenting essential data. Students who want to become teachers have oftentimes encountered courses in political denial. Throughout elementary and secondary schools they were presented the facts unproblematically as if they were true. In college their liberal arts and sciences courses many times simply delivered the facts in biology, physics, sociology, psychology, or literature. The idea that these courses presented only one narrow perspective on the field in question, that they left out competing forms of knowledge produced by scholars from different schools of thought or from different cultures, was never mentioned. The political assumptions behind the curricula they encountered were erased. To ask such students to start over, to relearn the arts and sciences in light of these political concerns, is admittedly an ambitious task. Even so, this is exactly what critical pedagogy does, and those of us in the field believe such an effort is worth the time invested. A first-year teacher cannot accomplish such a huge task in the first year of his or her practice, but over a decade one can. Critical pedagogy challenges you to take the leap.

An important aspect of the Great Denial is that politics should be kept out of education and that is what mainstream curricula do. Critical pedagogy argues that such pronouncements are not grounded on an understanding of power. The political dimensions of education should be pointed out in all teaching and learning—critical pedagogy included. We must expose the hidden politics of what is labeled neutral. Such calls are often equated with a pedagogy of indoctrination. The critical educator Henry Giroux (1988) responds to such charges, contending that such criticism is flawed. Giroux argues that it confuses the development of a political vision with the pedagogy that is used in conjunction with it. Advocates of critical pedagogy make their own commitments clear as they construct forms of teaching consistent with the democratic notion that students learn to make their own choices of beliefs based on the diverse perspectives they confront in school and society. Education simply can't be neutral. When education pretends to be politically neutral like many churches in Nazi Germany, it supports the dominant, existing power structure. Recognition of these educational politics suggests that teachers take a position and make it understandable to their students. *They do not, however, have the right to impose these positions on their students.* This is a central tenet of critical pedagogy.

In this context it is not the advocates of critical pedagogy who are most often guilty of impositional teaching but many of the mainstream critics themselves. When mainstream opponents of critical pedagogy promote the notion that all language and political behavior that oppose the dominant ideology are forms of indoctrination, they forget how experience is shaped by unequal forms of power. To refuse to name the forces that produce human suffering and exploitation is to take a position that supports oppression and powers that perpetuate it. The argument that any position opposing the actions of dominant power wielders represents an imposition of one's views on somebody else is problematic. It is tantamount to saying that one who admits her oppositional political sentiments and makes them known to students is guilty of indoctrination, while one who hides her consent to dominant power and the status quo it has produced from her students is operating in an objective and neutral manner. Critical pedagogy wants to know who's indoctrinating whom. These political dynamics won't go away and teachers must deal with them.

Critical Pedagogy Is Dedicated to the Alleviation of Human Suffering

Knowing and learning are not simply intellectual and scholarly activities but also practical and sensuous activities infused by the impassioned spirit. Critical pedagogy is dedicated to addressing and embodying these affective, emotional, and lived dimensions of everyday life in a way that connects students to people in groups and as individuals. In this context, the advocates of critical pedagogy are especially concerned with those groups and individuals who are suffering, whose lives are affected by the sting of discrimination and poverty. Acting on this concern

critical educators seek out the causes of such suffering in their understandings of power with its ideological, hegemonic (see Chapter 3), disciplinary, and regulatory dimensions.

Indeed, the very origins of critical pedagogy—the tradition that lays the groundwork for critical pedagogy and is concerned with power and its oppression of human beings and regulation of the social order—are grounded on this concern with human suffering. Herbert Marcuse, one of the founders of the Frankfurt School of Critical Theory who is discussed in Chapter 2, and Paulo Freire were profoundly moved by the suffering they respectively witnessed in post–World War I Germany and Brazil. Although I am committed to a critical pedagogy that continues to develop and operates to sophisticate its understandings of the world and the educational act, this evolving critical pedagogy in education should never, never lose sight of its central concern with human suffering. One does not have to go too far to find suffering. In the United States, suffering is often well hidden, but a trip to inner cities, rural Appalachia, or Native American reservations will reveal its existence. Outside of the United States, we can go to almost any region of the world and see tragic expressions of human misery. Advocates of critical pedagogy believe such suffering is a humanly constructed phenomenon and does not have to exist. Steps can be taken to eradicate such suffering if the people of the planet and their leaders had the collective will to do so. In recent years, however, market-driven, globalized economic systems pushed on the world by the United States and other industrialized nations via the World Trade Organization (WTO) and the International Monetary Fund (IMF) have exacerbated poverty and its attendant suffering.

Understanding at the theoretical level, both how diverse influences insidiously shape what we perceive and don't perceive about the world and how we can better cultivate the intellect, is a central dimension of critical pedagogy and must always be connected to the reality of human suffering and the effort to eradicate it. Sometimes scholarship and teaching operating exclusively on the theoretical level remove us from and anesthetize us to human pain and suffering. This insensitivity is unacceptable to the critical educator. In critical pedagogy the theoretical domain always interacts with the lived domain, producing a synergy that elevates both scholarship and transformative action.

Indeed, the very definition of a critical consciousness involves the development of new forms of understanding that connect us more directly to understanding, empathizing with, and acting to alleviate suffering. Sophisticated understandings and engagement in the struggle against inequality characterize a critical consciousness. Such a struggle engages the lived suffering that comes out of oppression while it studies its consequences in the realm of knowledge production (Barone, 2000; Giroux, 1997; Hicks, 1997; Madison, 1988; McLaren, 2000; 21st Century Schools, 2003).

Pedagogy That Prevents Students From Being Hurt

Critical Pedagogy mandates that schools don't hurt students—good schools don't blame students for their failures or strip students of the forms of knowledge they bring to the classroom. In a recent book I coedited with Alberto Bursztyn and Shirley Steinberg (2004), I began the introductory essay with the proclamation that "I don't trust schools." What I was trying to get across involved the understanding that those of us concerned with critical pedagogy have to be very wary of the goals schools embrace and the ways they engage particular individuals and groups. To exemplify my concern, I often ask students in my classes and audience members in my speeches if any of them have ever studied at any point during their schooling the story of the European colonization of Africa and the effects of the slave trade. The slave trade killed at the very least tens of millions of Africans; some scholars say two hundred million—estimates vary.

I often find that no one in a classroom or audience has encountered this human tragedy in any systematic detail in his or her schooling. In this context, I typically point out that I simply could not trust an institution that routinely ignored such information. The very idea that these millions of unnecessary deaths would not rate as one of the most important events of the last millennium is hard to understand. An institution that would not engage students in wrestling with the moral responsibilities accompanying acquaintance with such knowledge is both intellectually and ethically impaired. Something is wrong here. In no way do advocates of critical pedagogy blame teachers for this failure. They, too, have been victimized by the same social systems that have produced this situation. Indeed, their job is hard enough and so little respected that they don't need flack

from this domain. The arts and sciences programs in colleges and universities that were responsible for this aspect of teacher education failed them.

Understanding that education is always political as it supports the needs of the dominant culture while subverting the interests of marginalized cultures, critical pedagogy does not allow such omissions in the curricula it develops. In this context advocates of critical pedagogy work to make sure schools don't continue to be hurtful places. The same institutions that don't teach about the mass killings in Europe's African slave trade—and scores of other atrocities that could be listed here—also blame students for their academic problems. In many schools and especially those shaped by the George W. Bush administration's "No Child Left Behind" legislation in the early twenty-first century, teachers are discouraged from taking into account the social, cultural, and economic backgrounds of their students and the needs and interests that emerge from them.

The exclusion of the social, cultural, and economic ways of knowing from the development of curriculum often holds tragic consequences for students. Many educational leaders influenced by psychometrics (the discipline that measures intelligence) and mainstream versions of educational psychology construct schools around the belief that intelligence and academic ability are individual dynamics free from social, cultural, and economic influences. Since the time of Plato, theories of intelligence have been employed to justify socioeconomic disparity and scholarly inferiority. The "dregs" at the bottom have always been said to be deficient and/or pathological. Critical educators feel that it is an outrage to separate environmental factors from efforts to measure ability or intelligence.

It doesn't take a brain surgeon to uncover the process that occurs when a culturally different and/or poor student encounters the middle-class, white-culture-grounded practice of school and the intelligence-testing establishment. The middle-class mind-set often views poverty as a badge of failure. Many educational leaders and psychologists seem to be unconcerned with the psychic toll that declarations of failure inflict on marginalized children and adolescents. Advocates of critical pedagogy understand how hard it is to go day after day to a school where you are viewed as a failure in all aspects of your life. Should we be surprised when such students express hostility and anger about having to be in such schools or when they reject the value of academic work in their lives? In many ways such responses are logical reactions; they are strategies of self-protection in a hostile and hurtful environment. When tracking policies are added to this mix, the hurtful nature of schools is enhanced. Operating on the simple-minded assumptions of psychometrics and achievement and standards tests, students are deemed capable or incapable of academic work. Those who score poorly are relegated to the "slow" classes that serve to further undermine their academic performance (Beck, 1991; Grubb et al., 1991; Kincheloe and Steinberg, 1997; Kincheloe, Steinberg, and Gresson, 1996; Oakes, 1985).

Critical pedagogy will not stand for these mechanisms of social and educational stratification that hurt socially, linguistically, and economically marginalized students so badly. The cultural backgrounds of African American, Native American, poor Appalachian, and Latino students are often deemed by middle-class, white schools to be inferior to those of the dominant culture. Because of such perspectives, students from such backgrounds come to realize that success in school may come only with a rejection of their ethnic and/or class backgrounds and the cultural forms of knowledge that accompany them. Lilia Bartolomé (1996) refers to this process as the robbing of students' "culture, language, history, and values" (p. 233). Critical teachers work to foil this robbery by helping students recall what they already know. Such teachers take student knowledge seriously and examine it as part of their curriculum. Students who possess particular insight about a topic can become the teacher for a day and share their knowledge with other students in the class. Knowing that they possess valuable knowledge, such students begin to realize that they are capable of learning much more. With this realization, teachers work with students to delineate what else they can learn and how it can be useful in their lives.

The Importance of Generative Themes

Critical pedagogy is enacted through the use of generative themes to read the word and the world and the process of problem posing. Critical pedagogy applies Paulo Freire's notion of generative themes used to help students read the word and the world. This reading of the word and the world helped students

connect what they decoded on the printed page to an understanding of the world around them. Thus, a synergistic relationship emerged between word and world. After exploring the community around the school and engaging in conversations with community members, Freire constructed generative themes designed to tap into issues that were important to various students in his class. As data on these issues were brought into the class, Freire became a problem poser. In this capacity, Freire used the knowledge he and his students had produced around the generative themes to construct questions. The questions he constructed were designed to teach the lesson that no subject matter or knowledge in general was beyond examination. We need to ask questions of all knowledge, Freire argued, because all data are shaped by the context and by the individuals that produced them. Knowledge, contrary to the pronouncements of many educational leaders, does not transcend culture or history.

In the context of reading the word and the world and problem posing existing knowledge, critical educators reconceptualize the notion of literacy. Myles Horton spoke of the way he read books with students in order "to give testimony to the students about what it means to read a text" (Horton and Freire, 1990). Reading is not an easy endeavor, Horton continued, for to be a good reader is to view reading as a form of research. Thus, reading becomes a mode of finding something, and finding something, he concluded, brings a joy that is directly connected to the acts of creation and re-creation. One finds in this reading that the word and world process typically goes beyond the given, the common sense of everyday life. Several years ago, I wrote a book entitled *Getting Beyond the Facts* (2001a). The point of the title was to signify this going beyond, to represent a form of reading that not only understood the words on the page but the unstated dominant ideologies hidden between the sentences as well.

This going beyond is central to Freirean problem posing. Such a position contends that the school curriculum should in part be shaped by problems that face teachers and students in their effort to live just and ethical lives. Such a curriculum promotes students as researchers (Steinberg and Kincheloe, 1998) who engage in critical analysis of the forces that shape the world. Such critical analysis engenders a healthy and creative skepticism on the part of students. It moves them to problem-pose, to be suspicious of neutrality claims in textbooks; it induces them to look askance at, for example, oil companies' claims in their TV commercials that they are and have always been environmentally friendly organizations. Students and teachers who are problem posers reject the traditional student request to the teacher: "just give us the facts, the truth and we'll give it back to you." On the contrary, critical students and teachers ask in the spirit of Freire and Horton: "please support us in our explorations of the world."

By promoting problem posing and student research, teachers do not simply relinquish their authority in the classroom. Over the last couple of decades several teachers and students have misunderstood the subtlety of the nature of teacher authority in a critical pedagogy. Freire in the last years of his life was very concerned with this issue and its misinterpretation by those operating in his name. Teachers, he told me, cannot deny their position of authority in such a classroom. It is the teacher, not the students, who evaluates student work, who is responsible for the health, safety, and learning of students. To deny the role of authority the teacher occupies is insincere at best, dishonest at worst. Critical teachers, therefore, must admit that they are in a position of authority and then demonstrate that authority in their actions in support of students. One of the actions involves the ability to conduct research/produce knowledge. The authority of the critical teacher is **dialectical**; as teachers relinquish the authority of truth providers, they assume the mature authority of facilitators of student inquiry and problem posing. In relation to such teacher authority, students gain their freedom—they gain the ability to become self-directed human beings capable of producing their own knowledge.

dialectical authority

Involves studies that account for the importance of opposites and contradicitons within all forms of knowledge and the relationship between these opposites. Knowledge is not complete in and of itself. It is produced in a larger process and can never be understood outside of its historical development and its relationship to other information.

Teachers as Researchers

In the new right-wing educational order that exists in the twenty-first century, knowledge is something that is produced far away from the school by experts in an exalted domain. This must change if a critical reform of schooling is to ever take place. Teachers must have more say, more respect, in the culture of education. Teachers must join the culture of researchers if a new level of educational rigor and quality is ever to be achieved. In such a democratized culture, critical teachers are scholars who understand the power implications of various educational reforms.

In this context, they appreciate the benefits of research, especially as they relate to understanding the forces shaping education that fall outside their immediate experience and perception. As these insights are constructed, teachers begin to understand what they know from experience. With this in mind they gain heightened awareness of how they can contribute to the research on education. Indeed, they realize that they have access to understandings that go far beyond what the expert researchers have produced.

In the critical school culture, teachers are viewed as learners—not as functionaries who follow top-down orders without question. Teachers are seen as researchers and knowledge workers who reflect on their professional needs and current understandings. They are aware of the complexity of the educational process and how schooling cannot be understood outside of the social, historical, philosophical, cultural, economic, political, and psychological contexts that shape it. Scholar teachers understand that curriculum development responsive to student needs is not possible when it fails to account for these contexts. With this in mind, they explore and attempt to interpret the learning processes that take place in their classrooms. 'What are its psychological, sociological, and ideological effects?,' they ask. Thus, critical scholar teachers research their own professional practice (Kraft, 2001; Norris, 1998).

With empowered scholar teachers prowling the schools, things begin to change. The oppressive culture created in twenty-first-century schools by top-down content standards, for example, is challenged. In-service staff development no longer takes the form of "this is what the expert researchers found—now go implement it." Such staff development in the critical culture of schooling gives way to teachers who analyze and contemplate the power of each other's ideas. Thus, the new critical culture of school takes on the form of a "think tank that teaches students," a learning community. School administrators are amazed by what can happen when they support learning activities for both students and teachers. Principals and curriculum developers watch as teachers develop projects that encourage collaboration and shared research. There is an alternative, advocates of critical pedagogy argue, to top-down standards with their deskilling of teachers and the "dumbing-down" of students (Jardine, 1998; Kincheloe, 2003a; Norris, 1998; Novick, 1996).

Promoting teachers as researchers is a fundamental way of cleaning up the damage of deskilled models of teaching that infantilize teachers by giving them scripts to read to their students.

> Teacher says: Class, take out your pencils.
>> [teacher waits until all students have their pencils in hand.]
> Teacher then says: Class, turn to page 15 of your textbook.
>> [teacher waits until all students have turned to correct page.]
> Teacher says: Read pages 15–17. When you are finished, close your books and put your hands on the top of your desk. You have ten minutes.

Deskilling of teachers and dumbing-down of the curriculum take place when teachers are seen as receivers, rather than producers, of knowledge. A vibrant professional culture depends on a group of practitioners who have the freedom to continuously reinvent themselves via their research and knowledge production. Teachers engaged in critical practice find it difficult to allow top-down content standards and their poisonous effects to go unchallenged. Such teachers cannot abide the deskilling and reduction in professional status that accompany these top-down reforms. Advocates of critical pedagogy understand that teacher empowerment does not occur just because we wish it to. Instead, it takes place when teachers develop the knowledge-work skills, the power literacy, and the pedagogical abilities befitting the calling of teaching. Teacher research is a central dimension of a critical pedagogy.

Teachers as Researchers of Their Students

A central aspect of critical teacher research involves studying students, so they can be better understood and taught. Freire argued that all teachers need to engage in a constant dialogue with students that questions existing knowledge and problematizes the traditional power relations that have served to marginalize specific groups and individuals. In these research dialogues with students, critical teachers listen carefully to what students have to say about their communities and the problems that confront them. Teachers

help students frame these problems in a larger social, cultural, and political context in order to solve them.

In this context, Freire argued that teachers uncover materials and generative themes based on their emerging knowledge of students and their sociocultural backgrounds. Teachers come to understand the ways students perceive themselves and their interrelationships with other people and their social reality. This information is essential to the critical pedagogical act as it helps teachers understand how they make sense of schooling and their lived worlds. With these understandings in mind, critical teachers come to know what and how students make meaning. This enables teachers to construct pedagogies that engage the impassioned spirit of students in ways that moves them to learn what they don't know and to identify what they want to know (Degener, 2002; Freire and Faundez, 1989; Kincheloe and Steinberg, 1998).

It is not an exaggeration to say that before critical pedagogy can work, teachers must understand what is happening in the minds of their students. Freire, Giroux, McLaren, Shirley Steinberg, bell hooks, Patti Lather, Deborah Britzman, and Donaldo Macedo are all advocates of various forms of critical teaching who recognize the importance of understanding the social construction of student consciousness, focusing on motives, values, and emotions. Operating within this critical context, the teacher researcher studies students as living texts to be deciphered. The teacher researcher approaches them with an active imagination and a willingness to view students as socially constructed beings.

When critical teachers have approached research on students from this perspective, they have uncovered some interesting information. In a British **action research** project, for example, teachers used student diaries, interviews, dialogues, and shadowing (following students as they pursue their daily routines at school) to uncover a student preoccupation with what was labeled a second-order curriculum. This curriculum involved matters of student dress, conforming to school rules, strategies of coping with boredom and failure, and methods of assuming their respective roles in the school pecking order. Teacher researchers found that much of this second-order curriculum worked to contradict the stated aims of the school to respect the individuality of students,

action research

a form of research designed for practitioners that allows teachers, for example, to research practices, schools, students, communities, curriculum, and so on, for the purpose of improving their professional work.

to encourage sophisticated thinking, and to engender positive self-images. Students often perceived that the daily lessons of teachers (the intentional curriculum) were based on a set of assumptions quite different from those guiding out-of-class teacher interactions with students. Teachers consistently misread the anger and hostility resulting from such inconsistency. Only in an action research context that values the perceptions of students could such student emotions be understood and addressed (Armstrong, 1981; Kincheloe, 2001a; Oldroyd, 1985; Steinberg, 2000; Wood, 1988).

Social Change and Cultivating the Intellect

Critical pedagogy is interested in maintaining a delicate balance between social change and cultivating the intellect—developing a rigorous education in a hostile environment that accomplishes both goals. Freire always maintained that pedagogy has as much to do with the effort to change the world as with developing rigorous forms of analysis. In other words, a critical pedagogy is not only interested in social change but also in cultivating the intellect of teachers, students, and members of the larger society. There is nothing simplistic about this delicate and synergistic relationship. We cannot simply attempt to cultivate the intellect without changing the unjust social context in which such minds operate. Critical educators cannot just work to change the social order without helping to educate a knowledgeable and skillful group of students. Creating a just, progressive, creative, and democratic society demands both dimensions of this pedagogical process.

Freire and Horton were adamant about connecting these dimensions. Social change pursued in isolation can insidiously promote anti-intellectualism if critical educators are not careful. As Horton (Horton and Freire, 1990) put it, a teacher cannot be a coordinator or facilitator "if you don't know anything. What the hell are you around for, if you don't know anything? Just get out of the way and let somebody have the space that knows something" (p. 154). As Freire told me shortly before his death: "No teacher is worth her salt who is not able to confront students with a rigorous body of knowledge. This is not to endorse a banking education but to support the idea that teachers often provide students with knowledge that students then react to, reject, reinterpret, analyze, and put into action." Teachers, Freire and

Horton agreed, must model rigorous thinking and compelling ways of being a scholar for their students.

Often in my own writing about critical pedagogy I use the concept of complexity to help signify the importance of bringing together the goals of social change and the cultivation of the intellect. In doing so, I use the phrases "complex critical pedagogy" and "a critical complex education" (Kincheloe and Weil, 2001). Accomplishing these two goals is always complex and must be understood in great detail by critical teachers. In order to construct and enact a pedagogy that is socially transformative as well as rigorous in its cultivation of the intellect, teachers must be acutely aware of the complicated world of education with its diverse cultural settings and wide range of student backgrounds. Such goals cannot be accomplished without a compelling understanding of the goals themselves and the complicated context in which education takes place. Advocates of top-down standards, for example, assume that if we lay out the minimum content requirements that all students must meet and then teach everyone in the same way, schools will be improved. They don't seem to recognize the diverse needs and dispositions toward the schooling process that different students bring to the classroom. Would we teach the same skills and content in the same way to a group of students in a classroom where most students read below grade level as opposed to one where all students read above grade level? How do we develop and enact a pedagogy that takes into account this and a thousand other levels of diversity? Any pedagogy that doesn't address such issues is mere window dressing, a public relations campaign for particular political operatives.

Obviously, there are thousands of different ways to learn and critical teachers must gain an awareness of such cognitive differences in their efforts to teach in more sophisticated ways. Often these cognitive differences are connected to cultural issues such as race, ethnicity, socioeconomic class, gender, religious beliefs, and other factors. A critical complex pedagogy must understand the effects of these contextual factors, in particular the ways they affect school performance. Without such an understanding, cultural and cognitive *difference* are confused with academic *deficiency*. Learning to make this distinction and then developing a curriculum to address the difficulties students experience is a necessary teaching ability in a critical complex pedagogy.

In the twenty-first century, classrooms in this society are structured by multiple layers of complexity. Typically ignoring this reality, top-down, standards-oriented reforms often view the educational world as one homogenous group—everyone comes from an upper-middle-class, white, English-speaking background. Even relatively simple distinctions such as the difference between the goals of elementary and secondary education are often overlooked by the present standards conversation. Elementary educators teach all subjects and are expected to be content generalists. Of course, secondary teachers teach particular areas in the present school configuration and are expected to be content specialists. Elementary teachers are now being presented with stacks of content standards in a variety of fields with little, if any, help in integrating them or making sense of how these bodies of content might fit into an elementary education.

Secondary teachers are now being provided with large collections of top-down content standards in their disciplines. If such teachers possess the skills such standards dictate, then they are induced to discard their disciplinary knowledge and experience and embrace without question a body of externally imposed data. Such a pedagogy fails to produce transformative action or intellectual challenge. Teachers always deserve to be a part of the conversation about standards and educational reform, not deskilled functionaries who mechanically do what they are told by external inquisitors. In a complex critical pedagogy, teachers must not only engage in a dialogue with standards devisors but also need to buy into the logic of such a critical complex rigor if improvements are to be made. Advocates of a critical pedagogy must be prepared to convince teachers that such goals are worthy. Such advocates must be prepared to help teachers move from their present understandings to a more complex view of the teaching act that includes social transformation and the cultivation of the intellect. No educational reform can work if teachers are excluded from the negotiations about its development and implementation.

Marginalization and Critical Pedagogy

Critical pedagogy is interested in the margins of society, the experiences and needs of individuals faced with oppression and marginalization. It is not merely interested in the experiences and needs of students who come from the mythical center of

the social order. Thus, critical teachers seek out individuals, voices, texts, and perspectives that had been previously excluded. Mainstream scholarship and the education it supports often drop the margins from consideration in order to concentrate on the so-called typical. Critical pedagogy, thus, amplifies the voices of those who have had to struggle to be heard. Unfortunately, in contemporary U.S. society and its schooling, there are many excluded voices coming from multiple margins. Several times in the last few years, critical pedagogy itself has been accused of ignoring particular voices. The critical pedagogy that I am describing here must not marginalize the voices of any subjugated individual or group.

A complex critical pedagogy is always searching for new voices that may have been excluded by the dominant culture or by critical pedagogy itself. Poor, non-English as first language, gay, lesbian, and bisexual, physically challenged, nonathletic, nonwhite, overweight, shy, and short students often find themselves oppressed in various ways in school. Students who don't come from such groups and are deemed talented and popular in the school culture often find it very difficult to understand this oppression. From the privileged perspective of the dominant culture, it may be difficult to empathize with the travails of those who have been deemed to be "different." When one is a part of different privileged groups, he or she is less likely to notice the ways that the marginalized are judged by particular norms.

Advocates of critical pedagogy understand that all students can be silenced to some extent by top-down, memory-based classroom arrangements that dictate the issues to be studied, the nature of the lessons, and the arguments employed to support various positions. But marginalized students from the previously enumerated groups are vulnerable to personal humiliation by teachers, administrators, and other students. Such humiliation often follows from the assumption that a lack of familiarity with the habits, problems, values, rituals, and ways of seeing common to the school culture constitutes no mere difference but deficiency on the part of the marginalized. Critical teachers understand the anger, depression, and anxiety such practices incite in such students.

Antonia Darde described one middle-aged African American college student who experienced these emotions in school. In a journal the student kept for one of her classes she explained how

she had repressed her anger over her school experiences for years because she always worked to evade trouble with white people. Although she kept quiet for the first several weeks of the term, a class discussion in which white students expressed their resentment about being held accountable for the past racism of others pushed her over the edge. As she listened to white students explain that racism is a relic of history not found in the present, the student exclaimed: "Things may look better to you because you're white and middle class, but maybe you should come to my neighborhood in Watts. Things there are still a mess" (Darder, 1991).

After decades of silence, the student—by way of her own words—gained a new empowerment and developed a new public voice in racially mixed groups. Thinking back on the conversation, the student later wrote that she felt good about expressing her frustrations and rage. Reflecting on her school and work lives, she had come to understand that she had always put on two faces: one for African Americans and another for white people. Like countless other African Americans in offices and classrooms, she did what she had to do to survive in white-dominated institutions. Critical teachers appreciate the cultural dynamics at work in situations such as this one and operate to create safe classrooms that enable rather than repress marginalized students. In no way is this to imply that supporting such students is easy. When race, class, gender, sexual orientation, religion of teachers and students differ, numerous and complicated conflicts can develop. Critical teachers constantly have to deal with the ramifications of these differences.

In this context, advocates of critical pedagogy maintain that teachers must study the ways that a world that is unjust by design shapes the classroom and the relations between teachers and students. By doing this, teachers can begin to discern concrete manifestations of the abstract concept of a world unjust by design. Here critical teachers make use of this knowledge not to "save" marginalized students but to provide a safe space for them and to learn with them about personal empowerment, the cultivation of the intellect, and the larger pursuit of social justice. In a racial context, oftentimes the notion of saving students involves a paternalistic effort to help them become more culturally white. This is *not* what critical pedagogy is attempting to accomplish. Instead, critical pedagogy is profoundly concerned

with understanding subjugated forms of knowledge coming from these various oppressed groups and examining them in relation to other forms of academic knowledge.

Critical teachers explore non-Western, subjugated, and indigenous voices in order to better appreciate the nature and causes of human suffering and the process of domination. Such forms of knowledge are very important to the critical project because of the unique perspective they bring to scholars saturated with the Eurocentric, patriarchal, and elitist ways of seeing. As important as they are, however, indigenous forms of knowledge are not exempt from critique. Advocates of critical pedagogy always respect such forms of knowledge but refuse to turn them into icons that are too precious to analyze and interpret (McLaren, 2000; Semali and Kincheloe, 1999). Understanding such dynamics and putting them into practice in the everyday life of school is a central task of critical teaching. In this context, such understanding helps shape the nature of teacher-student interactions, the curriculum, the culture of the school, and educational purpose in general (Grange, 2003; Keesing-Styles, 2003; Kilduff and Mehra, 1997).

Such studies move critical educators to a larger awareness—so important in light of U.S. efforts at empire-building in the twenty-first century—of the sense of Western superiority embedded in knowledge production and curriculum development. The non-Western, subjugated, and indigenous forms of knowledge previously mentioned are viewed in this context as unsophisticated, backward, and unscientific. What the West has historically labeled reason has been associated with high levels of maturity of human civilization. Those who exercise reason enter a new stage of human maturity. Those who don't are viewed as depraved and underdeveloped. Thus, Western reason is a developmental notion. Different groups of people—races and nations, for example—can be located on a developmental continuum based on reason.

Such developmentalism is found at the individual level in schools as students are placed on a developmental continuum based on their capacity to employ reason. The point advocates of critical pedagogy are making in this context is that reason comes in many forms—the one used by many Western observers and educators is a particular form of reason that is particular to Western societies after the Scientific Revolution. To use one's own

worldviews to judge other peoples can be a dangerous enterprise. It can be used to justify the marginalization of groups who are different. There's no such thing as oppression, supporters of the status quo often argue, it's just that "those people" are inferior; they're not as intelligent and civilized as we are. Throughout history, Europeans have made such arguments from the Crusades against the heathen Muslims, the African slave trade and slavery, to the Third Reich's efforts to exterminate Jews, Gypsies, homosexuals, and physically challenged people.

The Importance of Positivism

Critical pedagogy focuses on the importance of positivism in shaping what goes on in education and knowledge production. The critique of positivism is central to critical theory and critical pedagogy. Positivism is an epistemological position. Epistemology is the study of knowledge, its production, the nature of truth, and the criteria we use to determine whether a statement is valid. Epistemology has shaped the education, the way we think, the way we see the world, and our view of ourselves. Epistemological questions might include: How do you know? Is that true? Is that a fact or an opinion? Is that an objective test? The epistemological position of Western Cartesian modernism is positivism. Few philosophical orientations have been so influential on the way we live our lives and shape education as has modernist positivism.

There is no difference, positivists argue, between the ways knowledge is produced in the physical sciences and in the human sciences—one should study sociology in the same way one studies physics. Social and educational knowledge about humans would be subjected to the same decontextualizing forces as the study of rocks. Positivist social and behavioral scientists continue to pull people out of their cultural settings and study them in laboratory-like conditions. They don't understand that we can't be understood outside of the context that helped shape us. Society, positivists maintain, like nature, is nothing more than a body of neutral facts governed by immutable laws. Therefore, positivists conclude that social actions should proceed with law-like predictability. In this positivistic context, education is also governed by unchanging laws. Thus, the role of the teacher is to uncover these laws and then act in accordance with them. For example,

educational laws would include universal statements regarding how students learn and how they should be taught.

The positivist educator, in other words, sees only one correct way to teach, and scientific study can reveal these methods if we search for them diligently. This is the logic, the epistemology on which top-down standards and other standardized forms of education are based. Everyone is assumed to be the same regardless of race, class, or gender. I know if I go into a poor area where I'm from in the Appalachian Mountains of East Tennessee with this positivistic framework I'm going to run into trouble. When I bring out the same curriculum and the same teaching strategies used in the wealthy suburbs of Scarsdale, New York, I'm going to find that because of the backgrounds of many of my poor Appalachian students, there will be problems. They're not going to be ready to study the same curriculum in the same ways as the New York students. This is not because of their inferiority—they are not inferior—but simply because they don't have the same experiences as the upper-middle-class students from Scarsdale. Good critical pedagogy dictates that I start where they are and teach them in ways that are culturally relevant to them.

In my book on social studies education (*Getting Beyond the Facts: Teaching Social Studies/Social Science in the Twenty-First Century*, 2001a), I list and discuss the characteristics of positivism. Critical teachers would do well to understand positivism and the ways it insidiously shapes schooling and what we know. Here is the list without extended discussion:

- All knowledge is scientific knowledge
- All scientific knowledge is empirically verifiable
- One must use the same methods to study the physical world as one uses to study the social and educational worlds
- If knowledge exists, it exists in some definite, measurable quantity
- Nature is uniform and whatever is studied remains consistent in its existence and behavior
- The factors that cause things to happen are limited and knowable, and, in empirical studies, these factors can be controlled
- Certainty is possible, and when we produce enough research, we will understand reality well enough to forgo further research

- Facts and values can be kept separate, and objectivity is always possible
- There is one true reality, and the purpose of education is to convey that reality to students
- Teachers become "information deliverers," not knowledge-producing professionals or empowered cultural workers.

There's an impudent dimension to critical pedagogy that says "who said teaching has to be done in this standardized way?" There's no one right way to teach. Such impudence is based on a cynicism toward the notion that positivistic ways of operating get us to the "right place" in research and education. We should use the research methods that are best suited to answering our questions about a phenomenon and the teaching methods that are designed for the special needs of the students we are teaching. Teaching and producing knowledge always encounter multiple inputs and forces. The best teacher in the world may not, for example, be able to reach a student on Thursday morning who watched her father beat up her mother on Wednesday night. The critical researcher-teacher does not allow these unexpected complexities to be dismissed by the excluding, reducing impulses of positivism. Refusing such reductionism is a subversive act in a school system shaped by positivist reforms such as "No Child Left Behind."

Advocates of a critical pedagogy understand that all human experience is marked by uncertainties and that order is not always easily established. "Order in the court" has little authority when the positivist judge is resting in *his* quarters. Indeed, the rationalistic and reductionistic quest for order refuses in its arrogance to listen to a cacophony of lived experience and the coexistence of diverse meanings and interpretations. The concept of understanding in the complex world viewed by critical teachers is unpredictable. Much to the consternation of many, there exists no final meaning that operates outside of historical and social context. As critical pedagogues create rather than discover meaning in the everyday world, they explore alternate meanings offered by others in diverse circumstances. If this weren't enough, they work to account for historical and social contingencies that always operate to undermine the universal positivist pronouncement of the meaning of a particular phenomenon. Jean Piaget may have studied how middle-class Swiss boys develop cognitively, but do African villagers from rural Malawi develop the same way? Critical psychologists don't

think so, and such scholars discern big problems when positivists claim that the Malawi children should. When they don't, they are deemed cognitively deficient, not just culturally different. When educators fail to discern the unique ways that historical and social context make for special circumstances, they often provide reductionistic forms of knowledge and teaching that impoverish our understanding of everything connected to them (Burbules and Beck, 1999; Cary, 1998, 2003; Marijuan, 1994).

The Force of Science to Regulate

Critical pedagogy is aware that science can be used as a force to regulate and control. Science—especially the social, behavioral, and educational—developed in a time of much upheaval in the European world. As nineteenth-century inventions, the social, behavioral, and educational sciences—sociology, psychology, economics, political science, and anthropology, in particular—were directed toward managing and regulating the emerging populations of the urban-industrial world. The landed, moneyed, and industrial classes were frightened by the prospect of a working-class revolution and hoped that such disciplines would help in the regulatory process. Indeed, the development of public schooling in the United States cannot be understood outside this desire to control the population. The social sciences, contrary to conventional wisdom, shaped the societies that they sought to study. Unlike the claims they put forward, they were not disinterested scientific observers seeking only objective knowledge.

With these dynamics in mind, advocates of critical pedagogy recognize the contributions of physical and social science but are always suspicious of this regulatory dimension. Thus, they always study science in cultural and historical contexts, asking questions of the uses to which it has been put and whose interests it serves. Critical observers understand that science—like any system of discourse and practice—involves more than can be seen on the surface. Science carries with it a social, cultural, political, and economic history replete with pain, suffering, and privilege. It is never wise, advocates of critical pedagogy warn, to take one way of seeing the world and assume that it provides a picture of what the world is really like—critical pedagogy included. Indeed, a key element of the type of critical pedagogy I'm promoting here involves the importance of gaining multiple perspectives (in this

context, see my work on bricolage, Kincheloe, 2001b; Kincheloe and Berry, 2004; Kincheloe and McLaren, 2004).

With this understanding of science as a regulative discourse, critical teachers are "on alert" to the ways Western elitist vantage points are normalized in education ("The Human Sciences," 1999; Kilduff and Mehra, 1997; Pickering, 2000). We see them at work in the world of art and art education when dominant power produces accepted modes of representing the world while excluding others (Cary, 1998, 2003). Concurrently, we see such dominant modes of perceiving in history, government, literature, and scientific curricula. Students

- study Western history and views of "others,"
- are exposed to little criticism of the structure of the nation's government,
- read the white male canon with a few gratuitous additions,
- are shielded from a view of science as a human construction by a particular cultural group at a specific historical time.

The promulgation of such ways of seeing is a form of education as regulation, reducing student and citizen resistance to the interests of dominant groups. Regulated individuals are more likely to accept their places in the workplaces of global capitalism. Teachers are not exempt from the dominant power's attempts to regulate. Critical pedagogy works to expose and confront the dominant power's appropriations of what were supposed to be democratic processes. The electronic world of the twenty-first century is vulnerable to power in ways never before imagined. Not only through schooling but also by way of television and other modes of communication, dominant power attempts to produce more compliant forms of consciousness and identity (Cannella and Kincheloe, 2002; Steinberg and Kincheloe, 1997). With nearly twenty-four-hour-a-day access to individuals in their most private spaces, the dominant power struggles to produce ways of seeing that allow it more freedom to operate. Thus, the regulatory power of science now uses media as well as schooling to accomplish its work.

The Importance of Understanding Context

Critical pedagogy is cognizant of the importance of understanding the context in which educational activity takes place.

The more teachers and students understand the various social contexts in which education takes place, the more we appreciate the complexity of the process. The more of these contexts with which teachers are familiar, the more rigorous and critical education becomes. The problems of teacher education and teaching are multidimensional and are always embedded in a context. The more research sociocognitives produce, for example, the more it becomes apparent that a large percentage of student difficulties in school results not as much from cognitive inadequacy as from socially contextual factors (Kincheloe, Steinberg, and Gresson, 1996; Kincheloe, Steinberg, and Villaverde, 1999; Lave and Wenger, 1991; Snook, 1999; Wertsch, 1991). Critical teachers need a rich understanding of the social backgrounds of students, the scholarly context in which disciplinary and counter-disciplinary forms of knowledge are produced and transformed into subject matter, and the political context that helps shape school purpose.

In positivistic schools, learners' lives are decontextualized. When they examine the contexts and relationships connecting learner, culture, teaching, knowledge production, and curriculum, teachers move into a more complex paradigm. In this "zone of complexity," learning is viewed more as a dynamic and unpredictable process. As a complex, changing, unstable system, it resists generalized pronouncements and universal steps detailing "how to do it." Complex systems interact with multiple contexts and possess the capacity for self-organization and creative innovation. Each teaching and learning context has its unique dimensions that must be dealt with individually. Our understanding of educational purpose is also shaped by the complexity of these contextual appreciations. Teachers who are aware of this complexity embrace an evolving notion of purpose ever informed and modified by encounters with new contexts (Capra, 1996; Kincheloe and Weil, 2001; Schubert, 1998).

Teachers act on these contextual insights to not only help understand the various educational forms of knowledge but to grasp the needs of their students. In the critical orientation, such concerns can never be separated from the sociopolitical context: macro in the sense of the prevailing **Zeitgeist** and micro as it refers to the context immediately surrounding any school. In this context, critical teachers listen for marginalized voices and learn

Zeitgeist
the German term for spirit of the times.

about their struggles with their environments. As such teachers delineate the effects of the contemporary political context shaped by corporations and economic interests, they build deep relationships with local communities, community organizations, and concerned individuals in these settings. With this in place, students gain new opportunities to learn, not only in classrooms but also in unique community learning environments. Here they can often address particular sociopolitical dynamics and learn about them in very personal and compelling ways (Cochran-Smith, 2000; Grimmett, 1999; Hoban and Erickson, 1998; Thomson, 2001; Vavrus and Archibald, 1998).

Critical educators place great emphasis on the notion of context and the act of contextualization in every aspect of their work. When problems arise, they stand ready to connect the difficulty to a wider frame of reference with a wide array of possible causes. When pedagogical problems fail to meet the criteria of an archetype, critical teachers research unused sources and employ the information acquired to develop a larger understanding of the interaction of the various systems involved with the problem. When teachers fail to perform such an act of contextualization, students get hurt. When teachers do not contextualize, they tend to isolate various parts of a pedagogical circumstance and call each a problem (Bohm and Edwards, 1991). They tinker with components of the problem but never approach its holistic nature. Educational data, for example, derive meaning only in the context created by other data. Context may be more important than content. These insights change the way educators approach their work.

Decades ago, John Dewey wrote about these contextual dynamics. In the second decade of the twentieth century, Dewey observed that many thinkers saw knowledge as self-contained, as complete in itself. Knowledge, he contended, could never be viewed outside the context of its relationship to other information. We only have to call to mind, Dewey wrote, what passes in our schools as acquisition of knowledge to understand how it is decontextualized and lacks any meaningful connection to the experience of students. Anticipating the notion of a critical pedagogy, Dewey concluded that an individual is a sophisticated thinker to the degree in which he or she sees an event not as something isolated "but in its connection with the common

technicalization

the focus on technique or how to do things rather than why to do things.

experience of mankind" (Dewey, 1916, pp. 342–343). To overcome the reductionism that has plagued teaching and allowed for its **technicalization** and **hyperrationalization**, critical educators must take Dewey's insights into account.

The Importance of Resisting the Dominant Power

hyperrationalization

the application of reason alone to analyses of the world in lieu of emotion, affect, and concerns of worth and justice.

Critical pedagogy is dedicated to resisting the harmful effects of dominant power. Advocates of critical pedagogy work to expose and to contest oppressive forms of power as expressed in socioeconomic class elitism, Eurocentric ways of viewing the world, patriarchal oppression, and imperialism around the world. In this context, white people must learn to listen to nonwhites' and indigenous people's criticism of them and of the cultural norms they have established and imposed on people of a lower socioeconomic class and non-European peoples at home and abroad. The struggle to resist the harmful effects of dominant power and the empowerment of marginalized and exploited peoples must include everything from engaging such individuals in a rigorous, empowering education to a more equitable distribution of wealth. Indeed, as Western societies have moved to the political right, traditional concerns about the welfare of the working class have faded. Too often in the contemporary global economy we find unemployed and underemployed individuals with insecure, temporary, part-time, and low-paying jobs. The exploitation of working people has intensified in the contemporary era, as free market economics and globalization have fragmented and disoriented the working class.

Too often, mainstream education teaches students and teachers to accept the oppressive workings of power—in the name of a neutral curriculum, in the attempt to take politics out of education. Critical pedagogy moves students, workers, and citizens to question the hidden political assumptions and the colonial, racial, gender, and class biases of schooling and media education. Critical pedagogy induces students to question these power plays that lead to human suffering. Many members of Western societies in the first decade of the twenty-first century see overtly political pronouncements as somehow inappropriate and out of place in institutions such as schools. Teachers, they say, should remain neutral. Students, however, need to understand the covert political

implications of almost everything that presents itself as objective information, disinterested science, and balanced curricula. Of course, advocates of critical pedagogy know where they're coming from: they are making a case for fairness, for delineation of both sides of a question. Students have been taught to believe that objectivity is an attainable virtue that should be practiced by everyone involved with education. They have never been exposed to the argument that education is never neutral and that when we attempt to remain neutral we fail to expose the political inscriptions of so-called neutrality. In the name of neutrality, therefore, students are taught to support the status quo. It is a highly complex and difficult task, but critical teachers believe we should resist this tyranny of alleged neutrality.

Such resistance is accomplished not only by speaking in gender terms about race, class, sexual, and colonial oppression. The curriculum of critical pedagogy "names names" as it focuses its attention on corporate power wielders (e.g., Enron), agents of colonialism (e.g., Donald Rumsfeld and his actions in relation to Iraq), and the promoters of specific types of race, class, gender, sexual, cultural, and religious prejudice (e.g., Rev. Franklin Graham and Rev. Jerry Falwell in relation to Muslims and Islam; Charles Murray and Richard Herrnstein in relation to African Americans, Latinos, and the poor of all races; and Michael Savage in relation to gays and lesbians). While names are named and conscious oppressors are delineated, critical pedagogues also appreciate the fact that many aspects of race, class, gender, sexual, cultural, and religious prejudice are not intentional and often take place in the name of good intentions.

Without an understanding of these specific dynamics, teachers are too often unable—even with love in their hearts and the best intentions—to protect students from the radioactive fallout of hidden structures of racism, class bias, patriarchy, homophobia, colonialism, and religious prejudice. Students of critical pedagogy must understand that college teacher education both in liberal arts and sciences and schools of education has often ignored these issues, focusing instead on inculcating a body of "neutral" facts into teachers' heads, rearranging the physical layout of the classroom, the format of the curriculum, lesson planning, and behavioral objectives. Too often such matters served only, in Donaldo Macedo's (1994) words, "to stupidify" those

who took them seriously, as they pushed questions of how both school purpose and teacher/student identities are shaped vis-à-vis larger socio-political and cultural formations off the table.

In the context of these questions of power, oppression, and struggle, advocates of critical pedagogy understand, even as they document the insidious operations of racism, class elitism, patriarchy, heterosexism, colonialism, and religious intolerance, that such structures have holes with numerous tunnels for escape. Even when educational purposes are consciously oppressive, Clint Allison (1995) reminds us, purposes and outcomes are not the same thing. Even though they have operated as tools of dominant power, schools are places that often teach literacy—an essential skill in the process of empowerment. Many students use those portions of education that they find applicable to their lives, concurrently identifying and rejecting hegemonic attempts to win their consent to "dumbing-down" perspectives.

Of course, these are the students who are deemed to have bad attitudes, who may be labeled surly and unteachable, but they also may be the students who are sufficiently empowered to lead pro-democracy and anticolonial movements in Western societies. Thus, proponents of critical pedagogy recognize the possibility for resistance, even successful resistance, to the forces of the dominant power. Because patriarchal, white supremacist, class elitist, colonial, and homophobic oppression is not **deterministic**, because it is mediated by countless factors, the dominant power's intentions may mutate in the kaleidoscope of everyday school life. In this context, critical teachers and students can seize opportunities to expose the oppressive workings of power and offer democratic, pluralistic, more power-sharing alternatives in their place.

determinism
asserts that all events have a cause and that everything in the world is regulated by laws of causation. In this context, humans are deemed to have little ability to change the flow of events. Thus, particular conditions are thought to produce certain results and there is no way to preclude such outcomes.

Understanding Complexity

Critical pedagogy is attuned to the importance of complexity in constructing a rigorous and transformative education. Because of the importance of complexity, I often refer to my version of critical pedagogy as a critical complex pedagogy (Kincheloe, 2001a; Kincheloe, Bursztyn, and Steinberg, 2004). Many observers have come to the conclusion over the last several decades that the simplicity of Cartesian rationalism and mainstream forms of knowledge production does not meet the needs of educators

and scholars. The web of reality is composed of too many variables to be taken into account and controlled. The scientist Ilya Prigogine labels this multitude of variables "extraneous perturbations," meaning that one extraneous variable, for example, in an educational experiment can produce an expanding, exponential effect. So-called inconsequential entities can have a profound effect in a complex nonlinear universe. The shape of the physical and social world depends on the smallest part. The part, in a sense, is the whole, for via the action of any particular part, the whole in the form of transformative change may be seen. To exclude such considerations is to miss the nature of the interactions that constitute reality. The development of a counter-Cartesian reconceptualization of critical pedagogy does not mean that we simplistically reject all empirical science. It does mean, however, that we conceive of such scientific ways of seeing as one perspective on the complex web we refer to as reality.

This theme of complexity is central to any critical pedagogy that works to avoid reductionism. Critical pedagogues who take complexity seriously challenge reductionistic, bipolar, true-or-false epistemologies. As critical teachers come to recognize the complexity of the lived world with its maze of uncontrollable variables, irrationality, non-linearity, and unpredictable interaction of wholes and parts, they begin to also see the interpretative dimension of reality. We are bamboozled by a science that offers a monological, one-truth process of making sense of the world. Complex critical scholars and cultural workers maintain that we must possess and be able to deploy multiple methods of producing knowledge of the world. Such methods provide us diverse perspectives on similar events and alert us to various relationships between events. In this complex context we understand that even when we use diverse methods to produce multiple perspectives on the world, different observers will produce different interpretations of what they perceive. Given a variety of values, different ideologies, and different positions in the web of reality, different individuals will interpret what is happening differently. Charles Bingham (2003) argues that we must understand this complexity in order to appreciate the complications of gaining knowledge. Humans, Bingham maintains, are not isolated agents in their efforts to acquire knowledge—they must receive help from others to engage in learning.

Bingham's notion of the relationship between knower and known changes the way we approach knowledge, learning, teaching, and social action. Indeed, critical activity in this complex process is not something employed by solitary students operating on their own. Critical agents use language developed by others, live in specific contexts with particular ways of being and ways of thinking about thinking, have access to some forms of knowledge and not others, and live and operate in circumstances shaped by particular dominant ideological perspectives. In its effort to deal with previously neglected complexity, the mode of critical pedagogy offered here appreciates the need to understand these contextual factors and account for them. Complex critical analysts are not isolated individuals but people who understand the nature of their sociocultural context and their overt and their occluded relationships with others. Without such understandings of their own contextual embedding, individuals are not capable of understanding from where the prejudices and predispositions they bring to the act of meaning making originate. Any critical activity that attempts to deal with the complexity of the lived world must address these contextual dynamics.

As we look back from the perspective of the first decade of the twenty-first century to the innovative scholarly work on epistemology and research of the last several decades, one gains understanding: producing knowledge about the world is more complex than we originally thought. What we designate as facts is not as straightforward a process as it was presented to us. Critical pedagogues with an understanding of complexity know that what most people consider the natural social world is a conceptual landmine wired with assumptions and inherited meanings. Critical researchers have learned that what is unproblematically deemed "a fact" has been shaped by a community of inquirers. Such uncritical researchers accept, often unconsciously, a particular set of theoretical assumptions. Engaging in knowledge work without a deep understanding of the tacit rules of the game is not a manifestation of rigor. Indeed, such a lack of knowledge of complexity profoundly undermines the effort to understand the world around us (Fischer, 1998; Horn, 2003). Great scholars in diverse historical and cultural settings have admonished individuals not to take fixed viewpoints and concepts as reality (Varela, 1999).

Roymeico Carter (2003a) extends this concept into the world of the visual. The complexity of researching the visual domain is often squashed by the formal methods of Cartesian aesthetics. Carter reminds us that the intricate layers of visual meaning must be studied from numerous perspectives as well as diverse cultural and epistemological traditions (Rose and Kincheloe, 2003). But such diversity of perception lets the cat out of the bag; it relinquishes control of how we are to see the world. According to Ilya Prigogine, complexity demands that researchers give up the attempt to dominate and control the world. The social and physical worlds are so complex that they can only be understood like human beings themselves: not machine-like, unpredictable, dependent upon context, and influenced by minute fluctuations (Capra, 1996). Thus, critical complex scholars focus their attention on addressing the complexity of the lived world, in the process understanding that the knowledge they produce should not be viewed as a transhistorical (not influenced by its historical context) body of truth. In this framework, knowledge produced is provisional and "in process." Critical scholars and educators know that tensions will develop in social knowledge as the understandings and insights of individuals change and evolve (Blackler, 1995).

A researcher, for example, who returns to an ethnographic study only a few years after completing it may find profound differences in what is reported by subjects. The categories and coding that worked five years ago may no longer be relevant. The most important social, psychological, and educational problems that confront us are untidy and complicated. As we wade through the swamp of everyday life, ways of seeing that fail to provide multiple perspectives at macro, meso, and micro levels do not provide the insights needed in a critical pedagogy. It is one thing to find out that schools do not provide many poor students a path to social mobility. It is quite another to take this macro finding and combine it with the meso dynamics of the ways particular schools and school leaders conceptualize the relationship between schooling and class mobility. It is also important that these findings be viewed in a context informed by everyday classroom and out-of-classroom interactions between teachers and students and students and their peers. Obviously, different research strategies will be used to explore the differing questions emerging at the different levels. Once data from these diverse layers are combined,

we begin to discern an emerging picture of the multiple dynamics of the relationship between socioeconomic class and education. Only a multidimensional, complex picture such as this can help us formulate informed and just strategies to address such issues.

Avoiding Empire Building

Critical pedagogy is aware of and opposed to contemporary efforts to build a new American Empire around the world. In the present era, emerging forms of U.S. colonialism and imperialism move critical pedagogues to examine the ways American power operates under the cover of establishing democracies all over the world. Advocates of critical pedagogy argue that such neocolonial power must be exposed, so it can be opposed in the United States and around the world. The American Empire's subversion of democratically elected governments from Iran (Kincheloe, 2004), Chile, Nicaragua, to Venezuela—when its real purpose is to acquire geopolitical advantages for future military assaults, economic leverage in international markets, and access to natural resources—is justified in the name of freedom. Critical teachers need to view their work in the context of living and working in a nation state with the most powerful military industrial complex in history. It is a complex that has shamefully used the monstrous terrorist attacks of September 11 to advance an imperialist agenda fueled by corporate accumulation by means of force. Indeed, the war on terror is a cloaking device to hide broader, imperialistic political and economic goals.

David G. Smith (2004) argues that such imperial dynamics are supported by particular epistemological forms. The United States is an epistemological empire based on a notion of truth that undermines the forms of knowledge produced by those outside the good graces and benevolent authority of the empire. Thus, in the twenty-first century, critical teachers must develop sophisticated ways to address imperialist conquests (whether accomplished through direct military intervention or indirectly through the creation of client states) and the epistemological violence that helps discipline the world. Smith refers to this violence as a form of "information warfare" that spreads deliberate falsehoods about countries such as Iraq and Iran. U.S. corporate and governmental agents become more sophisticated in the use of such epistoweaponry with every day that passes.

In many ways, September 11 was a profound shock to millions of Americans who obtain their news and worldviews from the mainstream, corporately owned media and their understanding of American international relations from what is taught in most secondary schools and in many colleges and universities. Such individuals are heard frequently on call-in talk radio and TV shows expressing the belief that America is loved internationally because it is richer, more moral, and more magnanimous than other nations. In this mind-set, those who resist the United States hate our freedom for reasons never quite specified. These Americans, the primary victims of a right-wing corporate-government-produced miseducation (Kincheloe and Steinberg, 2004), have not been informed by their news sources of the societies that have been undermined by covert U.S. military operations and U.S. economic policies (Parenti, 2002). Many do not believe, for example, the description of the human effects of American sanctions on Iraq between the first and second Gulf Wars. Indeed, the hurtful activities of the American Empire are invisible to many of the empire's subjects in the United States itself.

The hostile relations that now exist between the West (the United States in particular) and the Islamic world demand that critical pedagogues be very careful in laying out the argument we are making about this new era of U.S. imperialism in the world. The activities of the American Empire have not been the only forces at work creating an Islamist extremism that violently defies the sacred teaching of the religion. But American imperial misdeeds have played an important role in the process. A new critical orientation toward knowledge production, scholarship, and teaching based on this and the other dimensions of critical pedagogy can help the United States redress some of its past and present policies toward the diverse Islamic world and other nations victimized by U.S. aggression. While these policies have been invisible to many Americans, they are visible to the rest of the world. And, unfortunately, many Americans reading this book will pay for such national policies over the next few years.

In my chapter on U.S. imperialism in Iran in *The Miseducation of the West: Constructing Islam* (2004), I explore the inability of American leaders to understand the impact of empire-building in the Persian Gulf on the psyches of those personally affected by it. Indeed, the American public was ignorant of covert U.S.

operations that overthrew the democratically elected government of Iran, so a totalitarian regime more sympathetic to the crass needs of the American Empire could be installed. The citizens of Iran and other peoples around the Muslim world, however, were acutely aware of this imperial action and the contempt for Muslims it implied. When this was combined with a plethora of other U.S. political, military, and economic initiatives in the region, their view of America was less than positive. In the second Gulf War, American leaders simply disregarded the views of nations around the world—the Muslim world, in particular—when opposition to the American invasion of Iraq was expressed. History was erased as Saddam Hussein was viewed in a psychological context as a madman. Times when the United States supported the madman were deleted from memory. The empire, thus, could do whatever it wanted, regardless of its impact on the Iraqi people or the perceptions of others (irrational others) around the world. Critical teachers struggle to change these imperial policies.

Glossary

Action research—a form of research designed for practitioners that allows teachers, for example, to research practices, schools, students, communities, curriculum, and so on, for the purpose of improving their professional work.

Agency—a person's ability to shape and control his or her own life by freeing the self from the oppression of power.

Determinism—asserts that all events have a cause and that everything in the world is regulated by laws of causation. In this context, humans are deemed to have little ability to change the flow of events. Thus, particular conditions are thought to produce certain results, and there is no way to preclude such outcomes.

Dialectical authority—involves studies that account for the importance of opposites and contradictions within all forms of knowledge and the relationship between these opposites. Knowledge is not complete in and of itself. It is produced in a larger process and can never be understood outside of its historical development and its relationship to other information.

Hyperrationalization—the application of reason alone to analyses of the world in lieu of emotion, affect, and concerns of worth and justice.

Ideology—the traditional definition involves systems of beliefs. In a critical theoretical context ideology involves meaning that supports a form of dominant power.

Technicalization—the focus on technique of how to do things rather than why to do things.

Zeitgeist—the German term for "spirit of the times."

The Foundations of Critical Pedagogy

With these basic characteristics of critical pedagogy in mind, it is important to explore the ideas that have shaped critical pedagogy. Such background will provide us with a deeper understanding of this complex topic. This understanding will provide us with tools that will help implement a pedagogy that promotes social justice, cultivates the intellect, and expands the horizons of human possibility. There is so much human beings can do and accomplish that is not being done in the first decade of the twenty-first century. I can think of few things being more exciting than being a part of the larger effort to go where human beings have never gone before. Critical pedagogy takes us on that journey.

Critical theory forms the foundation for critical pedagogy. The notion of critical pedagogy—the concern with transforming oppressive relations of power in a variety of domains that lead to human oppression—that we're working with finds its origins in critical theory and evolves as it embraces new critical discourses in new eras. In Chapter 2 we trace an evolving critical pedagogy that studies the ways how new times evoke new manifestations of power, new consequences, and new ways of understanding

and resisting them. Concurrently, this evolving critical pedagogy devises new social arrangements, new institutions, and new forms of selfhood.

The Roots of Critical Pedagogy: The Frankfurt School of Critical Theory

Some seventy years after its development in Frankfurt, Germany, critical theory retains its ability to disrupt and challenge the status quo. In the process, it elicits highly charged emotions of all types—fierce loyalty from its proponents, vehement hostility from its detractors. Such vibrantly polar reactions indicate at the very least that critical theory still matters. We can be against critical theory or for it, but, especially at the present historical juncture, we cannot be without it. Indeed, qualitative research that frames its purpose in the context of critical theoretical concerns still produces, in our view, undeniably dangerous knowledge, the kind of information and insight that upsets institutions and threatens to overturn sovereign regimes of truth.

Critical theory is a term that is often evoked and frequently misunderstood. It usually refers to the theoretical tradition developed by the Frankfurt School, a group of scholars connected to the Institute of Social Research at the University of Frankfurt. However, none of the Frankfurt school theorists ever claimed to have developed a unified approach to cultural criticism. In its beginnings, Max Horkheimer, Theodor Adorno, Herbert Marcuse, and Walter Benjamin initiated a conversation with the German tradition of philosophical and social thought, especially that of Marx, Kant, Hegel, and Weber. From the vantage point of these critical theorists, whose political sensibilities were influenced by the devastations of World War I, postwar Germany with its economic depression marked by inflation and unemployment, and the failed strikes and protests in Germany and Central Europe in this same period, the world was in urgent need of reinterpretation. From this perspective, they defied Marxist orthodoxy while deepening their belief that injustice and subjugation shape the lived world (Bottomore, 1984; Gibson, 1986; Held, 1980; Jay, 1973). Focusing their attention on the changing nature of capitalism, the early critical theorists analyzed the mutating forms of domination that accompanied this change (Agger, 1992; Gall, Gall, and Borg,

1999; Giroux, 1983, 1997; Kellner, 1989; Kincheloe, 2001a; Kincheloe and Pinar, 1991; McLaren, 1997).

Only a decade after the Frankfurt school was established, the Nazis controlled Germany. The danger posed to the exclusively Jewish membership of the Frankfurt School and its association with Marxism convinced Horkheimer, Adorno, and Marcuse to leave Germany. Eventually locating themselves in California, these critical theorists were shocked by American culture. Offended by the taken-for-granted empirical practices of American social science researchers, Horkheimer, Adorno, and Marcuse were challenged to respond to the positivistic social science establishment's belief that their research could describe and accurately measure any dimension of human behavior. Piqued by the contradictions between progressive American rhetoric of egalitarianism and the reality of racial and class discrimination, these theorists produced their major work while residing in the United States. In 1953, Horkheimer and Adorno returned to Germany and reestablished the Institute of Social Research. Significantly, Herbert Marcuse stayed in the United States, where he would find a new audience for his work in social theory. Much to his own surprise, Marcuse skyrocketed to fame as the philosopher of the student movements of the 1960s. Critical theory, especially the emotionally and sexually liberating work of Marcuse, provided the philosophical voice of the New Left. Emerging in the 1960s, the New Left was politically influenced by the anticolonial liberation movements breaking out in Africa, Latin America, and Asia. The group supported the Civil Rights Movement in the United States and opposed the Vietnam War and American imperialism abroad. Concerned with the politics of psychological and cultural revolution, the New Left preached a Marcusian sermon of political and personal emancipation from the conventions of dominant power (Gibson, 1986; Hinchey, 1998; Kincheloe and Steinberg, 1997; Surber, 1998; Wexler, 1991, 1996a).

Many of the New Left scholars who had come of age in the politically charged atmosphere of the 1960s focused their attention on critical theory. Frustrated by forms of domination emerging from a post-Enlightenment culture nurtured by capitalism, these scholars saw in critical theory a method of temporarily freeing academic work from these forms of power. Impressed by critical theory's dialectical concern with the social construction of

experience, they came to view their disciplines as manifestations of the discourses and power relations of the social and historical contexts that produced them. The "discourse of possibility" implicit within the constructed nature of social experience suggested to these scholars that a reconstruction of the social sciences could eventually lead to a more egalitarian and democratic social order. Critical pedagogy clearly reflects these dimensions of critical theory.

Critical theory is a difficult animal to describe because (a) there are many critical theories, not just one; (b) the critical tradition is always changing and evolving; and (c) critical theory attempts to avoid too much specificity, as there is room for disagreement among critical theorists. To lay out a set of fixed characteristics of the position is contrary to the desire of such theorists to avoid the production of blueprints of sociopolitical and epistemological beliefs. Because of these facts, what I am offering in this primer is one idiosyncratic "take" on the nature of critical theory in the first decade of the twenty-first century. Please note that this is merely my subjective analysis, and there are many brilliant critical theorists who will find many problems with these descriptions. In this context, I offer a description of an ever-evolving critical pedagogy, a critical theory that was critiqued and overhauled by the **postdiscourses** of the last quarter of the twentieth-century and has been further extended in the first years of the twenty-first century (Bauman, 1995; Carlson and Apple, 1998; Collins, 1995; Giroux, 1997; Kellner, 1995; Peters, Lankshear, and Olssen, 2003; Roman and Eyre, 1997; Steinberg and Kincheloe, 1998; Weil and Kincheloe, 2003).

In this context, critical theory questions the assumption that societies such as the United States, Canada, Australia, New Zealand, and the nations in the European Union, for example, are unproblematically democratic and free. During the twentieth century, especially after the early 1960s, individuals in these societies were acculturated to feel comfortable in relations of domination and subordination rather than equality and independence. Given the social and technological changes of the last half of the century that led to new forms of information production and access, critical theorists argued that questions of self-direction and democratic egalitarianism should be reassessed. In this context, critical researchers informed by the postdiscourses

postdiscourses

the theoretical ways of understanding that developed in the last third of the twentieth century that questioned the assumptions about the world put forth by modernist, scientific Western frameworks. They would include postmodernism, poststructuralism, postcolonialism, and postformalism.

(e.g., postmodernism, critical feminism, poststructuralism) came to understand that individuals' view of themselves and the world were even more influenced by social and historical forces than previously believed. Given the changing social and informational conditions of late twentieth-century and early twenty-first-century media-saturated Western culture, critical theorists have needed new ways of researching and analyzing the construction of individuals (Agger, 1992; Flossner and Otto, 1998; Leistyna, Woodrum, and Sherblom, 1996; Smith and Wexler, 1995; Sünker, 1998; Steinberg, 2001; Wesson and Weaver, 2001). The following points briefly delineate my interpretation of a critical theory in the twenty-first century.

In this context, it is important to note that a social theory is a map or a guide to the social sphere. A social theory should not determine how we see the world but should help us devise questions and strategies for exploring it. A critical social theory is concerned in particular with issues of power and justice and the ways that the economy, matters of race, class, and gender, ideologies, discourses, education, religion, and other social institutions, and cultural dynamics interact to construct a social system (Beck-Gernsheim, Butler, and Puigvert, 2003; Flecha, Gomez, and Puigvert, 2003). Critical theory—in the spirit of an evolving critical pedagogy—is always evolving, changing in light of both new theoretical insights and new problems and social circumstances.

The list of concepts making up our description of critical theory indicates a critical pedagogy informed by a variety of discourses emerging after the work of the Frankfurt School. Indeed, some of the theoretical discourses, while referring to themselves as critical, directly call into question some of the work of Horkheimer, Adorno, and Marcuse. Thus, diverse theoretical traditions have informed our understanding of critical pedagogy and have demanded understanding of diverse forms of oppression including class, race, gender, sexual, cultural, religious, colonial, and ability-related concerns. In this context, critical theorists become detectives of new theoretical insights, perpetually searching for new and interconnected ways of understanding power and oppression and the ways they shape everyday life and human experience.

Thus, critical pedagogy and the knowledge production it supports are always evolving, always encountering new ways to

irritate dominant forms of power, to provide more evocative and compelling insights. Operating in this way, an evolving critical pedagogy is always vulnerable to exclusion from the domain of approved modes of research. The forms of social change it supports always position it in some places as an outsider, an awkward detective always interested in uncovering social structures, discourses, ideologies, and epistemologies that prop up both the status quo and a variety of forms of privilege. In the epistemological domain, white, male, class elitist, heterosexist, imperial, and colonial privilege often operates by asserting the power to claim objectivity and neutrality. Indeed, as discussed in Chapter 1, the owners of such privilege often own the "franchise" on reason and rationality. Proponents of an evolving critical pedagogy possess a variety of tools to expose such oppressive power politics. Such proponents assert that critical theory is well served by drawing on numerous liberatory discourses and including diverse groups of marginalized peoples and their allies in the nonhierarchical aggregation of critical analysts (Bello, 2003; Clark, 2002; Humphries, 1997).

Obviously, an evolving critical pedagogy does not promiscuously choose theories to add to the bricolage of critical theories. It is highly suspicious of theories that fail to understand the malevolent workings of power, that fail to critique the blinders of Eurocentrism, that cultivate an elitism of insiders and outsiders ("we understand Foucault and you don't"), and that fail to discern a global system of inequity supported by diverse forms of hegemony and violence. It is uninterested in any theory—no matter how fashionable—that does not directly address the needs of victims of oppression and the suffering they must endure. The following is an elastic, ever-evolving set of concepts included in our evolving notion of critical pedagogy. With theoretical innovation and a shifting *Zeitgeist* they evolve. The points that are deemed most important in one time period pale in relation to different points in a new era.

I.   *Critical enlightenment.* In this context, critical theory analyzes competing power interests between groups and individuals within a society—identifying who gains and who loses in specific situations. Privileged groups, critical pedagogists argue, often have an interest in supporting the status quo to protect their advantages; the dynamics of such efforts often become a central focus of

critical research. Such studies of privilege often revolve around issues of race, class, gender, and sexuality (Allison, 1995; Carter, 1998; Howell, 1998; Rodriguez and Villaverde, 2000). To seek critical enlightenment is to uncover the winners and losers in particular social arrangements and the processes by which such power plays operate (Dei, Karumanchery, and Karumanchery-Luik, 2004; Fehr, 1993; Pruyn, 1994, 1999).

2. *Critical emancipation.* Those who seek emancipation attempt to gain the power to control their own lives in solidarity with a justice-oriented community. Here, critical research attempts to expose the forces that prevent individuals and groups from shaping the decisions that crucially affect their lives. In this way, greater degrees of autonomy and human agency can be achieved. In the first decade of the twenty-first century, we are cautious in our use of the term *emancipation* because, as many critics have pointed out, no one is ever completely emancipated from the sociopolitical context that has produced him or her. Concurrently, many have used the term emancipation to signal the freedom an abstract individual gains by gaining access to Western reason—that is, becoming reasonable. Our use of emancipation in an evolving critical pedagogy rejects any use of the term in this context. In addition, many have rightly questioned the arrogance that may accompany efforts to emancipate "others." These are important caveats and must be carefully taken into account by critical researchers. Thus, as critical inquirers who search for those forces that insidiously shape who we are, we respect those who reach different conclusions in their personal journeys. Nonetheless, critical theorists consider the effort to understand dominant power and its effects on individuals to be vitally important information needed in the effort to construct a vibrant and democratic society (Cannella, 1997; Knobel, 1999; Steinberg and Kincheloe, 1998).

3. *The rejection of economic determinism.* A caveat of a reconceptualized critical theory involves the insistence that the tradition does not accept the orthodox Marxist notion that "base" determines "superstructure"—meaning that economic factors dictate the nature of all other aspects of human existence. Critical theorists understand in the twenty-first century that there are multiple forms of power, including the aforementioned racial, gender, sexual axes of domination. In issuing this caveat, however, an

evolving critical theory in no way attempts to argue that economic factors are unimportant in the shaping of everyday life. Economic factors can never be separated from other axes of oppression (Aronowitz and DiFazio, 1994; Carlson, 1997; Gabbard, 1995; Gee, Hull, and Lankshear, 1996; Kincheloe, 1995, 1999; Kincheloe and Steinberg, 1999).

4. *The critique of instrumental or technical rationality.* A reconceptualized critical theory sees instrumental/technical rationality as one of the most oppressive features of contemporary society. Such a form of "hyperreason" involves an obsession with means in preference to ends. Critical theorists claim that instrumental/technical rationality is more interested in method and efficiency than in purpose. It delimits its questions to "how to" instead of "why should." In a research context, critical theorists claim that many rationalistic scholars become so obsessed with issues of technique, procedure, and correct method that they forget the humanistic purpose of the research act. Instrumental/technical rationality often separates fact from value in its obsession with "proper" method, losing in the process an understanding of the value choices always involved in the production of so-called facts (Giroux, 1997; Hinchey, 1998; Kincheloe, 1993; McLaren, 1998; Ritzer, 1993; Stallabrass, 1996; Weinstein, 1998).

5. *The impact of desire.* A reconceptualized critical theory appreciates **poststructuralist** psychoanalysis as an important resource in pursuing an emancipatory research project. In this context, critical researchers are empowered to dig more deeply into the complexity of the construction of the human psyche. Such a psychoanalysis helps critical researchers discern the unconscious processes that create resistance to progressive change and induce self-destructive behavior. A poststructural psychoanalysis, in its rejection of traditional psychoanalysis's tendency to view individuals as rational and autonomous beings, allows critical researchers new tools for rethinking the interplay among the various axes of power, identity, libido, rationality, and emotion. In this configuration the psychic is no longer separated from the sociopolitical realm; indeed, desire can be socially constructed and used by power wielders for destructive and oppressive outcomes. In contrast, critical theorists can help mobilize desire for progressive and emancipatory projects. Taking their lead from feminist theory, critical researchers are aware of the patriarchal

---

poststructuralism

a social theoretical position that questions the universalizing tendencies of structural approaches to scholarship—for example, Piaget's universal stages of child development or Maslow's hierarchy of needs. Thus, poststructuralism emphasizes the historical and cultural contextual contingencies of all human experience— child development for boys and girls in isolated tribal groups in Botswana may be different than with Swiss boys from the middle and upper-middle classes. As it uncovers these dynamics, poststructuralism fosters resistance to the power they exert in the regulation and discipline of individuals.

inscriptions within traditional psychoanalysis and work to avoid its **bourgeois**, ethnocentric, and **misogynist** practices. Freed from these blinders, poststructural psychoanalysis helps researchers gain a new sensitivity to the role of fantasy and imagination and the structures of sociocultural and psychological meaning they reference. Such explorations clearly illustrate what we mean by an evolving critical pedagogy (Block, 1995; Britzman and Pitt, 1996; Gresson, 2004; Kincheloe, Steinberg, and Villaverde, 1999; Pinar, 1998; Pinar, Reynolds, Slattery, and Taubman, 1995).

6. *The concept of immanence.* Critical theory is always concerned with what could be, what is immanent in various ways of thinking and perceiving. Thus, critical theory should always move beyond the contemplative realm to concrete social reform. In the spirit of Paulo Freire, our notion of an evolving critical theory possesses immanence as it imagines new ways to ease human suffering and produce psychological health (A. Freire, 2001; Slater, Fain, and Rossatto, 2002). Critical immanence helps us get beyond egocentrism and ethnocentrism and work to build new forms of relationship with diverse peoples. Leila Villaverde (2003) extends this point about immanence when she maintains that critical theory helps us "retain a vision of the not yet." In the work of the Frankfurt School critical theory and the hermeneutics of Hans-Georg Gadamer (1989) we find this concern with immanence. Gadamer argues that we must be more cautious in our efforts to determine "what is" because it holds such dramatic consequences for how we engage "what ought to be." In Gadamer's view the process of understanding involves interpreting meaning and applying the concepts gained to the historical moment that faces us. Thus, immanence involves the use of human wisdom in the process of bringing about a better and more just world, less suffering, and more individual fulfillment. With this notion in mind critical theorists, critique researchers, educators, and political leaders who operate to adapt individuals to the world as it is. In the context of immanence, critical theorists are profoundly concerned with who we are, how we got this way, and where do we go from here (Kincheloe and Weil, 2001; Weil and Kincheloe, 2003).

7. *A reconceptualized critical theory of power: hegemony.* Our conception of a reconceptualized critical theory is intensely concerned with the need to understand the various and complex ways that

power operates to dominate and shape consciousness. Power, critical theorists have learned, is an extremely ambiguous topic that demands detailed study and analysis. A consensus seems to be emerging among critical pedagogists that power is a basic constituent of human existence that works to shape both the oppressive and productive nature of the human tradition. Indeed, we are all empowered and we are all unempowered in that we all possess abilities and we are all limited in the attempt to use our abilities. The focus here is on critical theory's traditional concern with the oppressive aspects of power. An important aspect of critical pedagogy, however, focuses on the productive aspects of power—its ability to empower, to establish a critical democracy, to engage marginalized people in the rethinking of their sociopolitical role (Apple, 1996; Fiske, 1993; Macedo, 1994; Nicholson and Seidman, 1995). In the context of oppressive power and its ability to produce inequalities and human suffering, Antonio Gramsci's notion of hegemony is central to critical research. Gramsci understood that dominant power in the twentieth century was not always exercised simply by physical force but also through social psychological attempts to win people's consent to domination through cultural institutions such as the media, the schools, the family, and the church. Gramscian hegemony recognizes that the winning of popular consent is a very complex process and must be researched carefully on a case-by-case basis. Students and researchers of power, educators, sociologists, all of us are hegemonized as our field of knowledge and understanding is structured by a limited exposure to competing definitions of the sociopolitical world. The hegemonic field, with its bounded social and psychological horizons, garners consent to an inequitable power matrix—a set of social relations that are legitimated by their depiction as natural and inevitable. In this context, critical researchers note that hegemonic consent is never completely established, as it is always contested by various groups with different agendas (Grossberg, 1997; Lull, 1995; McLaren, Hammer, Reilly, and Sholle, 1995; West, 1993).

8. *A reconceptualized critical theory of power: ideology.* Critical theorists understand that the formation of hegemony cannot be separated from the production of ideology. If hegemony is the larger effort of the powerful to win the consent of their "subordinates," then ideological hegemony involves the cultural forms,

the meanings, the rituals, and the representations that produce consent to the status quo and individuals' particular places within it. Ideology vis-à-vis hegemony moves critical inquirers beyond explanations of domination that have used terms such as propaganda to describe the way media, political, educational, and other sociocultural productions coercively manipulate citizens to adopt oppressive meanings. A evolving critical theory endorses a much more subtle, ambiguous, and situationally specific form of domination that refuses the propaganda model's assumption that people are passive, easily manipulated victims. Researchers operating with an awareness of this hegemonic ideology understand that dominant ideological practices and discourses shape our vision of reality (Lemke, 1995, 1998). Thus, our notion of hegemonic ideology leads to a nuanced understanding of power's complicity in the constructions people make of the world and their role in it (Kincheloe, 1998, 2002). Such awareness corrects earlier delineations of ideology as a monolithic, unidirectional entity that was imposed on individuals by a secret cohort of ruling-class czars. Understanding domination in the context of concurrent struggles among different classes, racial and gender groups, critical students of ideology explore the ways such competition engages different visions, interests, and agendas in a variety of social locales. These venues—for example, film, TV, popular music, sports, and so on—were previously thought to operate outside the domain of ideological struggle (Brosio, 1994, 2000; Steinberg, 2000).

9. *A reconceptualized critical theory of power: linguistic/discursive power.* Critical theorists have come to understand that language is not a mirror of society. It is an unstable social practice whose meaning shifts, depending upon the context in which it is used. Contrary to previous understandings, critical pedagogists appreciate the fact that language is not a neutral and objective conduit of description of the "real world." Rather, from a critical perspective, linguistic descriptions are not simply about the world but serve to construct it. With these linguistic notions in mind, critical pedagogists begin to study the way language in the form of discourses serves as a form of regulation and domination. Discursive practices are defined as a set of tacit rules that regulate what can and cannot be said, who can speak with the blessings of authority and who must listen, whose social constructions are valid and whose

are erroneous and unimportant. In an educational context, for example, legitimated discourses of power insidiously tell educators what books may be read by students, what instructional methods may be utilized, and what belief systems and views of success may be taught. In all forms of research, discursive power validates particular research strategies, narrative formats, and modes of representation. In this context, power discourses undermine the multiple meanings of language, establishing one correct reading that implants a particular hegemonic/ideological message into the consciousness of the reader. For example, Bruce Springsteen's "Born in the U.S.A." is a patriotic song—end of discussion. This is a process often referred to as the attempt to impose discursive closure. Critical theorists interested in the construction of consciousness are very attentive to these power dynamics. Engaging and questioning the use value of particular theories of power is central to our notion of an evolving critical pedagogy (Blades, 1997; Gee, 1996; Morgan, 1996; McWilliam and Taylor, 1996).

10. *Focusing on the relationships among culture, power, and domination.* In the last decades of the twentieth century, culture took on a new importance in the critical effort to understand power and domination. Critical theorists have argued that culture has to be viewed as a domain of struggle where the production and transmission of knowledge is always a contested process (Kincheloe and Steinberg, 1997; Steinberg and Kincheloe, 1997). Dominant and subordinate cultures deploy differing systems of meaning based on the forms of knowledge produced in their cultural domain. Popular culture, with its TV, movies, video games, computers, music, dance, and other productions, plays an increasingly important role in critical research on power and domination. **Cultural studies**, of course, occupies an ever-expanding role in this context, as it examines not only popular culture but also the tacit rules that guide cultural production. Arguing that the development of mass media has changed the way the culture operates, cultural studies researchers maintain that cultural epistemologies in the first decade of the twenty-first century are different from those of only a few decades ago. New forms of culture and cultural domination are produced as the distinction between the real and the simulated is blurred. This blurring effect of hyperreality constructs a social vertigo characterized by a loss of touch with

cultural studies

an interdisciplinary, transdisciplinary, and sometimes counterdisciplinary field of study that functions within the dynamics of competing definitions of culture. Unlike traditional humanistic studies, cultural studies questions the equation of culture with high culture; instead, cultural studies asserts that numerous expressions of cultural production should be analyzed in relation to other cultural dynamics and social and historical structures. These expressions include but are not limited to popular culture.

traditional notions of time, community, self, and history. New structures of cultural space and time generated by bombarding electronic images from local, national, and international spaces shake our personal sense of place. This proliferation of signs and images functions as a mechanism of control in contemporary Western societies. The key to successful counter-hegemonic cultural research involves: (a) the ability to link the production of representations, images, and signs of hyperreality to power in the political economy; and (b) the capacity, once this linkage is exposed and described, to delineate the highly complex effects of the reception of these images and signs on individuals located at various race, class, gender, and sexual coordinates in the web of reality (Carter, 2003b; Cary, 2003; O'Riley, 2003; Rose and Kincheloe, 2003; Sanders-Bustle, 2003; Thomas, 1997; Wexler, 2000).

11. *The centrality of interpretation: Critical hermeneutics.* One of the most important aspects of a critical theory-informed education and scholarship involves the often-neglected domain of interpretation. The critical hermeneutic tradition (Grondin, 1994; Gross and Keith, 1997; Rosen, 1987; Vattimo, 1994) holds that in knowledge work there is only interpretation, no matter how vociferously many analysts may argue that the facts speak for themselves. The hermeneutic act of interpretation involves in its most elemental articulation making sense of what has been observed in a way that communicates understanding. Not only is all research merely an act of interpretation, but, hermeneutics contends, perception itself is an act of interpretation. Thus, the quest for understanding is a fundamental feature of human existence, as encounter with the unfamiliar always demands the attempt to make meaning, to make sense. The same, however, is also the case with the familiar. Indeed, as in the study of commonly known texts, we come to find that sometimes the familiar may be seen as the most strange.

Thus, it should not be surprising that even the so-called objective analyses are interpretations, not value-free descriptions (Denzin, 1994; Gallagher, 1992; Jardine, 1998; Mayers, 2001; Smith, 1999). Learning from the hermeneutic tradition and the postmodern critique, critical theorists have begun to reexamine textual claims to authority. No pristine interpretation exists—indeed, no methodology, social or educational theory,

or discursive form can claim a privileged position that enables the production of authoritative knowledge. Human beings must always speak/write about the world in terms of something else in the world, "in relation to …". As creatures of the world, we are oriented to it in a way that prevents us from grounding our theories and perspectives outside of it. The critical hermeneutics that informs critical theory and critical pedagogy moves more in the direction of a **normative hermeneutics** in that it raises questions about the purposes and procedures of interpretation. In its critical theory-driven context, the purpose of hermeneutical analysis is to develop a form of cultural criticism revealing power dynamics within social and cultural texts.

Scholars familiar with critical hermeneutics build bridges between reader and text, text and its producer, historical context and present, and one particular social circumstance and another. Accomplishing such interpretive tasks is difficult, and researchers situated in normative hermeneutics push ethnographers, historians, **semioticians**, literary critics, and content analysts to trace the bridge-building processes employed by successful interpretations of knowledge production and culture (Gallagher, 1992; Kellner, 1995; Kogler, 1996; Rapko, 1998). Grounded by this hermeneutical bridgely building, critical analysts in a hermeneutical circle (a process of analysis in which interpreters seek the historical and social dynamics that shape textual interpretation) engage in the back-and-forth of studying parts in relation to the whole and the whole in relation to parts. Deploying such a methodology, critical hermeneuts can produce profound insights that lead to transformative action (Coben, 1998; Gadamer, 1989; Goodson, 1997; Kincheloe and Berry, 2004; Mullen, 1999; Peters and Lankshear, 1994).

12. *The role of cultural pedagogy in critical theory.* Cultural production can often be thought of as a form of education, as it generates knowledge, shapes values, and constructs identity. From the perspective of a book on critical pedagogy, such a framing can help critical teachers and students make sense of the world of domination and oppression as they work to bring about a more just, democratic, and egalitarian society. In recent years this educational dynamic has been referred to as cultural pedagogy (Berry, 1998; Giroux, 1997; Kincheloe, 1995; McLaren, 1997; Pailliotet, 1998; Soto, 1998). Pedagogy is a useful term that has traditionally been

normative hermeneutics
the art and science of interpretation and explanation regarding standards of behavior and prescriptions of such.

semioticians
scholars who study the nature and the social influence of signs, symbols, and codes.

used to refer only to teaching and schooling. By using the term cultural pedagogy, critical pedagogists are specifically referring to the ways dominant cultural agents produce particular hegemonic ways of seeing. In our critical interpretive context, the notion of cultural pedagogy asserts that the new "educators" in the electronically wired contemporary era are those who possess the financial resources to use mass media. This is very important in the context of critical pedagogy, as teachers in the contemporary era must understand not only the education that takes place in the classroom but also that which takes place in popular culture. This corporate-dominated, media-based pedagogical process has worked so well that few citizens complain about it in the first decade of the twenty-first century. Such informational politics doesn't even make the evening news. Can we imagine another institution in contemporary society gaining the pedagogical power that corporations now assert over information and signification systems? What if the Church of Christ was sufficiently powerful to run pedagogical "commercials" every few minutes on TV and radio touting the necessity for everyone to accept that denomination's faith? Replayed scenes of Jews, Muslims, Hindus, Catholics, and Methodists being condemned to hell if they rejected the official pedagogy (the true doctrine) would greet North Americans and their children seven days a week. There is little doubt that many people would be outraged and would organize for political action. Western societies have to some degree capitulated to this corporate pedagogical threat to democracy, passively watching an elite gain greater control over the political system and political consciousness via a sophisticated cultural pedagogy. Critical theorists are intent on exposing the specifics of this process (Drummond, 1996; Molnar, 1996; Pfeil, 1995; Steinberg and Kincheloe, 1997; Kincheloe, 2002).

Important Figures in the Emergence of Critical Pedagogy

With the basic ideas of critical pedagogy in mind, it is important to understand the work of a few important figures in the tradition. The following scholars have played an important role in shaping the tradition before, during, and after the work of Adorno, Horkheimer, Marcuse, and Benjamin in establishing critical theory.

W. E. B. Du Bois (1868–1963)

W. E. B. Du Bois was not a critical theorist and was not influenced by the Frankfurt School. Indeed, a significant portion of his scholarly work was produced before the development of critical theory. Nevertheless, Du Bois is one of the earliest figures promoting many of the same ideas that animate both critical theory and critical pedagogy. On many topics his ideas are still profoundly relevant and instructive for those seeking to develop an evolving critical pedagogy and a racially sensitive critical pedagogy in the twenty-first century. For these reasons we include him as an indispensable figure in the pantheon of scholars contributing to critical scholarship and action. His history of the slave trade written while he was a doctoral student in the 1890s is still viewed as one of the smartest and most comprehensive studies of the topic. Indeed, his scholarship on a variety of topics will inform critical pedagogists for generations to come.

The extensive and prescient work of Du Bois on education alone places him in the position of forerunner of critical pedagogy. Understanding that schooling should ground itself on a transformative vision of the society, we want to construct rather than simply reinforce the social arrangements of the status quo. Du Bois argued that the all-black schools of his time should aim to develop the latent power of students. Such students will become, he argued, people of "power, of thought—who know whither civilization is tending and what it means" (Du Bois, 1973, p. 14). Thus empowered, such black students—no matter how dramatic their disempowerment—gain the ability to resist politically, socially, and economically by acting in solidarity with one another.

Influenced by Du Bois, the prominent African American scholar Cornel West (1993) would pick up on this theme nearly a century later as he maintained that educators must develop the power of discernment among oppressed students. A powerful analytic moment is produced, West concluded in the spirit of Du Bois, when minority students gain a deep grasp of their present condition in light of the past. Such a moment highlights the ability of productive power to mitigate the effects of oppressive social structures by subjugated individuals' capacity to make meaning, interpret, and produce knowledge. African Americans, Du Bois maintained, had been situated as the "other" by slavery.

In this position they had been stripped of their cultural consciousness. A worthy education would restore self-consciousness, self-realization, and self-respect. It would allow black people to see themselves through their own eyes instead of solely through the eyes of white people—as in traditional forms of education. Du Bois's education was, in the language of critical theory, an emancipatory pedagogy with insights for the education of African Americans and all peoples in the contemporary era.

A careful reading of Du Bois's work reveals numerous parallels with what would come to be called critical pedagogy. For decades, white scholars viewed Du Bois's *Souls of Black Folk*, for example, as little more than an interesting description of black culture for a white reading audience. A more informed analysis reveals that the author constructs an unprecedented and carefully argued treatise on the nature of consciousness, self-consciousness, power, freedom, and resistance to oppression. These are the bread and butter issues of critical pedagogy—and Du Bois addresses them in ways that still hold profound insights into their complexity and enactment within a complex world. He well understood the need to view events in larger and diverse contexts, as illustrated by his work connecting race to European colonialism and the world economic system. In this framework his book *The Suppression of the African Slave Trade* (1896) is a classic.

Long before the advent of critical multiculturalism and critical multicultural education (Kincheloe and Steinberg, 1997), Du Bois understood the inseparability of race and class. In the 1890s he asserted that ghettoization is not the creation of poor African Americans but of social, political, and economic forces operating far away from the scene of the crime. He pointed out the existence of structural and institutional racism seventy years before the concepts were understood in mainstream sociology. Recognizing the folly of **social Darwinist** arguments made in the nineteenth century that attempts to help the poor are counterproductive, Du Bois called for the "democratization of industry," a concept that would later be called economic democracy. Proponents of economic democracy contend that political democracy cannot exist until wealth is more equally distributed (Kincheloe, 1999). In a neosocial Darwinist era, Du Bois's "democratization of industry" is as important a concept today as it was in the 1890s.

---

social Darwinism

the social theory devised by Herbert Spencer in the late nineteenth century that applied Charles Darwin's theory of evolution to human development. Like plants and animals in the biological world, human beings compete for survival in a social world shaped by the survival of the fittest.

In his concept of "double consciousness," Du Bois argued that if subjugated peoples are to survive they must develop an understanding of those who attempt to dominate them. In this context they understand the mechanisms of oppression and the ways they are deployed in mundane, everyday situations for best effect. This double consciousness or second sight is the ability to see oneself through the perception of others. It involves the ability to see what mainstream society sees and to see as well from vantage points outside the mainstream. This Du Boisian concept is central to critical pedagogy. A pedagogy of second sight is grounded on the understanding that a critically educated person knows more than just the validated knowledge of the dominant culture—she understands a variety of perspectives about the issues she studies. Subjugated perspectives, of course, are given high priority in this critical context.

Du Bois was also far ahead of the curve in the study of whiteness and white privilege. Early in his career Du Bois wrote about white privilege, specifying it in relation to the public defer- ence granted to whites, their unimpeded admittance to all pub- lic functions, the tendency of police officers to be drawn from the ranks of white people, their lenient treatment in court, and their access to the best schools. Whites in the United States. drew what Du Bois labeled the unearned "wages of whiteness." Such benefits comforted them with the knowledge that no mat- ter how far they fell down the socioeconomic ladder, they were still white. No matter how alienating and exploitative their work lives might be, they were still not slaves. Around Du Bois's work the whiteness scholarship that emerged in the 1990s coalesced. Such work drew on Du Bois's insights to induce white people to understand their privilege and listen to the wisdom of those people that whiteness has often silenced. In the spirit of Du Bois, whiteness scholars asked whites to see themselves as the oppressed and have historically viewed them in order to gain a new frame of reference on power and oppression in the society (Roediger, 1991; Kincheloe, Steinberg, Rodriguez, and Chennault, 1998; Rodriguez and Villaverde, 2000).

Du Bois also anticipated the work of poststructural theorists such as Michel Foucault in the area of genealogy and subjugated forms of knowledge—both of which are central concerns of criti- cal pedagogy. To understand ourselves as black people, Du Bois wrote in 1946, we must understand African history and social development. African forms of knowledge, he argued, constitute one of the most sophisticated worldviews the planet has witnessed. Foucault's concept of genealogy follows Du Bois's line, maintaining that excluded contents and meanings emerge in a state of insurrection against dominant forms of knowledge. In this context genealogy traces the formation of human consciousness (subjectivity). As Du Bois delineated in relation to African American consciousness, Foucault's genealogy helps us see ourselves at various points in the web of reality, ever confined by our placement but emancipated by our appreciation of our predicament.

Thus, empowered by our knowledge, we begin to understand and disengage ourselves from the power narratives that have laid the basis for the dominant way of seeing. In the context of subjugated forms of knowledge—forms that have been erased by dominant culture as primitive and/or invalidated by science—Du Bois viewed the African and African American past as a storehouse of insight for individuals struggling for equality. The methods used by our black ancestors, Du Bois posited, to fight slavery and oppression can be put to use in present struggles against racial tyranny. The blueprints for the black future, he theorized, must be built on a base of our problems, dreams, and frustrations: they will not appear out of thin air or be based exclusively on the experience of the other. In the context of subjugated knowledge and genealogy, Du Bois understood many decades before white analysts that the black past holds out great kinetic insurgent energy because it served the political function of destabilizing the existing order by revealing its social construction and its horrors.

In a celebration of subjugated educational knowledge, Du Bois wrote about traditional African education. In West Africa, he contended, education began very early as children accompanied their parents in their daily tasks. Early on children learned how to sow, reap, and hunt; young children learned the wisdom and folklore of the tribe; they learned the geography of the region. At the onset of puberty boys and girls learned about sex and emerged from this period with a graduation celebration that allowed them to sit on the tribal council with their elders. West African education, Du Bois concluded, was completely integrated with everyday life. No education existed in this context that was not concurrently usable for earning a living and for living a good life. In the

spirit of the critical celebration of subjugated knowledge, Du Bois argued that American education could learn lessons from Africa (McSwine, 1998). Indeed, Africans and African Americans in their genius had a message for the world, he proclaimed.

Du Bois's paradigm-busting body of work has been left out of the critical canon far too long. The critical pedagogy that I promote here embraces Du Bois as one of the most important architects of critical pedagogy in general and in relation to race and racism in particular. He created an alternate paradigm for sociology and history that was suppressed until after his death. He even anticipated the critique of positivism—delineated in Chapter I—in the early decades of the twentieth century. Contrary to the work of eminent sociologists and historians of the time, Du Bois wrote, human experience is not machine-like and scholarship cannot be disinterested and neutral, for it is always informed by particular, albeit hidden, values. He even anticipated my "innovative" work in multimethod research (Kincheloe, 2001; Kincheloe and Berry, 2004). Indeed, what many contemporary scholars have called "**bricolage**," Du Bois employed in 1899 in his compelling work, *The Philadelphia Negro*. In this study, Du Bois employed research strategies as varied as historiography, survey research, ethnography, urban mapping, urban ecology, geography, criminology, and demography.

Du Bois was never afraid to engage in research for the purpose of furthering social action—a central dimension of knowledge work in critical pedagogy. Scoffing at mainstream scholars' claims of disinterestedness in their work, Du Bois set the standard for emancipatory forms of research long before the term was used by the Frankfurt School. Not surprisingly, Du Bois's work was suppressed for decades and considered by many as a form of dangerous knowledge. No critical pedagogy can be complete or free itself from charges of being a white discourse without the towering presence of Du Bois. His work serves as a foundation for the work of critical pedagogy in the twenty-first century (Du Bois, 1973; Kincheloe and Steinberg, 1997; McSwine, 1998; Monteiro, 1995; Yale-New Haven Teachers Institute, 1993).

---

bricolage

French term for the work of a handyman/handywoman who uses numerous available tools to complete a task. Norman Denzin and Yvonna Lincoln have recently used the term to describe multimethodological forms of research.

Antonio Gramsci (1891–1937)

Antonio Gramsci was a political activist in Italy who worked for left-wing causes and worker movements in the second and third decades of the twentieth century. Despite his election to the Italian Parliament, Gramsci was arrested by the new fascist government in Italy and sentenced to twenty years in prison. He died in prison in 1937 before finishing his time. During his decade in prison, Gramsci wrote profusely, producing what came to be known as his prison notebooks. In these writings Gramsci provided an in-depth study of Italian fascism and strategies for defeating it. These are very important ideas in the twenty-first century as we see the emergence of fascist-like movements in the United States and around the industrialized world. The notebooks were not published in Italy until the late 1940s and not translated into English until the late 1950s. Thus, Gramsci's influence in North America was not experienced until well into the 1960s. The most famous notion emerging from the notebooks involved Gramsci's concept of hegemony. As discussed previously in the delineation of critical theoretical concepts, hegemony is a central concept of critical pedagogy in its effort to understand power. Hegemony, Gramsci wrote from prison, involves the process used by dominant power wielders to maintain power. The key dimension of this process is the manipulation of public opinion to gain consensus. When hegemony works best the public begins to look at dominant ways of seeing the world as simply common sense.

In the United States, Ronald Reagan in the 1980s and George W. Bush in the first decade of the twenty-first century have used the concept of hegemony to win consent for their right-wing policies. In both cases, religion was employed to gain the allegiance of individuals whose economic interests were not served by free market policies and the dismantling of access to education and the public space. We are Christians just like you, Reagan and Bush proclaimed, and we are here to protect you from the godless forces in our country (feminists, homosexuals, dangerous minority groups, intellectuals) that are attempting to turn America away from its traditional values. In this context, Reagan, Bush, Dan Quayle, William Bennett, Lynn Cheney, and other right-wing Americans focused on the importance of the cultural domain in building their power base. Religion was just one element of the strategy, as these politicos focused attention on the political and moral dynamics of TV and movies. Gramsci understood these strategies as they played out in fascist Italy

in the 1920s and 1930s. Marx and Lenin had contended that power is maintained via control of the state and the means of production (the economy). In his theory of hegemony Gramsci argued that in modern industrial societies, it was also necessary to control culture.

Culture is controlled not by way of coercive force but through the winning of consent. Many white fundamentalist Christians gave their consent to Reagan and Bush with the promise of particular psychic benefits. With George W. Bush in power we can remain confident, many people contended, that white, heterosexual Christians will maintain control of the nation. "With Bush we won't have gay marriage, affirmative action, feminism, or anti-Christians taking prayer out of our schools. We'll have curricula in schools that respect our national heritage and allow criticism of it. Our history, culture, language, and religion won't be diluted by multicultural information and other forms of revisionism." This elevation of the importance of culture, Gramsci argued, also increased the need for intellectuals in modern societies. Organic intellectuals, Gramsci wrote, are individuals who resist hegemony and help bring their fellow citizens a sense of historical consciousness of themselves and the society. These organic intellectuals were to be distinguished from traditional intellectuals, Gramsci concluded, whose charge is to maintain existing power relations, to create and deliver sanitized information that supports the existing hegemonic order.

One can quickly discern how important Gramsci's work is for the evolution of critical theory and especially for critical pedagogy. Of course, the role of the critical pedagogue is in part a reflection of Gramsci's characterization of the organic intellectual. By the late 1960s and 1970s, Gramsci's work was exerting a profound influence on those contributing to the critical traditions. His concepts of hegemony and organic intellectuals in particular played a central role in the development of cultural studies at the Centre for Contemporary Studies at the University of Birmingham in England. Much of the work produced at the center on the impact of popular culture in the hegemonic struggle was directly influenced by Gramsci. This work is very important to the development of critical pedagogy (Browning, 2002; Coben, 1998; Forgacs, 1988; "Gramsci Archives," 2003; Spencer, 2003).

Lev Vygotsky (1896–1934)

Vygotsky is a central figure in the development of a critical psychology, a critical learning theory that can be employed in a critical pedagogy. Born to a middle-class Jewish family in Orsha, Belorussia, Vygotsky contracted tuberculosis from his mother. His life was cut short by the disease; he died at the age of thirty-eight. Always upset with the decontextualized individualistic focus of mainstream psychology, Vygotsky called for a sociocultural psychological approach that accounted for the way individual cognition is socially and culturally mediated. By social and cultural mediation, Vygotsky meant that individual behavior cannot be removed from the context in which it takes place. Thus, psychology should always be studied in a cultural-historical context, he maintained. In this psychology scholars understand that there is a close connection between the social context in which individuals live and their psychological processes. Thus, when psychometricians administer IQ tests, they are not merely measuring individual cognitive ability but also the cultural relationship between the social context of the learner and the social context in which the test was developed. Cultural disjunctions often will be missed by the test administrators and mistakenly interpreted as a lack of cognitive ability on the part of the test-taker.

Thus, for Vygotsky the rigorous study of social context was a key dimension of his psychology. Without an understanding of the relationship between social context and cognitive behavior, psychologists were bound to make profound mistakes in studying mental processes. It was in this context that his well-known concept of the zone of proximal development (ZPD) emerges. In a sense, the ZPD represents the social context in which learning takes place. This social context shapes the range of potential each student has for learning. With the aid of the ZPD, critical teachers can better understand why some students might do well in a class and others do poorly. Instead of capitulating to the cognitive nihilism of a psychological theory that posits such ability levels are biological and hereditary in nature and thus unchangeable, the notion of the ZPD assures us that a large percentage of academic difficulties have little to do with innate cognitive ability. Instead, one's cultural exposure becomes profoundly important. Does the student's out-of-school life put her in contact with people who read? Does she interact regularly with individuals who value the

role of academic learning in one's life? Does she have access to people who can encourage and answer her questions about academic matters? Does she have access to resources that she can use to help her explore forms of academic knowledge? The answers to such questions help us understand the nature of particular students' ZPD.

So, in the most elementary dimension of Vygotsky's work, critical teachers learn that educators must understand the social, cultural, political, ideological, and economic forces that affect cognitive development. Appreciating this complex process, individuals can begin to see the ways their consciousnesses have been constructed, their relationship to schooling produced. Thus, understanding this dimension of Vygotsky's work, critical teachers can encourage students to see themselves and how they became themselves from the perspective of other people. In this context we all gain the benefit of self-knowledge and thus the ability to change ourselves in say, emancipatory ways—ways that empower us to resist the oppressive effects of dominant power. Here we become aware of the ways that self is constructed via relationship to others. With this knowledge we can begin to reconstruct our own ZPDs so as to become more than we are right now. This is a central dimension of critical pedagogy.

Because of his heavy emphasis on the social dimension of consciousness and learning, Vygotsky parted company with Piaget. In this context, Vygotsky was critical of Piaget's testing of the problem-solving ability of individual students working alone. Vygotsky contended that the ability a student developed working with an adult in forming concepts would be a much better barometer for revealing the present state of her intellectual abilities. Because individual ability always emerges from modes of collective living, psychological measures that neglect this social dimension are dangerous. Another way Vygotsky deviated from Piaget involved his perspective on cognitive developmentalism. For Vygotsky, developmentalism was more a research methodological concept that merely applied to the systematic evolution of cognitive functions. Vygotskian developmentalism reflected his belief that psychological or any other phenomena could only be studied and understood via a study of its origin and its history. Piaget's concept of development as the systematic movement from one discrete cognitive stage to another was dismissed by the great Soviet psychologist. Vygotsky saw cognitive development as anything but systematic, as individuals depending on their ZPDs and social encounters experienced uneven cognitive growth characterized by potholes in the road, setbacks, drastic changes, and unexpected epiphanies.

Another key aspect of Vygotsky's psychological work involves his emphasis on the importance of artifacts, especially artifacts external to the individual, in cognitive activity. In this context, Vygotsky extended the idea that humans use tools to interact with nature and to transform themselves. Thus, what and how we learn is always dependent on the artifacts or tools available. And which tools are available to us is contingent on our social context. Thus, he argued, it is especially through our tools that cognition is socially mediated. In cognitive activity, Vygotsky noted, the most important tools tend to be sign systems—for example, language, numbers, writing, ideographs, and so on. When humans learn and internalize such sign systems, cognitive and behavioral change is facilitated. A key aspect of a modern ZPD involves an individual's access to such sign systems and to individuals who adeptly model their usage.

Thus, central to Vygotsky's psychology is the use of language in the development of thinking. It is not surprising that one of his most important books was entitled, *Thought and Language.* In this context, he maintained that higher mental functions are always connected to the mediation of language. Through linguistic mediation, individuals are able to sophisticate their self-directed thought processes. To understand Vygotsky's critical psychology, one must appreciate his efforts to study the development of language in relation to thought. Thus, because of human beings' ability to use tools such as language to change their social context and themselves, they are not simply at the mercy of social and historical processes. Through the mediation of such tools, humans gain agency (Cole and Scribner, 1978; Cole and Wertsch, 2003; John-Steiner and Souberman, 1978; Kozulin, 1997; Nicholl, 1998; Samaras, 2002; Subbotsky, 2003; Vygotsky, 1978, 1997; Wertsch, 1991).

Paulo Freire (1921–1997)

With Freire, the notion of critical pedagogy as we understand it today emerges. Born in Recife, Brazil, in 1921 Freire

learned about poverty and oppression through the lives of the impoverished peasants around whom he lived. Such experiences helped construct a devotion to work that would improve the lives of these marginalized people. Beginning his educational work in Recife, Freire became the most well-known educator in the world by the 1970s. Peter McLaren (2000) has called Freire the "inaugural philosopher of critical pedagogy" (p. 1). Indeed, all work in critical pedagogy after him has to reference his work. His work with the Brazilian poor was viewed as dangerous and subversive by wealthy landowners and the Brazilian military. When the military overthrew the reform government of the country in April of 1964, progressive activities were shut down and Freire was jailed for his insurgent teaching. After serving a seventy-day jail term, Freire was deported. He continued his pedagogical work in Chile and later, under the umbrella of the World Council of Churches, throughout the world.

Not only have scholars in education employed Freire's work, but individuals working in literary theory, cultural studies, composition, philosophy, research methods, political science, theology, sociology, and other disciplines have used it as well. In this context, Freire reconstructed what it means to be an educator, as he upped the ante of what professional educators need to know and do. After Freire a progressive educator cannot be viewed as a technician, a functionary carrying out the instructions of others. Educators in the Freirean sense are learned scholars, community researchers, moral agents, philosophers, cultural workers, and political insurgents. As discussed in Chapter 1, Freire taught us that education is always political and teachers are unavoidably political operatives. Teaching is a political act—there's no way around it. Freire argued that teachers should embrace this dimension of their work and position social, cultural, economic, political, and philosophical critiques of dominant power at the heart of the curriculum. His notion of critical praxis characterized as informed action demanded curricular and instructional strategies that produced not only better learning climates but a better society as well.

Freire used a variety of strategies to produce this ambitious undertaking. In order to help students develop wider conceptual lenses to view their lives and social situation, Freire developed what he called codifications—pictures and photographs as part of a research process directed at the students' social, cultural, political, and economic environment. The pictures in this codification process depicted problems and contradictions in the lived worlds of students. Freire induced the students to step back from these pictures, to think about what they told them about their lives. What are the unseen forces and structures that are at work in these images, covertly shaping what is going on in the areas they depict? In this context students began to see their lives and the hardships they suffered in a new way. They began to understand that the way things presently operated was not the only option available. The possibility for positive change embedded in this understanding is the key to Freire's educational success. Students were motivated to gain literacy in order to take part in changing both their own lives and the society. The process of learning was inseparable from individual empowerment and social change. They could not achieve the goals they sought without knowing how to read and write. Because the dominant classes did not want students from the peasant class to succeed with their academic studies, Freire's students knew that they had to excel in their studies in order to overcome the oppressors.

Such experiences helped Freire understand in profoundly concrete terms the ways that schooling was often used by dominant interests to validate their own privilege while certifying the inferiority of students marginalized by social and economic factors. Understanding schools as impediments for the education of the poor, Freire sought numerous ways for students to intervene in this dehumanizing process. Freire referred to this process of intervention as liberatory action. Indeed, liberation in the Freirean articulation requires more than a shift of consciousness or an inward change. Instead, he argued, liberation takes place in the action of human beings operating in the world to overcome oppression. There is nothing easy about this process, he warned his readers. Liberation is akin to a painful childbirth that never completely ends, as oppression continuously mutates and morphs into unprecedented forms in new epochs. Thus, liberation is not merely a psychological change where an individual comes to feel better about herself. Freirean liberation is a social dynamic that involves working with and engaging other people in a power-conscious process.

Social change in the context of liberation and emancipation, according to Freire, is possible—even in right-wing times. Since

the world has been constructed by human beings, then it can reconstructed by human beings. Nothing human made is intractable, and because this is so, then hope exists. History can be made by individual human beings with radical love in their hearts and a vision of what could be. Human beings can become so much more than they are now, Freire always maintained, in the spirit of this critical hope. In many ways Freire is critical pedagogy's prophet of hope. Oppression, he understood, always reduces the oppressed understanding of historical time to a hopeless present. We are all oppressed from time to time by this hopeless presentism that tells us time and again: "things will never change." Throughout history these hopeless moments have been followed by radical changes. Such a "long view" is, of course, hard to discern in the black hole of despair. Freire's historical hope was paralleled by a pedagogical hope shared between students and teachers. In this domain of hope, Freire brought the belief to his students that in the framework of his historical hope we can learn together in the here and now. As he put it, students and teachers

> … can be curiously impatient together, produce something together, and resist together the obstacles that prevent the flowering of our joy. … Hope is a natural, possible, and necessary impetus in the context of our unfinishedness. Hope is an indispensable seasoning in our human, historical experience. Without its, instead of history we would have pure determinism. (1998, p. 69)

Undoubtedly, one of the most important dimensions of Freire's pedagogy involved the cultivation of a critical consciousness. Liberation and critical hope cannot be attained, he contended, until students and teachers address the nature of a naïve consciousness and the maneuvers involved in moving from a naïve to a critical consciousness. To make this complex move, Freire posited, individuals need to understand reality as a process rather than a "static entity." In this process-oriented mode teachers and students begin to understand historically how what is came to be. In this frame teachers and students can begin to imagine ways that release the future from the dictates of the past. They develop a consciousness that imagines a future that refuses to be "normalized and well-behaved." For the naïve thinker, education involves molding oneself and others to this normalized past. For the critically conscious thinker, education involves engaging in the continuous improvement and transformation of self and reality.

Again, this is no easy task. The oppressed, Freire frequently reminds his readers, have many times been so inundated by the ideologies of their oppressors that they have come to see the world and themselves through the oppressor's eyes. "I'm just a peasant, or a hillbilly, or a black kid from the ghetto, or a woman, or a man from the Third World, or a student with a low IQ; I have no business in higher education." Exposure to oppression often opens the eyes of the oppressed to its nature, but it can also, Freire cautioned, distort one's self-perceptions and interpersonal interactions. In such a context, critical consciousness is elusive because the oppressed are blinded to the myths of dominant power—the ones that oppress them and keep them "in their place." Such myths—for example, African Americans and other nonwhite peoples are not as intelligent as individuals from European backgrounds—must be confronted and exposed for what they are—vicious lies. Such confrontation and the plethora of insights that emerge in the process constitute what Freire labels "conscientization"—the act of coming to critical consciousness. In this movement from naïveté to critical pedagogy individuals grasp the social, political, economic, and cultural contradictions that subvert learning. Teachers and students with a critical consciousness conceptually pull back from their lived reality so as to gain a new vantage point on who they are and how they came to be this way. With these insights in mind, they return to the complex processes of living critically and engaging the world in the ways such a consciousness requires.

Thinking about critical consciousness, Freire talked about the inseparability of learning and being (ontology). Learning from Freire's perspective is grounded in the learners' own being, their interaction with the world, their concerns, and their visions of what they can become. In this ontological context Freire made some important points. All teachers, of course, should honor the being and the experiences of the oppressed—but they should never take them simply as they are.

How have ideology and other forms of power shaped the identity and experiences of the oppressed? Identity is always in process; it is never finalized, and as such it should not be treated as something beyond the possibility of change. Here Freire makes a pedagogical argument that has often been missed by many of his followers. Understanding the student's being and experiences

opens up the possibility for the teacher to initiate dialogues designed to synthesize his or her systematized knowing with the minimally systematized knowing of the learner.

Thus, Freire argues that the teacher presents the student with knowledge that may change the learner's identity. Freire here emphasizes the directive status of the teacher. Thus, he contends that the authority of the teacher is based on the knowledge and insight she brings to class. Freirean authority exists not simply because she is the teacher but because of what she has to offer the students. There is a vast difference between this type of authority that respects the being and experiences of students and authoritarianism. Authoritarianism views student subjectivity as irrelevant, as it attempts to make deposits of information in student mind banks. What the information means to them and how they might use it are irrelevant in authoritarian pedagogy. The student's role is to demonstrate that she learned the information and can give it back to the teacher in the same form it was provided to her. The ontological dimension of the student's being is not applicable in banking pedagogy.

In this pedagogical context, Freire injects his concept of literacy. The ability to use the printed word is essential to Freire's effort to reshape the world. As students become literate they are empowered to change themselves and to take action in the world. In this empowered literate state, learners employ generative themes (discussed in Chapter I) around which they can organize insurgent action. As they read the word and the world, students read their reality and write their lives. Such reading by itself, Freire warned, is of little use if not accompanied by transformative action for justice and equality. His ideas on literacy struck a positive nerve with many people, as in the first decade of the twenty-first century, one can find Freirean literacy programs around the world. Many people were fascinated by the way Freire positioned literacy as a way of life where one used reading and writing skills as tools to care for other people. This critical notion of literacy as a way of life and the larger concept of education as a political act must not be lost in efforts to implement Freire's work. Ever since his initial work appeared, there has existed a tendency for teachers to tame Freirean pedagogy in ways that move to two ends of a critical pedagogy curriculum (Freire, 1970, 1972, 1978, 1985).

On one end some teachers attempt to depoliticize his work in ways that make it simply a amalgam of student-directed classroom projects. On the other end of the continuum some teachers have emphasized the political dimensions but ignored the rigorous scholarly work that he proposed. These latter efforts have resulted in a social activism devoid of analytic and theoretical sophistication. Academic work that cultivates the intellect and demands sophisticated analysis is deemed irrelevant in these antiintellectual articulations of Freire's ideas. With these problems in mind the struggle to implement a Freirean critical pedagogy should never seek some form of "purity" of Freirean intent. Indeed, Paulo insisted that we critique him and improve upon his ideas. Living up to many of his pedagogical principles without sanctifying and canonizing him and his work is a conceptual tightrope that those of us who admired him must always walk. The walk is always worth it. Few have embodied the impassioned spirit as intensely as Freire did in his pedagogy (Aronowitz and Giroux, 1991; Giroux, 1988, 1997; McLaren, 2000; Peters, Lankshear, and Olssen, 2003; Mayo, 2000; Roberts, 2003; Slater, Fain, and Rossatto, 2002; Steiner, Krank, McLaren, and Bahruth, 2000).

Stanley Aronowitz

From union organizer and adult educator to a professor in college and university classrooms, Stanley Aronowitz has worked as a critical educator during the last forty years. As a union and community organizer, Aronowitz operated under the assumption that "organizing" was mainly a critical educational activity. Always concerned with raising suspicions with his students about the value of mainstream forms of intellectual labor, Aronowitz has seen his main pedagogical function as providing a good reading list to his students. In his writing, organizing, and teaching, he has remained dedicated to delineating the practical uses of theory. Theory in Aronowitz's articulation is nothing arcane or esoteric but a very straightforward activity—the attempt to provide coherence to a system of concepts and ideas while introducing students to the pleasures and benefits of philosophy, history, and social theory. In this process, he argues, students develop rigorous habits associated with learning.

It is revealing, Aronowitz argues, that this type of intellectual activity, this critique, has acquired a bad name in the United

States and in Western democratic capitalist societies. Such transformative intellectual work is being replaced by an instrumentalist
orientation to politics and social issues. Many social activists
have become increasingly impatient with speculative reason. No
doubt these groups may attempt to mobilize their constituents
to protest and resist policies established by dominant power blocs
and advance proposals to solve current problems caused by the
state and corporate leaders and visited upon communities and
workplaces. But most rarely engage in reflective thought about the
various lifeworlds they inhabit or about their own social practice.
As a result the often heroic and self-sacrificing work of political
organizers in various sectors tends to follow what C. Wright Mills
once called the "main drift" in which public activity is severely
circumscribed and forced into channels that Michael Harrington
once described, approvingly, as "the left wing of the possible."

In this context, Aronowitz describes his critical pedagogy as
necessarily utopian because "I urge my students to place themselves in the right-wing of the impossible." It is right wing, he says,
because he believes that knowledge should have a practical intent,
that is, directed to changing the conditions of everyday life and
addressing the problem of power even if its uses are deferred to an
indefinite future. In this work, Aronowitz found a kindred spirit
in Paulo Freire—whom he knew and worked with on a personal
basis. In his writings Aronowitz insists that Freire's "pedagogy"
was not primarily a "method" of teaching but a radical democratic
philosophy of education. It was radical because it sought to enable
the excluded, not only in economic terms but also in political and
social terms, to take control over their own lives.

Freire, Aronowitz maintains, elaborated on Marx's reminder
that representative government is heteronomous and that classes/
social movements form when people refuse to be represented
by others and insist on their autonomy and their sovereignty.
Influenced by Freire's educational philosophy, Aronowitz reminds
his readers and students that Freire's critical pedagogy is deeply
shaped by Marxism, by phenomenology, and by psychoanalytic
theory. Freire constantly reminded the multitude of his acolytes
and admirers, Aronowitz points out, that education was an activity
that entailed, among other things, the critical appropriation of the
best social thought. Such entailment connotes a necessary dimension that, sadly, has been occluded as his ideas have migrated

from revolutionary situations to the corroded environments of the leading Western countries.

Exercising his profound insight about the development and use of critical pedagogy, Aronowitz insists that in the twenty-first century we live in a period when the need for new concepts has never been more urgent. The rush of contemporary events has challenged the old formulae of socialist revolution, the primacy of the industrial working class, and the certainties of Marxism and anarchism. At the same time, he continues, we are witnesses to a torrent of right-wing **pronunciamentos of "endings"** combined with smug statements from our state intellectuals that this America is "the best of all possible worlds." In this new world of the twenty-first century, Aronowitz issues a challenge to those of us who believe that world can and should be transformed. We have an obligation, he tells us, to revisit the doctrinal verities inherited from the past and to abandon those ideas that no longer advance an understanding of the present and future. Thus, the significance of critical pedagogy for Aronowitz resides, in the first place, in its blunt declaration that education is a political practice. This political practice involves, among other things, the act of assisting the oppressed and exploited from every social stratum to articulate—linguistically as well as politically—their own demands and create their own forms of social and political organization, and of course, to render their own critique of their lifeworlds and of the larger social forces shaping them (Aronowitz, 1973, 1981, 1988, 1992, 1993, 2001; Aronowitz and DiFazio, 1994).

---

pronunciamentos of "endings"

referring to the notion that history, ideology, and political evolution have ended because liberal democratic capitalists states have produced a social order that can never be improved.

Henry Giroux

It is with Giroux's work in the late 1970s and 1980s that the concept of critical pedagogy as we know it today takes shape. Bringing together Freire's work, the cultural capital of Pierre Bourdieu, the radical democratic work of Aronowitz, and the critical theory of the Frankfurt School, Giroux establishes critical pedagogy as a domain of study and praxis. In the late 1970s and early 1980s, radical educational scholarship had fallen victim to a reductionistic determinism that maintained that schools were hopelessly subordinate to the dictates of social, political, and economic power. While correcting liberal educational analysts who simplistically celebrated the democratic functions of schooling,

Giroux chastised the radicals for reducing schooling to its oppressive functions in a capitalist society. Giroux sought an avenue out of determinism by illustrating how schooling can be a force for both domination and emancipation. In the spirit of a democratic pedagogy, Giroux searches for those instances in classroom, when conscientization is possible. Thus, the critical pedagogy Giroux establishes is a discourse of educational possibility.

No romantic, Giroux has a hard-boiled sense of possibility that always takes place within an understanding of a logic of domination that in the late twentieth century was deployed into every social sphere, no matter how private. It is in this context that the work of Max Horkheimer, Theodor Adorno, and Herbert Marcuse became so important to Giroux's delineation of critical pedagogy. Critical theory provided Giroux in the early 1980s with a mode of critique that reshaped and extended the notion of the political. The political domain in the critical theoretical tradition moves into both everyday social relations and the realm of consciousness and psyche. This move was necessary for critical educators to make sense of the way power was beginning to operate in popular culture via the register of affect and emotion. Indeed, this understanding changed the topography of critical scholarship well into the twenty-first century.

Giroux's passion revolves around the struggle for a critical democracy both in the United States and the world at large. This critical or radical democracy, as he employs the term, involves the effort to expand the possibility for social justice, freedom, and egalitarian social relations in the educational, economic, political, and cultural domains. Thus, Giroux's critical pedagogy deploys both critique and possibility in the struggle to expose the forces that undermine education for a critical democracy. In the age of Ronald Reagan, Giroux's introduction of Frankfurt School critical theory into educational scholarship struck a responsive chord with those offended by the right-wing use of schooling and other social institutions to reeducate Americans. This reeducation project involved countering the liberation movements that emerged from the anticolonial rebellions in Africa, Asia, and Latin America. Adeptly using critical theory to expose the right wing's use of education in this larger project, Giroux in the early 1980s exposed modes of domination tacitly operating in educational spaces both in and out of school.

culture of postivism

Positivism asserts that natural science constitutes all legitimate human knowledge. In this context, the culture of positivism refers to a "way of seeing" dominance in American culture that employs positivist science as a means of social regulation. Education in this culture becomes a tool of dominant power that operates to peressure the status quo.

Giroux understood that somewhere in the relationship among power, ideology, and schooling the crisis of historical consciousness was intensified. With the help of the work of Horkheimer and Adorno, Giroux described a **culture of positivism**—an irrational rationality marked by an emphasis on prediction and technical control. When combined with the rejection of the interpretive dynamics of hermeneutics, this culture of positivism mutated into a dominant ideological form of oppression. Only one way existed to interpret the meaning of a text or to present information to students—and that one way was the perspective of dominant forms of power. In this culture of positivism, schooling emerges as a form of social regulation that moves individuals toward destinies that preserve the world as it now is. Reflection on how identity is shaped by power or analysis of "what is" via "what should be" is subverted by positivistic culture. The development of consciousness of historical forces and their relationship to the classroom and everyday life in general has no place in the technocratic rationality of the culture of positivism.

In this same period Giroux's theoretical infrastructure was taking shape. Throughout the 1980s, as his familiarity with the emerging postdiscourses deepened, Giroux fine-tuned his insights concerning the ways individuals deal with power and the relationship of these dynamics to the production of subjectivity. His early fascination with British cultural studies—especially the work of Raymond Williams, Richard Johnson, and Stuart Hall—led Giroux to connect his study of subjectivity, power, and pedagogy to issues of language, discourse, and desire. He made use of the best of twentieth-century educational scholarship—including the progressivism of John Dewey, the transgressive pedagogy of Paulo Freire, and the insights of William Pinar and the curriculum reconceptualists—to transcend the notion that power is merely the distribution of political and economic resources. Employing and extending this battery of theoretical sensibilities, Giroux conceptualized power as a concrete set of practices that produces social mechanisms through which distinct experiences and personal identities are shaped.

By the end of the 1980s, Giroux was working with cultural studies scholars in the effort to legitimize popular culture as an academic concern. As a primary producer of pleasure, popular culture is a powerful pedagogical agent for representing the world

in ways that both disempower and empower. Frankfurt School critics had long maintained that culture is a political entity. Operating on this assumption, Giroux set out to bring cultural studies insight into the analysis of popular culture as a pedagogical locale. Refusing to merely mimic cultural studies' emphasis on the popular, Giroux refocused cultural studies around his long-time concern with radical democracy. He thereby moved to the center stage of cultural studies, as his innovative work within the field raised larger questions of justice, liberty, and equality.

Using the interdisciplinary and transdisciplinary tools of cultural studies to translate theory into democratic practice, Giroux expanded the intellectual envelope in his search for new modes of academic enterprise. In this way, his work in the 1990s and first decade of the twenty-first century has provided new understandings of the pedagogical process, new insight into pleasure, new maps of desire, and fresh interpretations of the relation among reason, emotion, and domination. Ironically, Giroux helped return cultural studies to its pedagogical roots—as exemplified by Raymond Williams's studies of adult education and the roles of democracy and social change in the academic process. No understanding of critical pedagogy is complete without insight into the seminal role of Henry Giroux (Aronowitz and Giroux, 1991; Giroux, 1981, 1983, 1988, 1992; Giroux and McLaren, 1989; Giroux and Simon, 1989).

Michael Apple

The inequity of American society has always been a dominating concern in the life of Michael Apple. From the time he worked as a volunteer in literacy programs for southern African American children whose public schools had been closed to avoid the possibility of court-ordered integration to his multifaceted work in the twenty-first century, Apple has been convinced of the need to study the effects of power and inequality in education. Schools, Apple has consistently contended, cannot be separated from political and economic life. Indeed, he argues that the entire process of education is political in

- the way it is funded
- its goals and objectives
- the manner in which these goals and objectives are evaluated

- the nature of the textbooks
- who attends and who doesn't
- who has the power to make these and other decisions.

Because of this political dimension, Apple contends that schools will always be positioned in political struggles concerning the meaning of democracy, whose culture is legitimate, and who should benefit from governmental actions. With these concerns at the forefront of his work, Apple has made central contributions to critical scholarship in curriculum studies and teaching as well as in educational theory and policy.

In his work in curriculum and teaching in the 1980s, Apple studied education as a process of labor. In this context he analyzed the ways that particular right-wing reforms operated to deskill teachers, removing the need for professional decision making and diagnostic expertise in technicist forms of rationalized practice. In this pedagogical context Apple studied curricular forms of knowledge and their relationship to larger political, economic, social, and cultural dynamics. How did school forms of knowledge reflect power in these domains, he asked. How does curricular knowledge get validated in the commerce of everyday life in capitalist societies? What is the role that such knowledge plays in maintaining extant social, economic, political, and cultural arrangements? After rigorous study of these and other questions, Apple contends that education in the United States works not only to benefit the privileged socioeconomic classes but also to extend gender hierarchies and the privilege of diverse groups already in power. Teachers' attempts to address this inequity are mitigated, he posits, by external modes of control of pedagogies and materials by external regulatory agents.

Operating in a context marked by a conservative resurgence in Western societies, Apple has worked tirelessly to provide his students and his readers with an understanding of the political right. The moving force behind so-called neoconservative and neoliberal educational policy is not so new at all. Instead, Apple contends, it evolves from an age-old conservative belief in the value of social hierarchy. Conservatives, whether in neoconservative or neoliberal suits, believe we live in a meritocratic society that appropriately rewards educational excellence and economic ingenuity. Those who do poorly in schools and in their economic life simply do not have "the right stuff" and have nobody to blame

but themselves. Thus, in this right-wing articulation, inequality is fair. According to Apple, conservatives have been overwhelmingly successful over the last twenty-five years in promoting this perspective in the educational conversation. Their success, he argues, can be best understood as a "conservative restoration."

This conservative restoration has been made possible by a coalition of market economists, old humanists calling for a reassertion of the Euro-canon in the curriculum, and neoconservative intellectuals. A central feature of the restoration in education involves an attack on democratic schooling in the framework of a larger free-market privatization project. What is sobering about the restoration, Apple argues, is that it is the most powerful and successful political reeducation movement of the last century of American life. In this context, in the twenty-first century right-wing elites now possess the hegemonic ability to establish once and for all what constitutes official knowledge via their political economic power. Corporations now firmly control both the media and the production of school textbooks. In this control they have established a knowledge industry that emphasizes the traditional family, free-market economic policy, a narrow view of patriotism, Christianity, and a business needs-driven school curriculum.

In light of the theoretical dimensions of critical pedagogy, Apple has promoted these perspectives, maintaining along the way that educational theorists should never "academize the political." Theory, he contends, should never become an academic pursuit of its own. There are positive dimensions to theorizing, Apple asserts: "We absolutely need to constantly interrogate our accepted perspectives," he writes. But Apple grows impatient with such theorizing when it is not explicitly connected to the most central political, economic, and cultural issues of the day. In this context, he warns, we should never theorize from on high, above the fray of everyday educational experiences and human suffering. The linguistic turn of the theoretical postdiscourses, he concludes, may have empowered us to view the world as a text. This, however, does not imply that we should ever lose sight of the gritty dimensions of life and the human pain that inevitably accompanies them (Apple, 1979, 1982, 1988, 1999; Apple and Weis, 1983; Carlson and Apple, 1998).

bell hooks

Born in rural Kentucky, bell hooks as a child was aware of the degradation and devaluation of black women. Racist and sexist stereotypes, she maintains, continue to play a significant role in constructing the identity and behavior of African American women in the United States. With these understandings embedded in her consciousness, hooks as a young woman began to examine the racial dynamics of the women's movement. Arguing that no common bond among all women existed, hooks took the women's movement of the 1970s to task for ignoring the role of racism in the oppression of women. Because the white and often upper-middle-class orientation of the early feminist movement had turned off many women of color, hooks worked with a number of other black women to help refocus white feminist attention. In this context, hooks and other women of color moved many feminists toward an effort to challenge an entire system of domination. The problem for many women, she wrote, is not simply male gender prejudice but their placement in a larger oppressive system. In theoretical terms hooks maintained that feminism must be more than a call for equal rights for women. In the contemporary context it must be able to identify and eradicate the ideology of domination that expresses itself along the axes of race, class, sexuality, colonialism, and gender.

hooks's theoretical concerns have made a profound impact on the development of critical pedagogy. Her own pedagogy, she contends, is informed by anticolonial, critical, and feminist theories. There is no way one can or should separate feminist theoretical notions of pedagogy from Freirean theory and pedagogy. Weaving feminism and Freirean thought together, hooks is unsure where one stops and the other begins. Freire, hooks contends, was far more concerned with the plight and the needs of the disenfranchised than were many of the white bourgeois feminists I encountered. This once again illustrates the idea that one's actions in pursuit of resistance to oppression are more important than one's race, class, or gender—one's positionality. In an era in which we see a regeneration of white supremacy, a growing apartheid that separates white people from people of color, the well-to-do from the have-nots, and men from women, hooks's admonitions strike a resonating chord. Advocates of

critical pedagogy cannot call for justice in one domain and remain oppressors in another.

With these notions in mind, hooks encourages educators to appreciate the narrow boundaries that shape the way knowledge is produced and transmitted in the classroom. Such processes reflect the ideology of domination that has undermined American claims to democracy for centuries. Students, she posits, are more than ready to break through these ideological barriers to knowing. They are excited by the possibility of relearning the world and exposing the ideological filters that perverted their studies the first time around. In this context hooks calls for teachers to teach in a manner that works to transform consciousness and creates an atmosphere of open expression that is the mark of an emancipatory education. Such an exciting pedagogy can emerge only when teachers and educational leaders develop loyalties that transcend their race, ethnicity, socioeconomic class, religion, and nation. In such a context teachers develop a global perspective that allows one to see self as others see it. Such a perspective encourages teachers to criticize one's ethnicity, class, religion, or nation when it is complicit with oppression. In the twenty-first century, hooks's perspectives become more important than ever (hooks, 1981, 1984, 1989, 1991, 1994).

Donaldo Macedo

Donaldo Macedo has been a central figure in critical pedagogy over the last twenty years. His work with Paulo Freire broke new theoretical ground in its attempt to develop a critical understanding of the ways in which language, power, and culture contribute to the positioning and formation of human experience and learning. He is known as Freire's chief translator and interpreter in English. Macedo's published dialogues with Paulo Freire are considered classic work for their elucidation not only of Freire's own theories of literacy but also for the way in which they have added a more critical and theoretically advanced dimension to the study of literacy and critical pedagogy. His coauthored book with Paulo Freire, *Literacy: Reading the World and the Word,* is central to critical literacy in that it redefines the very nature and terrain of literacy and critical pedagogy.

In addition to his seminal work with Freire, Macedo has played a central role in constructing a literacy of power for use

in critical pedagogy. Contrary to popular belief and dominant ideology, schools do not always serve the best interests of their students. Schools as well as the cultural pedagogies of media and other social institutions too often perpetuate ignorance or, as Macedo puts it, stupidification. As schools and other institutions fragment knowledge and deny contextual understanding, students find their ability to make connections between school information, their lived worlds, and relations of power and privilege more and more difficult. Macedo's work directly challenges the educational experts who seek to keep issues of power and social struggle outside the purview of education. As Macedo argues, questions of power vis-à-vis socioeconomic class relations, gender dynamics, and racial discrimination are suppressed by many mainstream political and educational leaders. What does class analysis have to do with education, hegemonic educators ask, when we live in a classless society? Such positions, Macedo asserts, conveniently ignore questions of ethics. As long as such questions are suppressed and a literacy of power is ignored, schools will remain tools of the status quo.

Macedo ties this literacy of power directly to what he describes as an emancipatory literacy. An **emancipatory literacy**, Macedo posits, involves students becoming knowledgeable about their histories, experiences, and the culture of their everyday environments. In addition, they also must be able to discern the dominant culture's codes and signifiers in order to escape their own environments. In an educational context shaped by an emancipatory literacy, therefore, teachers must constantly teach a dual curriculum. A language of possibility, Macedo argues, permeates this two-tier curriculum that both empowers students to make sense of their everyday life and gain the tools for mobility valued in the dominant culture. In this context, Macedo writes that students celebrate who they are while learning to deal with ways of seeing and being that are not their own. In this way students from marginalized backgrounds can make their own history (Freire and Macedo, 1987; Macedo, 1994; Macedo and Bartolome, 2001).

emancipatory literacy involves revealing the ways dominant power operates in a manner that allows an individual and groups to act in resistence to its efforts to oppress them.

Peter McLaren

Beginning his career in education as an elementary school teacher in Toronto, McLaren achieved notoriety with the 1980

publication of his teaching diary, *Cries from the Corridor: The New Suburban Ghettoes*. The book became a best-seller in Canada and catalyzed a national debate on the state of Canada's inner-city schools. Entering graduate school after this success, McLaren reported that his reading of critical theory, cultural studies, and feminist studies taught him that teachers had to be grounded both theoretically and politically. In this context, he developed the belief that critical teachers had to engage in the difficult work of developing a coherent philosophy of praxis. The ideas took shape in his *Schooling as a Ritual Performance: Towards a Political Economy of Educational Symbols and Gestures*—a very important ethnography of education—and *Life in Schools: An Introduction to Critical Pedagogy in the Foundations of Education*—a resource now in its third edition used to introduce critical pedagogy to numerous teachers and other scholars.

These praxis-related insights moved him to become less focused on the classroom per se and more directed toward political, cultural, and racial identity, antiracist multicultural education, the politics of whiteness, white supremacy, modes of resistance and popular culture. During this period—the early and mid-1980s—McLaren, as a professor of education along with Henry Giroux at Miami University (Ohio), focused on the larger relevance of critical pedagogy involving its capacity to expose life's permanent conditions of oppression and exploitation. In the last half of the decade, McLaren researched the relevance of postmodernism for inclusion in the discourse of critical pedagogy. In 1986 he published the first article in education journals on the relationship between postmodernism and pedagogy.

In McLaren's revolutionary critical pedagogy critical educators seek to realize in their classrooms democratic social values and to embrace their possibilities. Consequently, McLaren argues that they need to go outside of the protected precincts of their classrooms and analyze and explore the workings of capital in the larger society. Critical revolutionary pedagogy sets as its goal the reclamation of public life under the assault of corporatization and privatization. Here McLaren offers no blueprint but a contingent utopian vision that offers direction not only in "unpacking the apparatus of bourgeois illusion" but also in diversifying the theoretical repertoire of the critical educator so that new questions can be generated along with new contexts in which to

raise them. Here McLaren's emphasis is not only on denouncing the injustices of neoliberal capitalism and serving as a counterforce to neoliberal ideological hegemony but also on establishing the conditions for new social and economic arrangements.

Peter is at his best when describing the globalitarian world with its unacceptable and ever-increasing disparity of wealth. His work in this domain documents the economic and environmental effects of the North American Free Trade Agreement (NAFTA) on Latin American nations such as Mexico—disease, birth defects, and an intensification of poverty. All of this is occurring at the same time that many political and educational leaders are proclaiming the virtues and victory of the unfettered free market. In the name of freedom they demand that the peoples of the world submit to the demands of the market. As the U.S. government provides grants of public money to corporations, budget cuts gut programs designed to help the victims of unregulated capital. McLaren warns us that such a reality cannot continue indefinitely without some type of violent explosion. McLaren's work is a secular prayer that calls for action in the present that will avert the intensification of the major human tragedy known as globalization (McLaren, 1989, 1995, 1997, 2000; McLaren, Hammer, Reilly, and Sholle, 1995).

Ira Shor

Growing up as a Jewish kid in the South Bronx, Ira Shor quickly came to understand the lived experience of being white working class as well as the specificities of racial and ethnic discrimination in New York in the 1950s and 1960s. These experiences, like those of so many other men and women now involved in critical pedagogy, shaped his sociopolitical perspectives and his conception of the role of a teacher. With these ideas in mind, Shor became fascinated with the work of Paulo Freire, and to some degree Shor's critical pedagogy has always been intimately involved with what it means to apply Freire in the classrooms of North America. In this context, Shor has carefully worked to integrate critical notions of social critique with techniques of pedagogy in ways that create new educational possibilities. Joined together these two notions help produce a thoughtful, just, and democratic education. Such an education engages students in a way that subverts the exploitation of the subordinate classes, the

manner in which social structures reproduce themselves in the everyday life of the classroom, and the process by which authority regulates the poor.

Keeping these ideas in the front of his consciousness, Shor calls for (and employs in his own teaching) a dialogical pedagogy. In such a teaching the teacher starts with student experience—student responses to themes, texts, and/or problems. In this context the teacher engages students in a critical discourse about these issues. Such a pedagogy, Shor maintains, disconfirms a teacher-centered, authoritarian form of teaching and replaces it with a dialogical one. Indeed, teaching of this kind helps focus critical pedagogy's questioning of the status quo as it enacts its democratic dimension. At the very core of his democratic, decentralized pedagogy, Shor is dedicated to the proposition that the classroom is the venue for the construction of knowledge, not merely for its inculcation. This assertion is inseparable from his profound discomfort with the teacher-driven, authority-dependent nature of many classrooms claiming a variety of ideological positions—critical pedagogy included.

In this context, Shor insists that teachers develop an epistemological relationship to subject matter. Entering into this relationship, teachers monitor students' forms of knowledge and interpretations of subject matter and experience, expressing their own insights at appropriate times in this process of student engagement. Critical teaching of this variety is a compelling art form in the hands of an adept teacher such as Shor. When it is running on all cylinders, Shor posits that a "third idiom" is created. Such an idiom is distinct from both the everyday language of students and the academic language of teachers. It is a critical language constructed as a synthesis of these different ways of thinking and talking in the lived world of the classroom. As such it comes out of the conflicts and the collaborations of teachers and students and emerges as something new—a power-mediated hybrid discourse.

In some ways, Shor's work in critical pedagogy has become, in a right-wing socioeducational *Zeitgeist*, a guidebook for resistance to the standardization and deskilling of contemporary schooling. In an era of hyperbanking pedagogy, Shor challenges the relationship between information-transmitting teachers and passive student receivers. Such challenges position him as the

critical pedagogical champion of the democratic classroom. Up front about both its benefits and its difficulties, he is unafraid to speak and write of his own failures in the complex process. Positioning oneself as a teacher in opposition to the hegemonic culture inscribing classrooms is never a comfortable role for teachers or students. In this sometimes discomforting role, Shor asserts, one must struggle to find strategies that encourage rather than discourage students from thinking of themselves as critical agents shaping their own education. When students are able to think of themselves as such empowered agents, Shor maintains that both students and teachers develop their capacities as democratic agents and social critics—everyone becomes involved in the learning process. Achieving the best balance of teacher and student input into the critical classroom is central to Shor, as he pushes the boundaries of the democratic classroom as a sophisticated form of group process (Shor, 1980, 1987, 1992, 1996; Shor and Freire, 1987; Shor and Pari, 1999a, 1999b).

Jesus "Pato" Gomez (1952-2006), Ramon Flecha, and CREA

Jesus "Pato" Gomez was one of the world's premier scholars on critical pedagogy and love. Gomez who was a professor of Research Methods in Education at the University of Barcelona, much in the spirit of his dear friend Paulo Freire, he studied the power of a revolutionary love to address unequal power relationships among diverse individuals. As many of us who knew him recognize, not only was Pato's scholarship a great testimony to his genius as a critical pedagogue, but his revolutionary pedagogy was also seen simply in the way he lived his life. He was gifted in his ability to teach critical pedagogy through the example of his everyday love for people, his omnipresent *joie de vivre*, his informed empathy, and his critical interconnection with the people he knew.

I wish I could have been privy to his conversations with Paulo Freire about radical love and its relationship to critical pedagogy's scholarship and activism. Pato and I discussed these conversations and I listened carefully to every dimension of what he told me—but I still would like to have been there to listen to the dialogue between the two greatest advocates and practitioners of radical love I was ever privileged to meet. Always concerned with the role of affect in critical pedagogy, Gomez and Freire

spoke about writing a book on revolutionary love and critical
affect entitled "Pedagogy of the Shine in the Eyes." Their time
on earth was too limited, though, and it was not to be.

It is important to note in this critical pedagogical context
that Gomez's love was never trite in the "love conquers all" school
of thought. Pato's truly was a critical love that recognized the
need to interrogate love, to theorize it in the critical theoretical
tradition. In this critical love domain, much of his scholarship and
activism involved love-related issues such as the origins and causes
of gender violence. This historicization of love was central to his
work and led him to pedagogies that helped adolescents think
about and construct the modes of critical analyses needed to
overcome contemporary patriarchal tendencies that often led to
oppressive, often violent, and degrading "romantic" relationships.
In this critical context, Pato worked to develop romantic relationships and modes of love that were life-affirming and empowering.
His book, *El Amor en la Sociedad del Riesgo* (*Love in a High Risk Society*)
delineates many of these ideas.

In this book and others Gomez questioned popular roman-
ticized assumptions that love is a fairy tale-like dynamic that
suddenly overcomes human beings no matter how dehumanizing
or unhealthy the relationship may be for one or both of the lov-
ers involved. Promoting a critical pedagogy of love that engaged
students in a power-literate and ideologically informed understanding of love, Pato sought to engage diverse people in questioning whether certain social practices associated with love were
liberating or oppressive. As individuals recognize the way power
permeates all dimensions of human experience, Pato believed
that they could develop ways of loving in pedagogy in particular
and in life in general that led to passionate and enhanced modes
of living.

In the last years of his life Gomez took the ways he studied
love and applied them to interdisciplinary research methodologies—what Pato labeled the "communicative methodology of
research." This methodology—similar in many ways to the bricolage that will be discussed later in this book—was used in a
number of influential research projects including ones that dealt
with the oppression and liberation of Romani peoples (Gypsies)
living in Spain and various countries in Europe. In his communicative methodology Gomez worked to make sure that so-called

subjects of research were included in the interpretive and analytical dialogue with university-based researchers and scholars. Pato's sensitivity to the genius and forms of knowledge of oppressed peoples and the subjugated perspectives they bring to research of any type laid the foundation for his critical multiperspectival research. This sensitivity was present in every dimension of his life, work, and play and serves as a beacon to all of us who presume to engage in critical pedagogy. As his beloved friend/Basque brother Ramon Flecha said of Pato: "he was too intelligent, too creative, too revolutionary, and too sensitive for the current structures of our universities." I hope that universities, research, and pedagogy in general move in the direction theorized and lived by Pato in the coming years.

Ramon Flecha is one of the preeminent critical pedagogical scholars in the world today. A professor of Sociological Theory at the University of Barcelona, Flecha has worked tirelessly since the 1960s to help implement the groundbreaking critical work of Paulo Freire. Working with Freire for over twenty years, Flecha helped establish Freirean literary circles with nontraditionally educated working class peoples in the factories and shops of Barcelona in the early 1970s. Continuing this work into the present, Flecha's labors in this domain have helped create one of the most successful examples of critical pedagogy operating in informal settings to help teach the word and the world. Having visited CREA (Center for Social and Educational Research with which Flecha's—as was Gomez's—work is connected at the University of Barcelona) several times, Flecha and his fellow critical scholar/activists have shown Shirley Steinberg and me a compelling example of how "critical pedagogy in the streets" can change the lives of thousands of individuals.

CREA is one of the premier critical pedagogical research and social action centers in the world. The center has produced research and organized social action movements that have not only transformed education in Barcelona and Spain but throughout Europe in general. The group's major domain of study involves the investigation of sociopolitical inequities and the development of pragmatic ways of addressing and surmounting such injustices. Cofounder of the European Research and Development Institutes for Adult Education and a member of the European Society for Research on the Education of Adults, the center's

work has influenced critical research in North American and Latin American venues. CREA has sponsored numerous research studies involving social justice, political action, and education. Any student of critical pedagogy should be familiar with the emancipatory work that CREA has produced and is presently completing.

Flecha has been deeply concerned with the inclusion of the voices and insights of those people not traditionally educated and included in academic and public policy conversations. It was quite obvious when we attended the twentieth-anniversary celebration of the establishment of the literacy circles that Ramon had been so central in founding and nurturing, that something very special was happening. Several of the older people who had learned to read and become scholars in Flecha's critical adult education were excited to speak to me as an American critical pedagogy scholar about their love of the work of Antonio Gramsci.

After the ceremony over dinner we began our excited conversation about Gramsci's notions of the organic intellectual, the social role of intellectuals, hegemony, and so on, I enthusiastically responded to the questions of the wonderful worker/scholars with whom I was dining. After several responses to their questions, I asked their opinions on the topics discussed. The responses to my queries were life changing for me. I realized I was privileged to be sitting with a group of the most learned Gramsci scholars I had ever met. Their readings of Gramsci vis-à-vis their life experiences and what they had learned in Flecha's literacy circles had turned them into scholar-activists with unique insights into the work of Gramsci (and many other theorists and topics) that needed to be shared with the critical world. I already understood the brilliance of what Ramon Flecha had set in motion, but I had little idea just how powerful it was until that moment. In addition to such compelling critical work, Flecha has published numerous books including *Contemporary Sociological Theory* (with Jesus Gomez and Lidia Puigvert) with Peter Lang.

Deborah Britzman

Deborah Britzman began working in critical pedagogy in the early 1980s. In 1986, in collaboration with Catherine Walsh and Juan Aulestea, she organized the First Working Conference on Critical Pedagogy at the University of Massachusetts. The conference supported three strands of educational practice not often in discussion with one another: adult education, bilingual education, and teacher education. Although teacher education did have a critical strand of research, it was typically isolated from social theory, other branches of education, and larger political and philosophical discussions. To address this isolation, Britzman invited Maxine Greene to speak to the teacher education strand of the conference. In this context, she engaged in conversations with some of the main proponents of critical pedagogy at the time: Paulo Freire, Henry Giroux, Peter McLaren, Madeleine Grumet, Roger Simon, Elizabeth Spellman, and John Bracey.

It was in this context that Britzman made presentations that would evolve into one of her best-known works: *Cultural Myths in the Making of a Teacher: Biography and Social Structure in Teacher Education* (1986). In this piece, Britzman applied to education some of the basic concerns of Frankfurt School Critical Theory, arguing that there was a way out of the technocratic, individualistic manner in which mainstream teacher education operated. This work would be expanded into Britzman's influential first book, *Practice Makes Practice: A Critical Study of Learning to Teach.* Along with engaging the research discussions of critical pedagogy, *Practice Makes Practice* became an influential work in critical pedagogy because of its consideration of the inner world of the teacher.

With this concern in mind, Britzman connected the problem of self-knowledge with social structural constraints, in the process highlighting some of the main issues of critical pedagogy. Focusing on the ways secondary education abstracts knowledge from its social context, extends the perpetuation of marginalization through the construction of canons, and harbors implicit values in the curriculum that constrain teacher voice, Britzman pushed the boundaries of critical pedagogy. The concept of voice in Britzman's conception was not merely a personal phenomenon but a social struggle with authority, knowledge, and power. The key dynamic at work in Britzman's scholarship in this era involved addressing the existential dilemmas that all teachers must confront as they learn to teach.

Another dimension of Britzman's work in critical pedagogy has involved integrating the epistemological and ontological dilemmas of race, sexuality, class, and gender into the problem

of teaching and learning. Here Britzman explored the role of critical pedagogy in encouraging teachers and students to critique their everyday world and the resistance this often elicited. In this context she focused on the psychology of denial, the refusal of many privileged individuals to believe that social inequality matters in their world or the world of others. Britzman asked how this affects critical pedagogy. Pushing the psychological dimension of critical pedagogy, Britzman explored questions of sexuality in relation to teachers, students, and the curriculum. Employing psychoanalysis and queer theory, she explored what she labeled "difficult knowledge" in teaching and learning as a part of a larger process of dealing with traumatic history. This work continues to play an important role in the field, as younger scholars engage it in many diverse contexts.

Britzman's study of difficult knowledge led her to yet another major contribution to critical pedagogy—the use of Freudian and Kleinian psychoanalytic theory in liberatory work. In this context, Britzman has worked to radically extend what counts as education, contending that pedagogical study should always have second thoughts on questions of interiority, self-other relations, and the production of subjectivity. Critical pedagogy, she posits, has often left the psychology of teaching to others, incorrectly assuming that psychology is too grounded in programs of subjection and normalization to be of any use. While clearly the history of psychology in education has been devastating to large populations through its categorizations of emotional disorders, IQ testing, and behaviorist orientations to learning theory, psychoanalysis, Britzman maintains, is of a different order and well worth a second look. Britzman has consistently reminded critical pedagogy of the power, beauty, and controversies of psychoanalysis, the need to study its discarded content, its dreams, and its breakdowns, and the necessity of the attempt to understand the unconscious in education and in critical pedagogy itself (Britzman, 1991, 2003).

Philip Wexler

Philip Wexler has written extensively about his "kinship" to the critical pedagogy movement. He is a critical social analyst, with a long-standing specialization in education. He was educated in "classical" sociological theory, anthropology, social

statistics and cognitive psychology. Despite his "establishment" education and involvement in the mainstream of sociology of education (as editor of the American Sociological Association journal in education, *Sociology of Education*), he was early drawn to critical social theory, in the work of the Frankfurt School, and in so-called "Western Marxism," generally. He was among the few mainstream sociologists to apply this tradition to social theory and research in education, and also to do comparative field research in education, from the vantage point of a class analysis of everyday school life (*Becoming Somebody*).

Wexler has traveled into unmapped critical pedagogical territory in his analysis of the nature of individuality vis-à-vis the larger themes of criticality and a diversity of socio-cultural resources. In *Holy Sparks: Social Theory, Education, and Religion*, Wexler bravely ventures into affect-centric hyperreality, searching for untapped emancipatory possibilities. In this book and also in *The Mystical Society: Revitalization in Culture, Theory, and Education*, he maintains that a decentered revolution, of sort, has already taken place grounded on a form mysticism that reshapes (revitalizes, in Wexler's words) the lives of those ensnared in the commodified, regulated, hegemonized culture of contemporary globalized society. In the same way that affective dynamics can be employed by dominant power to oppress individuals and social groups, they can also be used to make certain dimensions of life matter in ways that assert human agency and group solidarity.

Making use of what is available on the contemporary political and cultural landscape, Wexler recognizes that the transformation of selfhood is central to the mystical revolution that has in many ways already occurred. Knowing, this Wexler works to connect particular critical principles to this commitment to the revitalization of the self in the interests of larger social change. Connecting his commitment to both critical social theory and education to this possibility, Wexler has increasingly drawn upon mystical religious and spiritual traditions as a cultural resource in the development of social analysis and social and educational critique (to the surprise, and even consternation of some of his longtime scholarly friends and colleagues).

As a student of comparative religion with an especial emphasis on the study of Jewish mysticism, in Kabbalah and Hasidism, Wexler continues his work searching for the relevance of these

starting places for a critical theory of the individual, society, and education. Using such sources, Wexler's analysis of neomysticism and what he labels, enlivenment, moves his readers into a confrontation with the resacralization of cultural codes, the globalizing synthesis of diverse cultural expressions that expose the ethnocentrism of European science and epistemology, and a new historicism that reengage the premodern, the ancient, and the archaic.

Patti Lather

Patti Lather's work in critical education has revolved around the intersections, fissures, and distinctions characterizing the relationship between feminist and critical pedagogy, feminist ethnography, and poststructualism. Over the last fifteen years, the disjunction between critical pedagogy and feminist pedagogy has become a source of interest and tension that profoundly affects the future of the discipline in the twenty-first century. Lather in the 1990s focused masculinized articulations of critical pedagogy and their tendency to marginalize issues of gender in the field. In this context, Lather maintains that the "return to Marxism" articulated by some advocates of critical pedagogy in recent years reinforces her thesis that critical pedagogy has operated as a masculinized space, a venue in which male leftist academics could claim praxis. Lather posits that this "return to Marxism" has come to view the postdiscourses as a form of accommodation to dominant sociopolitical and educational powers. The critique of postmodernism and poststructuralism coming from the return-to-Marxism camp of critical pedagogy, she contends, has focused on feminist poststructuralism. This has created yet another layer of gendered trackings in the work of critical and feminist theory and practice.

Central to the importance of Lather's work in critical pedagogy have been her compelling exposes of the ways the postdiscourses, neo-Marxist modes of seeing, and different articulations of feminism can help critical pedagogists locate the fingerprints of power on research methods and modes of knowledge production. In this context, Lather has provided numerous insights into the ways critical researchers can reconceptualize the research act. Laying the foundation for this reconceptualization in *Getting Smart* in 1991, Lather followed up in 1998 with *Troubling the Angels.*

In this book, Lather created a "multivoiced" work that experimented with interweaving concurrent multiple meanings and interpretations on the same page. The book successfully demonstrated ways of representing the complexity of the interpretive process and new directions in conveying that complexity to the reader.

The subversive quality of Lather's work is omnipresent, as she consistently labors to undermine the validated expert status of mainstream academic practice. Indeed, some of her most creative work has involved the development of new forms of research validity that explode the hegemonic dynamics of positivist internal and external validity. In this context, she has moved critical pedagogy to a more contingent epistemological stance, as she problematizes any facile closure in relation to questions of truth and the effort to represent reality. The critical theoretical notion of emancipation, Lather contends, is a dangerous terrain that can contain within it tacit forms of oppression. In an educational context, this oppressive dynamic of emancipatory action becomes profoundly dangerous, as its transmission-based pedagogies can work to disempower and marginalize in the name of justice and equality.

Antonia Darder

Antonia Darder is internationally recognized for her contributions as a radical educator in the critical pedagogy tradition. Her work has focused on comparative studies of racism, class, gender, and society. Her teaching examines cultural and global issues in education with an emphasis on identity, language, and popular culture, as well as the philosophical foundations of critical pedagogy, Latino and Latina studies, and social justice theory.

Her strong commitment and identity as a working class Puerto Rican woman of color is rooted in her personal history of survival. During the first twenty-six years of her life, she lived in poverty. As a young single mother with three children and on welfare, she began her studies at a community college in 1972. She became first a pediatric nurse and then a licensed psychotherapist, working with poor and working-class Spanish-speaking families. Always at the heart of her work, was the question of self-determination and community empowerment.

It was at a conference exploring Paulo Freire's work that Darder first met Paulo Freire, Henry Giroux, Peter McLaren, Donaldo Macedo, Ira Shor, and others considered central figures in the evolving critical pedagogy movement in the United States at that time. And although she had been involved in a variety of movement and community struggles since 1975, this meeting indeed was to dramatically change the course of her scholarship and serve as the intellectual foundation for the contributions she was to make to the field.

The unexpected meeting catapulted her work into a deep critical engagement with questions related to oppressed cultures, languages, and schooling. The outcome was the publication in 1991 of her classic text, *Culture and Power in the Classroom.* Antonia's work infused the critical education discourse with a perspective that was shaped at the margins of the existing white, male-dominated domain of the field. Her scholarship has attempted to join her theoretical understanding of schooling and politics with her life as a Puerto Rican activist-scholar—an identity that continues to be anchored in her history as a working-class woman of color.

Among her groundbreaking works are found three important texts that defined her contribution. *Reinventing Paulo Freire: A Pedagogy of Love* was named outstanding book in curriculum for 2001–2002 by the American Educational Research Association. The book sought to rethink Freire's theories within the context of U.S. public schooling. The *Critical Pedagogy Reader* (coedited with Rodolfo D. Torres and Marta Baltodano), the first major compilation of a variety of seminal articles on critical pedagogy and schooling, was a featured text of the International Conference on Curriculum in London in 2005. Finally, *After Race: Racism After Multiculturalism* (coauthored with Torres) has been recognized internationally as a forthright critical analysis of the significance of class in an understanding of how racism functions within U.S. capitalist society.

In conjunction with her scholarly efforts as an educator and public intellectual in the critical pedagogical tradition, Darder has also been active in a variety of grassroots struggles tied to educational rights, workers' rights, bilingual education, women's issues, and immigrant rights. In 1998, she was instrumental in founding the *California Consortium of Critical Educators* (CCCE), a member supported progressive teachers' organization committed to a critical vision of schooling, intimately linked to the radical educational tradition in the United States.

Moreover, with an eye on the development of a critical pedagogy of dissent, Darder currently works with students on the production of *Liberacion! The Nexus of Local and Global Politics, Art, and Struggle*, a public affairs program on community radio and on the *Public* I, a radical independent monthly publication. Darder's strong community involvement is in concert with her deep belief in the need for critical scholars, researchers, and teachers to move outside the comfort zone of the university and schools. Through her lived activism, she reinforces in daily life the importance of working consistently in solidarity with those involved in community struggles to transform oppressive conditions and social structures that stifle our self-determination and disrupt our opportunities to love, create, and dream as free subjects of history.

John Willinsky

The basic operating principle of John Willinsky's approach to critical pedagogy has been to help students become better students of their own education. This is the point, after all, of their principal contact with the institutional forces and ideologies that govern their lives. This former schoolteacher and now professor of education at Stanford, after a long career at Canadian universities, has examined this educational process in terms of a number of educational traditions with an eye to equipping teachers with a better understanding of how education has been shaped to reflect governing ideas. The primary focus of his curriculum work has been on literacy and literature teaching, gradually broadening out to include curriculum studies and more recently, basic questions of access to knowledge. For example, Willinsky has worked with ideas of how literature has been taught in the schools, looking at how the progressive politics of Louise Rosenblatt's approach were sidetracked by an emphasis on aesthetic experience (Willinsky 1991), while developing materials for a feminist teaching of Romeo and Juliet, which also encouraged students to consider how literature is used in the schools (Willinsky and Bedard, 1989).

On the question of language teaching and the teaching of standard English, he undertook a book-length critique of

the editing that went into the *Oxford English Dictionary* over the last 150 years, establishing the degree to which this standard was constructed around a number of shifting suppositions that started with a commitment to basing English's order on its literary achievement with all of the prejudices which that body of work reflect, with this editorial emphasis gradually shifting over the course of the twentieth century to political, business, and technical developments in the language (Willinsky, 1994). Extending his focus beyond issues of language, Willinsky's work on imperialism's educational legacy drew him across the curriculum, to considerations not only of literature, but of the teaching of race in biology, the great divide between Asia and Europe in geography, the concept of the West and freedom in history (1998), with the classroom implications of this approach worked out in his teaching in a high school English class by having the students construct a class set of a multilingual, multicultural poetry anthology for the use of the school, with the students going farther in their postcolonial critique of the school than he had realized during the class (2006a).

Finally, Willinsky's work has moved into a critical pedagogy of the public sphere with his research and development work on enabling scholarly journals, particularly in developing countries, to become part of the people's right to know and right to use that knowledge to help effect change, doing so by making freely available open source online systems for publishing journals that reduce costs and support various open access publishing models for journals (Willinsky 2006b). In terms of where Willinsky has ended up, at this point, is then a critical pedagogy based not on what needs to be taught, but on a larger, critical sense of what can be learned, and how that can be unduly restrained by the prevailing political economy of knowledge. The PKP (Public Knowledge Project)—the open access publishing undertaking conceived by Willinsky under which this work has been conceived and promoted—is changing the face of academic publishing in a way that helps reconstruct and promote critical pedagogical goals.

Shirley Steinberg

Shirley Steinberg was introduced to critical pedagogy in the 1980s by David G. Smith, her professor and advisor at the

University of Lethbridge in Alberta, Canada. Intrigued by the radical personal approach as exemplified by Paulo Freire, she began to define her own teaching through dialogue and improvisational theater. As a high school drama teacher, she turned from the traditional, script-driven performance to working with her students in a collective environment. Informed by Keith Johnston's concept of Theatre Sports, Augusto Boal's *Theatre of the Oppressed*, and the pedagogy of Freire, she and her students developed socially conscious, autobiographical theatrical "happenings." Loosely based on the Canadian notion of the theatrical collective, she developed "anthologies" which allowed students to combine research, personal narrative, and the arts in casual performances that invited audience participation. Steinberg's first performance/happening, *An Anthology of Girls,* was in 1986 at the "Girls, Women, and Giftedness International Conference" in Lethbridge, Alberta. Acutely aware of the impact of performance on not only the audience but also on the performers, she has used the theatrical anthology within schools and community groups as an effort to bring about social consciousness and change.

Steinberg's own research began to expand as she began to combine the feminist notion of positionality, William Pinar's notion of autobiography, and her own humorous interpretations of popular culture. Writing with an offbeat, postmodern, Catskillish approach to research, she adopted the notion of research bricolage (she profoundly shaped my notion of bricolage) as she unlayered the levels of each artifact she investigated. Noted especially for her notion of *kinderculture,* Steinberg maintains that the curriculum of childhood is most affected by the cultural texts that surround children and youth. She is also well known for her work in multicultural education and diversity, contributing to the field in her recent edited collection, *Multi/intercultural Conversations: A Reader* (Steinberg, 2001).

Insisting on placing her own position within the text as she interprets and theorizes, Steinberg's analytical approach disallows any possibility of hidden agenda as she delves into her subject. In her work in queer studies, for instance, she declares that she is a "misplaced drag queen" (Steinberg, 1998). While discussing teacher efficacy, she brings to text her own experiences with "Mrs. G." (Steinberg, 1992, 1996), and as she deconstructs

the multicultural implications of Mattel's Barbie, she reveals "my life is out of control" as she becomes engaged in her own research subject (Steinberg, 1997). Never shying from controversial and heated subjects, her work in film reading vis-a-vis a critical media literacy continues to be provocative and edgy (Steinberg, 2002a, 2004). The founding and senior editor of *Taboo: The Journal of Culture and Education*, she has encouraged marginalized writers including youth and graduate students to produce both artistically radical and theoretical work. Her recent work focuses on the incorporation of critical pedagogy through cultural studies (Steinberg, 2004; Macedo and Steinberg, 2007) in both the formal and informal educational environment. Currently, she is the Director of The Paulo and Nita Freire International Project for Critical Pedagogy at McGill University where she has worked to establish a highly creative and innovative venue for the movement of critical pedagogy into a new phase of its existence.

Ana Cruz

Ana Cruz was born in Manaus, the heart of Amazonas, Brazil, and, because of a committed teacher/sociologist/activist, was exposed to the work of Paulo Freire already in high school. Proud of her multiracial identity, Cruz embraces her black/native Indian/white heritage. She was raised in a middle-class family, but she was not isolated from the unique environment of Manaus with its distinctive ecological setting, conspicuous cultural diversity, oppression, and instances of utter poverty. Cruz has taught elementary school, high school, adult education, and College/University in Brazil and in the United States.

In her current position preparing two-year college students to become teachers, she is a fervent exponent of critical pedagogy. She is not hesitant to expose these students to Freire's work with the goal of increasing their ability to think critically, to reflect upon social reality, and to become agents of social change. Cruz's Foundations of Education course embraces Freire's "Teachers as Cultural Workers" where she stresses the importance of commitment in order to become an effective teacher. Instigating a quest for self-knowledge, Ana requests her students to constantly reflect upon: Who am I? What are my beliefs? How are these beliefs/values eventually affecting my teaching? How do I relate to people who are different from me?

In the Technology for Teachers course, Cruz emphasizes critical thinking by addressing issues of access to technology—the digital divide—and the implications of virtual reality on social relationships. In addition, she has developed several exercises/ projects to increase students' awareness of how their commitment (or lack thereof) to the teaching profession can build up or destroy learners in their quest for knowledge and understanding of their place in the world.

Cruz's research is strongly influenced by Freire's work (e.g., the oppressor-oppressed relationship, the internalization of the oppressor's views by the oppressed, and the process of gaining consciousness). Critical pedagogy/critical theory inform her research in Music and Deafness, where she investigates the power relationships within the **Deaf** community and the relationships to the hearing world. Her focal point is the issue of dominance and control in music based on auditory skills, the hegemonic relationships between the individuals involved. Here she demonstrates the significance of **plural pathways** in experiencing music (Cruz, 1997a) and of accessibility to music education by those who are Deaf (Cruz, 1997b). The research also highlights how the development of critical consciousness is important for Deaf people interested in engaging in music, because it seems that a large segment of the Deaf culture has identified with the ideologies of the oppressor (normally hearing).

Deaf people, therefore, interested in music have to confront outside pressures (from the normally hearing culture) and inside pressures (from the Deaf culture) that follow ideological concepts espousing music as an identifier of the normally hearing and not suitable for the Deaf. Following Freire (1970), critical consciousness can liberate Deaf people from the state of being oppressed, freeing them from accepting a view of themselves constructed by the oppressor, and enabling them to change their reality—in this case that they can have a meaningful relationship with music. The Deaf should not be excluded, based on ideologies, from engaging in musical activities, but it should be their own decision, empowered by knowledge, whether they want to pursue these activities or not. Cruz seeks to provide a space where a Deaf person can have a voice to construct and/or deconstruct his/her life world of music through **enabling meaning.**

Glossary

Bourgeois—middle class, conventional, unimaginative, and selfish.

Bricolage—French term for the work of a handyman or handy-woman who uses numerous available tools to complete a task. Norman Denzin and Yvonna Lincoln have recently used the term to describe multimethodological forms of research.

Cultural studies—an interdisciplinary, transdisciplinary, and sometimes counterdisciplinary field of study that functions within the dynamics of competing definitions of culture. Unlike traditional humanistic studies, cultural studies questions the equation of culture with high culture. Instead, cultural studies asserts that numerous expressions of cultural production should be analyzed in relation to other cultural dynamics and social and historical structures. These expressions include but are not limited to popular culture.

Culture of positivism—positivism asserts that natural science constitutes all legitimate human knowledge. In this context, the culture of positivism refers to a "way of seeing" dominance in American culture that employs positivist science as a means of social regulation. Education in this culture becomes a tool of dominant power that operates to preserve the status quo.

Deaf—a person who belongs to a community who shares the same culture, beliefs, and language (American Sign Language—ASL) pertinent to deaf people (deaf: someone who cannot hear).

Emancipatory literacy—involves revealing the ways dominant power operates in a manner that allows an individual and groups to act in resistance to its efforts to oppress them.

Enabling meaning—the meaning constructed by a Deaf person rather than one assigned to the person by others.

Normative hermeneutics—the art and science of interpretation and explanation regarding standards of behavior and prescriptions of such.

Plural pathways—a combination of residual hearing, feeling, moving, seeing, and so on used by many Deaf persons to experience music. (*Direct pathway* involves the hearing sense, the *dominant* way of experiencing music by normally hearing people.)

Postdiscourses—the theoretical ways of understanding that developed in the last third of the twentieth century that questioned the assumptions about the world put forth by modernist, scientific Western frameworks. They would

include postmodernism, poststructuralism, postcolonialism, and postformalism.

Poststructuralism—a social theoretical position that questions the universalizing tendencies of structural approaches to scholarship—for example, Piaget's universal stages of child development or Maslow's hierarchy of needs. Thus, poststructuralism emphasizes the historical and cultural contextual contingencies of all human experience—child development for boys and girls in isolated tribal groups in Botswana may be different from the development of Swiss boys from the middle and upper-middle classes. As it uncovers these dynamics, poststructuralism fosters resistance to the power they exert in the regulation and discipline of individuals.

Pronunciamentos of "endings"—referring to the notion that history, ideology, and political evolution have ended because liberal democratic capitalist states have produced a social order that can never be improved.

Semioticians—scholars who study the nature and the social influence of signs, symbols, and codes.

Social Darwinism—the social theory devised by Herbert Spencer in the late nineteenth century that applied Charles Darwin's theory of evolution to human development. Like plants and animals in the biological world, human beings compete for survival in a social world shaped by the survival of the fittest.

Critical Pedagogy in School

As critical pedagogy explores the cosmos of power and its efforts to regulate human beings, it turns its analytical gaze to schools and classrooms. Questions that are too infrequently asked emerge in this context:

- What is the sociocultural role of schooling?
- What is the relation between this role and dominant power blocs?
- How does this relationship affect the construction of the curriculum?
- Is education in a democracy different than education in a totalitarian state?
- How do critical teachers negotiate these power dynamics?
- In an era of top-down standards and standardization of instruction, how do teachers teach critically?
- How does a teacher resist an oppressive curriculum in an age of tight control of teachers?
- What does a teacher need to know to successfully engage in a critical pedagogy?
- How do we recognize a pedagogy of social control?

In the context of such questions, John Covaleskie (2003) writes: "a pedagogy that commits to making children receptive and docile is also one that denies human dignity and freedom." In Chapter 3, we will explore teaching and teacher education in the context of critical pedagogy. It is important for teachers, students in teacher education, teacher educators, and educational leaders to think about the contemporary state of teaching and teacher education from new conceptual frameworks.

Dealing with the Contemporary Situation

Too often, when examining curriculum development and school operation, critical teachers observe modes of knowledge distributed to teachers and students that feign neutrality but covertly support particular political interests. Students are not encouraged to study multiple points of view or learn that both within U.S. society and around the planet there are profoundly different interpretations of historical, scientific, literacy, political, social, and economic issues than the ones offered in their textbooks, content standards, and curriculum guides. Students are typically not taught about the complex nature of interpretation and the assumptions embedded in and power imprinted on all knowledge. Many political and educational leaders deem such profoundly important dimensions of learning unimportant. Indeed, many power wielders view such insights as downright frightening, as critical teachers begin to uncover the slippery base on which school knowledge rests. Knowledge production and curriculum development are always and forever historically embedded and culturally inscribed processes. In this context, critical educators are suspicious of any curriculum that presents itself as the truth without at least some reflection in light of differing perspectives.

Critical pedagogues maintain that the contemporary discourse about American education has not been very interested in understanding the dynamics of knowledge production or theories of knowledge. In the culture of contemporary schooling, there exists a reductionistic impulse to take knowledge at face value. Few question "how information got here." There is no need for the development of interpretive ability in this context—students either learn the "subject matter" or they don't. On the basis of their innate ability and work ethic, it is argued, students either pass or fail. Advocates of critical pedagogy maintain that the key to becoming a scholar resides at this level of interpretation—not in stuffing volumes of unproblematized data in mental filing cabinets. Such dynamics are infrequently discussed in twenty-first century public educational discourse because little questioning of educational purpose takes place—little is allowed under the auspices of twenty-first-century political leaders. The role schools play in the historical construction of the self is not an important topic of study in contemporary U.S. culture. The dominant culture's conversation about education simply ignores questions of power and justice in the development of educational policy and classroom practice.

Those who study these features of power have come to understand the ways it shapes a student's relationship to and capacity to succeed in schooling. As a rural student from the southern Appalachian Mountains, I ran into college professors who felt that someone from my background could not do well in school. As a member of a subculture with particular cultural markers, I "wore" my relationship to dominant power. I was an outsider seeking "certification" by the academy. On numerous occasions, I was told by different professors after handing in an essay or research paper that they knew I had plagiarized the work because "someone like me" was not capable of producing such writing. For reasons that maybe only a psychoanalyst might understand, I chose to continue pursuing academic work. I was lucky and privileged, however, because I possessed the confidence that I could become a scholar. Most students who find themselves in such disempowered situations don't have the confidence to continue.

Understanding this lack of confidence alerts critical teachers to one of many subtle ways that power vis-à-vis the domains of race, class, gender, geographical place, religion, and so on operates to "collate" students, to sort and rank them. When technologies of power such as standardized testing and curricular standardization are in place, possibility decreases that marginalized students will gain the confidence to reshape their relation to power or even reshape power's relationship to them. Critical educators have worked hard to try to get these understandings of power across to teachers, administrators, educational leaders, and the public. In the twenty-first century, such understandings

about schools as political locales for struggle and resistance seem profoundly out of touch with the right-wing *Zeitgeist*. Complex critical thinkers work diligently to develop new ways to make these power-related points. As Juan-Miguel Fernandez-Balboa (2003) maintains, "One of the first steps in the empowerment of people is to help them realize that their status is due, to a great extent, to systemic forces (e.g., institutional meritocracy) designed to keep them ignorant and resigned."

When I teach about power, schooling, and critical thinking, I often make use of Pierre Bourdieu's notion of "cultural capital" to illustrate these ideas. In the same way that money is a form of "economic capital," membership in the dominant culture affords individuals ways of knowing, acting, and being (cultural capital) that can be "cashed in" in order to get ahead in the lived world. These ways of knowing, acting, and being often are thought of under the categories of manners, deportment, taste, style, accent, proper grammar, level of affect, and so on. Those, like myself, who come from social and cultural locations outside of dominant culture may possess particular abilities but are marginalized because we don't understand the codes of dominant cultural capital. My students become more adept critical analysts when they understand the ways cultural capital is deployed to keep the marginalized in a subordinate position and the privileged in a dominant one. From the perspective of power wielders, this reproduction of the status quo takes place within the boundaries of common sense: "We wouldn't want someone like her in our corporation, company, department," *ad infinitum.*

As teachers, critical theorists work to both develop intellect and expose these power-related dynamics that prop up the status quo, undermine social mobility, and produce discourses, and ideologies that justify such antidemocratic practices. Majorie Mayers and Jim Field (2003) are helpful in this context as they write about the unassailable knowledge of textbooks. Textbooks in a democratic education are always open to challenge and critical teachers must stand ready to take issue with them. Taking inspiration from Mayer's and Field's questioning stance toward the sanctity of textbooks, critical teachers demand that a variety of opinions and perspectives be brought to schools. Such a demand is not merely some affirmation of diversity that insists on fairness. While fairness is obviously important, the critical perspective referenced here brings an awareness that the way curricular exclusions are executed is typically an insidious process that takes place under a flag of objectivity. We have to appeal to a broader and more complicated concept than fairness in this context. Here critical pedagogues have to understand the epistemological dimensions of knowledge production referenced in Chapter 1 and the ways diverse viewpoints are excluded by modes of positivism. Expert: "This sociological knowledge has been produced by objective social scientists." Questioner: "But it doesn't include any recognition of the role of poor women in this social process." Expert: "The inclusion of lower-socioeconomic-class women in this study was outside the purview of the research design. Next question."

The Need for a Critical Teacher Education

It is hard not to get discouraged in twenty-first-century teacher education. My colleagues in teacher education in the City University of New York (CUNY) system, for example, work so hard with teaching responsibilities, student teaching and field observations, administrative demands, service work to the community and their disciplinary specialties, and their scholarly work that they have little time left for themselves. And all of this for so little financial reward and, importantly, so little respect. With this in mind, I am painfully aware of what I'm asking them and teacher educators like them around the country to do: they need to take the diverse critical forms of knowledge we discussed in Chapters 1 and 2 and make professional education more rigorous and demanding. Teacher education students and practicing teachers need to gain a more complex conceptual understanding of the multiple contexts in which education takes place and the plethora of forces shaping the process. My colleagues in education need to help their colleagues in the arts and sciences understand these dynamics and their relevance for curriculum development in their portion of teacher education.

A critical teacher education as it problematizes knowledge distances itself from that which can be easily known. In this way, the teacher education advocated here brings students to a place they may have never been before in higher education: a terrain of discomfort where knowledge is too complex to simply give it out for use on multiple choice texts or convergent questions. On

this complex epistemological landscape the assumptions teacher candidates bring to the classroom about teaching are challenged, analyzed, and debated. The easy process of seeking a comfortable consensus must be abandoned. Too often in colleges of education the consensus that is proclaimed is a pseudoagreement. Once we dig deeper around the notion that "all of us agree that social justice should be a foundational principle on which we build our teacher education program," we find profound disagreement. In university arts and sciences far too few professors understand what curriculum development that accounts for issues of social justice might look like.

Indeed, some of the conceptions of what social justice looks like in a teacher education curriculum are incompatible, even contradictory. In an age of intellectual mediocrity in which the public conversation about such issues is truncated—where it exists at all—the attempt to deal with such concerns is at least uncomfortable. Indeed, even the ways we raise questions about such issues privilege particular ways of operating over others (Cochran-Smith, 2000; Noone and Cartwright, 1996). The ways we ask questions about social justice, for example, can exclude any authentic concern with its meaning and application in a program. Integrating the concept of social justice into a critical program is difficult, often contentious, and demands a rethinking of everything a school of education and schools of arts and sciences do. Moreover, social justice is just one of many concerns in the critical rethinking of contemporary teacher education.

Where Do Questions Come From? Ideological Undercurrents and the Forms of Knowledge of Teaching

The questions we ask about teacher education drive the form it takes. The more we know about the different forms of knowledge and about the relationship between power and knowledge, the more we realize that the questions we ask validate specific ways of thinking about teacher education while invalidating others. Questions are grounded in particular paradigms, value structures, epistemologies, and political orientations. Critical teacher educators must develop the ability to name the hidden assumptions within such questions, the value conflicts implicit within differing inquiries. The questions that bombard teacher educators from the public discourse are diverse to the point that they complicate the process of professional education. When some journalists (and educators) maintain that there is consensus around questions of what the outcomes of schooling and teacher education should be, they are not only suppressing the implicit diversity in the questions asked about education but hiding particular ideological and pedagogical inscriptions in the maneuver.

In such proclamations of consensus, dialogue is truncated. The complexity of education in a democratic society is diluted and reductionistic truths replace rigorous analysis. We do not all agree on the answers to questions such as

- Should there be national content standards?
- What is the best way to teach reading?
- What should a teacher know, and what skills should he or she possess?
- What is an educated person?
- How should teachers make use of their knowledge of a student's background?

The way we conceptualize teacher education depends, of course, on what questions we ask and how we answer them. Often I have heard students and teachers react negatively to critical pedagogy by saying the proponents don't give any empirical proof of whether or not it works. What they don't understand is that many questions about education don't involve empirical proof. How does one apply empirical knowledge to this question: should teachers help students develop a literacy of power? Different educational questions require different types of knowledge. A brief survey of such forms of knowledge in teacher education is helpful in our effort to explain the nature and benefits of a critical pedagogy.

Normative Knowledge

Normative knowledge concerns "what should be" in relation to moral and ethical issues about education. What constitutes moral and ethical behavior on the part of teacher educators and teachers? How do we develop a vision of practice that will empower educators to embrace these behaviors without fear of reprisals? Such questions begin the critical theoretical work

necessary to the development of a democratic, egalitarian sense of educational purpose. Such normative knowledge is central to the effort to establish just and rigorous colleges of education and liberal arts and sciences. Such knowledge is not produced arbitrarily but in relation to particular social visions, power relations, and cultural/historical contexts.

Empirical Knowledge

Empirical knowledge comes from research based on data derived from sense data/observations of various aspects of education. Throughout this book, I have expressed reservations about the positivist version of empirical knowledge and its uses—but not about the concept of empirical knowledge itself. A critical teacher education demands more sophisticated forms of observational forms of knowledge of education. A thicker, more complex, more textured, self-conscious form of empirical knowledge takes into account the situatedness of the researcher and the researched—where they are standing or are placed in the social, cultural, historical, philosophical, economic, political, and psychological web of reality. Such insight respects the complexity of the interpretive dimension of empirical knowledge production. With these hermeneutical cautions in mind, critical teachers need to be acquainted with a wide variety of empirical studies of school and society.

Political Knowledge

Political knowledge is closely associated with normative knowledge, as it focuses on the power-related aspects of teacher education and teaching. In the context of political knowledge, the charges of politicization grow louder and often more strident. Critical teacher educators maintain, however, that it is impossible to conceptualize curriculum outside of a sociopolitical context. No matter what form they take, all curricula bear the imprint of power. When teacher education students are induced to study the curriculum outside of such horizons, they are being deceived by a claim of neutrality concerning the production of knowledge. The culture of positivism defines the curriculum as a body of agreed-upon forms of knowledge being systematically passed along to students as an ever-evolving but neutral, instructional process. Of course, critical teachers challenge such hegemonic assertions.

Ontological Knowledge

Ontological knowledge has to do with what it means to *be* a teacher in light of the forces that shape our teacher persona. There is nothing new in asserting that the ways one teaches and the pedagogical purposes one pursues are directly connected to the way teachers see themselves. At the same time, the ways teachers come to see themselves as learners, in particular, the ways they conceptualize what they need to learn, where they need to learn it, and how the process should take place shape their teacher persona (CPRE, 1995). Such a persona cannot be separated from the various forms of knowledge delineated here and the larger notion of "professional awareness." Too infrequently are teachers in a university, student teaching, or in-service professional education encouraged to confront why they think as they do about themselves as teachers—especially in relationship to the social, cultural, political, economic, and historical world around them. Teacher education provides little insight into the forces that shape identity and consciousness. Becoming educated, becoming a critical complex practitioner necessitates personal transformation. It necessitates analysis of one's teacher self in light of the historical role of teachers.

Experiential Knowledge

Experiential knowledge involves information and insight about practice, about managing a classroom. Too often and in a variety of contexts, such knowledge is not viewed as important or worthy of study. Advocates of critical pedagogy need to take these forms of knowledge seriously and place them neither above nor below other forms of knowledge about education. Forms of knowledge about practice are inherently problematic, however, because the nature of what constitutes practice is profoundly complex. There are many different forms of educational practice:

- classroom teaching
- teacher leadership involving areas of curriculum and instruction
- educational administration
- educational policy making
- teacher education
- knowledge production in education
- political activism.

Too often in teaching and teacher education, the only type of practice signified by the term involves classroom teaching. We have to be very careful about this type of reductionism as we work to develop and put into practice a critical teacher education and a critical pedagogy.

Thus, the form of teacher education advocated here recognizes that not only are there numerous forms of practice but that all of them are complex. Donald Schon (1995) has used the term "indeterminate zones of practice" to signify the uncertainty, complexity, uniqueness, and contested nature of any practice. In its complexity, the critical notion of educational practice avoids universal rules about how to do it correctly. There are as many brilliant forms of practice as there are brilliant practitioners.

Look to the overhead projector, class; here are the five steps to writing on the chalkboard:

- always keep chalk longer than two inches readily available in the chalk tray,
- before writing adjust shades to minimize glare on board,
- hold the chalk at a forty-five-degree angle relative to the board,
- write letters at least five inches tall,
- dust hands before leaving the board so not to wipe them inadvertently on clothing.

I actually endured this universal positivistic lesson in an undergraduate teacher education class in 1971. I am still trying to recover.

Reflective-synthetic Knowledge

Reflective-synthetic knowledge involves bringing all of our forms of knowledge of teaching together so they can be employed in the critical pedagogical act. Acknowledging our debt to Donald Schon's notion of the reflective practitioner, a critical teacher education includes a reflective-synthetic form of educational knowledge. Because our purpose is not to indoctrinate practitioners to operate in a particular manner but to help them think about practice in more sophisticated ways, a central dimension of teacher education involves reflecting on and examining all of these forms of knowledge in relation to one another. A reflective-synthetic knowledge of education involves developing a way of thinking about the professional role in light of a body of forms of knowledge, principles, purposes, and experiences. In this process educators work to devise ways of using these various forms of knowledge to perform our jobs in more informed, practical, ethical, democratic, politically just, self-aware, and purposeful ways. At the same time, they work to expose the assumptions about knowledge embedded in various conceptions of practice and in the officially approved educational information they encounter.

With these forms of knowledge in mind, teaching moves to new intellectual, emancipatory, and pragmatic domains. For example, the way in which we answer the question of whether there should be national content standards depends on normative issues of educational purpose. Is our purpose to inculcate a body of data in the minds of students? And if we answer that question affirmatively, then what kind of data might that involve? In this context, political questions arise: Who gets to choose what data are included and excluded? On the basis of what criteria would such choices be made? Here these normative and critical questions certainly reflect my own values and priorities. Other questions reflect other values and priorities. None of them are neutral, objective questions. Indeed, they are merely the first questions that arise—there are many more, especially when we get into the role of teacher education in this context.

Consider the question of how the role of schooling in a democratic society differs from that in a nondemocratic society. Here is another question with empirical, normative, critical, ontological, experiential, and reflective-synthetic dimensions. By nature, a question about democracy is a critical question because it always involves issues of power and its distribution. The empirical dimension of the question involves studies of education in both democratic and nondemocratic societies. Knowing what we know about empirical research, critical teachers would have to study how the studies were designed and what criteria were used to designate a democratic or nondemocratic education. The question raises experiential concerns about how we put into practice a democratic education: What do democratic classrooms look like? How does a teacher operate in democratic classrooms?

An ontological aspect of the question induces us to ask—how do I become a democratic teacher? How does that

designation change my teacher persona? From a critical perspective, our reading of positivist-driven education both historically and contemporaneously involves the assertion that it is hard to distinguish such a pedagogy from education in totalitarian societies. Although I am not willing to make a final generalization, several interviews with individuals who attended elementary and secondary school in the former Soviet Union reveal that they had more contact with diverse political ideas than many of their U.S. counterparts. Given the dominant political opinion in the United States in the first decade of the twenty-first century, I would guess that my perspective on this issue is not part of a wider public consensus.

Moving to a Critical Complexity: Teaching an Evolving Critical Pedagogy

Teachers working in a critical context rebel against the view of practitioners as information deliverers, as deskilled messengers who uncritically pass along a canned curriculum. Highly skilled scholarly teachers research their students and their communities and analyze the curricular topics they are expected to cover. In light of such inquiry, these teachers develop a course of study that understands subject matter and academic skills in relation to where their students come from and the needs they bring to school. Such an act is highly difficult, requiring a wide range of knowledge and abilities as well as subtle pedagogical skills. If nothing else, it is complex. When this complexity is added to the complications of a deep understanding of knowledge and its production, the job of teaching becomes a profoundly sophisticated task.

Critical educators and policy makers who appreciate complexity in the way it is employed here know that the physical world and social reality answer analysts' questions much like the oracle at Delphi—enigmatically. Rarely do standardized and/or standards-driven schools take into account issues of complexity such as:

- the ambiguity of language and its less-than-transparent meanings
- the ways individual minds rarely perceive phenomena and their meanings in the same way

- meaning-making is not simply a rational process
- the boundary between rationality and irrationality is blurred
- the construction of a neutral curriculum is an impossibility
- researchers coming from different value positions will produce often-contradictory information about a particular artifact or text
- the nature of the disagreements about the benefits of Western reason.

The importance of understanding these issues contributing to educational complexity revolves around the conceptual and cognitive limitations of that which comprises mainstream schoolwork. The addition of the insights of complexity theory to critical pedagogy is an important dimension of the concept of an evolving critical pedagogy (as described in Chapter I). In my own work in critical pedagogy, I refer to this merging of critical pedagogy and complexity theory as a complex critical pedagogy. When educators don't understand critical pedagogy and the evolving critical pedagogy of complexity, the analytical abilities of, say, an Albert Einstein would not be recognized as legitimate or relevant (see Kincheloe, Steinberg, and Tippins, 1999, for an expansion of these ideas). Einstein would not have been a good student in schools shaped by top-down technical standards because he was not proficient at memorizing data. When it came to viewing the world from unprecedented angles, viewing contradictions within accepted bodies of knowledge, developing thought experiments where "what would happen if …?" questions were raised, transferring learning in one domain to another, or applying particular forms of knowledge to problems in the lived world, however, Einstein was undoubtedly a genius. These complex abilities were not simply ignored in Einstein schools, they were not viewed as worthy of knowing. Unfortunately, in the technical-standards-driven schools of the early twenty-first century, they are still unrecognized. Such recognitions are central to an understanding of both critical pedagogy and a complex critical pedagogy, as they reflect the complexity we seek.

If schools are ever to be worthy of the patronage of young Einsteins—and there are millions of students capable of Einsteinian achievements in a variety of fields—they must begin

to identify the nature of the new forms of knowledge and scholarly abilities teachers need to teach using a complex critical pedagogy. Colleges of education must play a central role in this identification and preparatory process; school districts and state departments of education must develop incentives for educators to immerse themselves in the complex task of acquiring, practicing, and teaching these high-level abilities. Laying the conceptual foundations for these two tasks is a basic goal of a complex critical pedagogy. One of the central understandings of these conceptual foundations involves exposing the logic behind the organization of many existing schools and the positivistic standards that guide them.

The Slippery and Complex Relationship Between Theory and Practice

Because critical pedagogy is all about connecting theory to practice, it is important to discuss the relationship between the two dynamics. Too often in existing forms of teacher education, theory and practice are designated in a positivist manner that views theory as the discrete domain of the university and practice the province of elementary and secondary schools. In this rationalistic articulation, theory serves as a direct guide to practice—a concept taken directly from the assumption that scientific knowledge produces universal theories that are developed for their practical utility. In a critical complex context, practice attempts to escape from the practical domain where theory is applied. Max van Manen (1999) problematizes this notion of practice, developing a variety of notions of the concept: "professional practice, moral practice, pedagogical practice, radical practice, discursive practice, and an epistemology of practice." The concept has a more complex meaning, he adds, than expressed in the phrase "operationalizing the techniques and competencies of classroom teaching."

In this context, critical complex teacher educators add the notion of **praxis**, the complex combination of theory and practice resulting in informed action. Here the effort to contextualize modes of thinking is a form of practice necessary to all professional activity. Critical complex teacher educators attempt to engage students in questions about the relationships between particular thoughts and actions as they confront lived experience.

praxis
involves a process of action-reflection-action that is central to development of a consciousness of power and how it operates.

As critical teacher educators challenge the legitimacy of particular forms of knowledge and theory, for example, they encourage students to reconsider the social and educational goals and forms of practice that might have been developed around the acceptance of such knowledge and theory (Joshua, 1998). Such recognition moves us to a new appreciation of the multidimensionality of the theory and practice relationship.

deskilling teachers

teachers and other professionals often fall into a state of degraded professional practice when hyperrationalized reforms remove the conceptualization of the professional task from its execution. Deskilling positions teachers as low-level functionaries in the educational workplace who simply follow the dictates of their administrative superiors.

Freed from the notion that educational theory produces generalizations about a narrowly defined teaching practice that can be mass-produced as curriculum guides for **deskilling teachers**, a critical complex teacher education constantly attempts to preclude too much coziness between theory and practice. In a critical pedagogical context, I argue that the theory-practice relationship involves the negotiation of more desirable ways of thinking and acting. Proceeding cautiously in such a negotiation, the tentative nature of the relationship is always emphasized. As we ponder the connections between theory and practice, we reflect on the generally accepted assumptions that drive teacher education and teaching. In our critical stance, we disrupt the common wisdom by exploring the contradictions between theory and practice. Just developing a theoretical language or a theoretical critique is never sufficient; the relation between the act of theorizing and professional practice is far more complex (Pinar and Grumet, 1988; van Manen, 1999).

On this tentative terrain, critical complex teacher educators must tread carefully. Of course, the development of theory-driven conceptual frameworks that help us implement critical complex professional education is essential. Interaction with such frameworks is important to everyone involved with a teacher education program—students in particular. The salient point here is that the theoretical framework never tells us exactly what to do—how exactly to construct the student teaching experience, for instance (Pinar and Grumet, 1988; Vavrus and Archibald, 1998). There is always an interpretive (hermeneutic) dimension that precludes such facile resolution of the nature of the theory-practice relationship. The role of the critical complex teacher educator is to view practice through the lenses of the theoretical framework and the theoretical framework through the lenses of practice. In this process, the kinetic energy of each is intensified, but the exact nature of their relationship is unresolved. The interaction

is catalytic, not fixed. Teacher educators and teachers emerge more informed from their understanding of the dynamics of the interaction. Students profit as such a critical complex theory and practice take into account the individuality of learners and the social context in which learning takes place. Critical teachers don't teach to some positivistic mean.

Extending our concern with the interaction of theory and practice, it is important for teacher educators and students to focus on the benefits of social theory. The questions asked and the concerns raised in this primer have been driven by particular social theoretical dynamics—critical ones, of course. What, many of my students ask, is a social theory supposed to do? Understanding social theory helps individuals place themselves and their worldviews within social, cultural, historical, economic, and philosophical frameworks. When such lenses are brought to teacher education, teachers and students begin to analyze and reconstruct their "ways of being" in the social cosmos and in the institution of education. A critical social theory identifies conflicting interests and the cultural politics emerging from this competition. These cultural politics shape every dimension of schooling from the curriculum to interpersonal relationships between different groups. Social theory helps us identify these power dynamics in a way that allows us to work more adeptly for a democratic and socially responsible education (Apple, 1999; Giroux, 1997; Hinchey, 1998; Kincheloe and McLaren, 2004; McLaren, 2000).

In this social theory-grounded context, professionals are better equipped to engage in conversations about the role of teacher education in the process of social change. In such a conversation, social theoretical understandings help everyone understand the ways teacher education and schooling tacitly contribute to the maintenance of the status quo with its unjust power relations. With this in mind, teacher educators bring a critical hermeneutical understanding to their work. As we know from Chapter 2, this term implies that we develop rigorous ways of understanding the world so we can change it in just and democratic ways. Ever since positivists applied physical science methods to social science and educational research, there has been a struggle to address those aspects of the human condition that need not just counting but understanding. The hermeneutic dimension of research

attempts to appreciate this question of meaning by focusing on the interpretive aspects of the act of knowledge production. In the instrumental rationality of many colleges/schools/departments of education, this hermeneutic dimension is often dismissed. Understanding that all knowledge is an interpretation, a critical complex teacher education places great emphasis on the hermeneutic dimension (Geeland and Taylor, 2000; Purpel, 1999; Scering, 1997; Shaker and Kridel, 1989; Steiner, Krank, McLaren, and Bahruth, 2000; Sumara, 1996; Zuss, 1999).

Learning from the critical hermeneutic tradition, teacher educators learn to reexamine claims to authority in knowledge production and professional expertise. No pristine interpretation exists in educational research or skill development. No methodology, social or educational theory, or discursive form can claim a privileged position that enables the production of uncontested knowledge. Educational knowledge producers must always speak/write about the world in terms of something else in the world, "in relation to." As creatures of the world, we are oriented to it in a way that prevents us from grounding our theories and perspectives outside of it. Thus, whether we like it or not, we are all destined, as interpreters, to analyze from within its boundaries and blinders. Within the limitation, however, the interpretations emerging from the hermeneutic process can still move us to new levels of understanding. With this in mind, critical complex teacher educators can begin to understand educational knowledge from an angle that allows them unanticipated insights into where it came from and whose interests it serves (Carson and Sumara, 1997; Ellis, 1998; Gallagher, 1992; Jardine, 1998; Mayers, 2001).

With this theoretical-interpretive dimension established, teacher educators can begin to bring previously excluded knowledge forms to professional education:

- African American studies
- Feminist epistemologies
- Indigenous forms of knowledge
- Phenomenology
- Critical theory
- Semiotics
- Discourse analysis
- Psychoanalysis

- Queer theory
- Political economic studies
- Postcolonial studies
- Poststructural analysis.

As teacher educators and teachers learn these rigorous modes of analyses, they gain new competence in the production of reflective-synthetic forms of knowledge. They learn to see anew, to discern the role of values and power in knowledges originally presented as innocent. With their 3-D glasses, teachers who grasp these theoretical constructs can interpret and make meanings around the complex interaction of theory and practice. In this context, everyone involved with teacher education sees that there are diverse and conflicting ways to conceptualize any pedagogical activity. As such complexity is noted, outside experts can no longer provide reductionistic answers for $20,000 dollars a pop. Teachers will emancipate themselves from top-down management schemes with their obligatory canned curricula, teacher scripts, and outside evaluations (Edwards, 2000; Foote and Goodson, 2001; Snook, 1999).

Glossary

Deskilling teachers—teachers and other professionals often fall into a state of degraded professional practice when hyper-rationalized reforms remove the conceptualization of the professional task from its execution. Deskilling positions teachers as low-level functionaries in the educational workplace who simply follow the dictates of their administrative superiors.

Praxis—involves a process of action-reflection-action that is central to the development of a consciousness of power and how it operates.

CHAPTER FOUR

Critical Pedagogy and Research

An evolving critical pedagogy holds profound implications for knowledge production and research in education and many other fields. Drawing on a critical complex epistemology that examines the social, historical, cultural, economic, educational, and political cosmos from the perspectives of particular, often marginalized racial/cultural groups, an evolving criticality challenges the master narratives and the dominant discourses of more traditional academic disciplines. In this context, educational research moves into a critical domain as it challenges dominant race, class, gender, sexual, and colonial ideologies that have inscribed both these disciplines and various social institutions.

The study of such ideologies constitutes one dimension of critical pedagogy's larger analysis of power and the complex ways it shapes the experiences of Africans and peoples of African descent, indigenous peoples from around the world, Latinos/Hispanics, Asians/Asian Americans and other groups constructed around categories such as gender, sexuality, and one's relationship to colonialism. Thus, models of power have become profoundly important in the critical pedagogy, especially as understanding

them helps critical educators/researchers better comprehend and act to subvert structures and inscriptions of social and cultural inequality. Central to the scholarship of our notion of an evolving criticality has been an interdisciplinary orientation that is eclectic in its methodology and theory as it seeks new and better ways to accomplish the goals of diverse domains of study.

This chapter is directly related to this **multilogicality,** this multiperspectival critical pedagogy, and its use of multiple methodological and theoretical tools. In the effort to better understand structures and inscriptions of power and the ways they promote social and cultural inequality, I promote the notion of the bricolage (Kincheloe and Berry, 2004). Connecting the methodological and theoretical eclecticism of the bricolage with a **critical multiculturalist** concern with the development of a literacy of power to help understand and take action in opposition to relations of inequality, this chapter contributes to the critical pedagogical goal of producing knowledge that leads to the ending of human suffering. Students of critical pedagogy will find these concerns relevant to their scholarly, cultural, and political work. In this attempt to extend thought and action the chapter examines

- Ways social/cultural diversity expresses itself in the epistemological realm as it analyzes strategies that criticalists can employ to transcend Cartesian-Newtonian reductionism.
- More textured and rigorous (not in the positivistic sense) models of knowledge production.
- New modes of exposing and understanding the impact of tacit social forces, structures, and discourses overlooked by monological research methods.
- Multilogical articulations of epistemology, social theory, and methodology, and their uses in critical pedagogy.
- Subjugated and indigenous forms of knowledge and the diverse forms of meaning making and knowledge production they bring to an evolving criticality.
- New frames from which to conceptualize and extend the concept of interdisciplinarity.
- Multiple perspectives that help students of education devise more compelling interpretations of the data they confront.

- Ways of deploying the multidimensional "power of difference."
- Modes of expanding what multiperspectival research in a multilogical criticality can become.
- The process a researcher might employ to enter the bricolage and engage its insight into conceptualizing and designing inquiry.

It is important to note in this context that the bricolage is not designed to create an elite corps of expert researchers in critical pedagogy who deploy their authority over others by excluding them from the conversation about knowledge production. When critical scholars establish an exclusive "critical elite," they have fallen prey to the same power inequalities that motivated the founding of critical pedagogy in the first place. When such domains of exclusion take shape around categories of status, class, race, gender, sexuality and/or institutional affiliation, critical scholars have no moral or intellectual authority to produce knowledge in relation to the traditional concerns of education. Bricoleurs, as described here, are acutely aware of the dangers of such reproductions of inequality even among those studying and ostensibly challenging it. Thus, the critical bricoleurs imagined in this chapter come from a wide diversity of social, cultural, and ethnic backgrounds, academic disciplines, educational and academic institutions, vocational roles, and activist groups.

Building the Critical Multiculturalist Theoretical Base in an Evolving Criticality

In 1997 in *Changing Multiculturalism*, Shirley Steinberg and I offered an evolving notion of critical multiculturalism that attempted to address and avoid the problems of more mainstream articulations of multiculturalism. Unimpressed by what was labeled multiculturalism and multicultural education, we drew upon critical theory and the tradition of an evolving criticality (Kincheloe and McLaren, 2004; McLaren and Kincheloe, 2007) along with a variety of scholarship from diverse ethnic studies, cultural studies, sociology, and education to produce our critical multiculturalism. Critical multiculturalism is concerned with how individuals are discursively, political economically, ideologically,

and culturally constructed as human beings. Indeed, critical multiculturalism wants to promote an awareness of how domination takes place, how dominant cultures reproduce themselves, and how power operates to shape self and knowledge.

This position makes no pretense of neutrality as it openly proclaims its affiliation with efforts to produce a just, egalitarian, and democratic world that refuses to stand for the perpetuation of human suffering (Kincheloe and Steinberg, 1997). Critical multiculturalism is uncomfortable with the term *multiculturalism* but works to redefine it in the contemporary era. Indeed, the first decade of the twenty-first century cannot be understood outside the framework of fast capitalism, transnational corporations, corporatized electronic and ideologically inscribed information, mutating, and more insidious forms of racism and ethnic bias, and a renewed form of U.S. colonialism and military intervention designed to extend the political, economic, and cultural influence of the twenty-first century American Empire (Kincheloe and Steinberg, 2004).

In particular, a critical multiculturalism is profoundly concerned with what gives rise to race, class, gender, sexual, religious, cultural, and ability-based inequalities. Critical multiculturalists focus their attention on how power has operated historically and contemporaneously to legitimate social categories and divisions. In this context, we analyze and encourage further research on how in everyday, mundane, lived culture these dynamics of power play themselves out. It is at this ostensibly "innocent" level that the power of patriarchy, white supremacy, colonial assumptions of superiority, heterosexism, and class elitism operate. Critical multiculturalism appreciates both the hidden nature of these operations and the fact that most of the time they go unnoticed even by those participating in them and researching them. The invisibility of this process is disconcerting as the cryptic nature of many forms of oppression makes it difficult to convince individuals from dominant power blocs that they exist. Such subtlety is matched by cognizance of the notion that there are as many differences within groups as there are between them (Du Bois, 1973; Macedo, 2006; Sleeter, 1993; Yudice, 1995).

In the twenty-first century, the increased influence of right-wing power blocs have elevated the need for a critical multiculturalist approach to knowledge production. The geopolitical and military operations to extend the American Empire have been accompanied by disturbing trends in knowledge production that hold alarming implications for the future—the future of research in particular. Critical multiculturalists are aware that such knowledge work possesses a historical archaeology in Western culture and U.S. society. In this context, David G. Smith (2006) contends that the U.S. Empire is constructed not only around territorial and natural resource claims, but in hyperreality, epistemological claims as well. Tracing the epistemological claims of the empire, Smith studies Western knowledge from the **cognito** of Descartes to Adam Smith's economics of self-interest. With the merging of Descartes' rationalism with Adam Smith's economics, the West's pursuit of economic expansionism is justified by the concept of liberty. An evolving critical pedagogy cannot ignore these dynamics at the end of the first decade of the twenty-first century.

Multicultural researchers who employ the bricolage described in this chapter have carefully examined this Enlightenment reason and its relation to oppression and social regulation. Proponents have maintained for centuries that it is this form of reason that frees us from the chaos of ignorance and human depravity. It is this reason, they proclaimed, that separated us from the uncivilized, the inferior. Smith (2006) argues that it is this notion that supports a philosophy of human development or developmentalism used in a variety of discourses to oppress and marginalize the cultural others who haven't employed such Western ways of seeing and being. Often in their "immaturity" these others, this rationalistic developmentalism informs us, must be disciplined, even ruled in order to teach them to be rational and democratic.

The right-wing developmentalist story about the contemporary world situation conveniently omits the last 500 years of European colonialism, the anticolonial movements around the world beginning in the post-World War II era and their impact on the U.S. civil rights movement, the women's movement, the antiwar movement in Vietnam, Native American liberation struggles, the gay rights movement, and other emancipatory movements that inform our critical multiculturalism and have been traditional concerns of criticality. In an other work I have argued that the reaction to these anticolonial movements have set the tone and content of much of American political, social, cultural, and educational experience over the last three

decades (Gresson, 1995, 2004; Kincheloe, 2001a; Kincheloe and Steinberg, 1997; Kincheloe, Steinberg, Rodriguez, and Chennault, 1998; Rodriguez and Villaverde, 2000). At the end of the first decade of the twenty-first century, these forces of reaction seemed to have gained a permanent foothold in American social, political, cultural, and educational institutions. In this context, all forms of critical study find themselves in a precarious position.

The future of knowledge is at stake in this new political economic and cultural landscape. Few times in human history has there existed a greater need for forms of knowledge work that expose the dominant ideologies and discourses that shape the information accessed by many individuals. The charge of critical multiculturalists in a larger critical pedagogical context in this Zeitgeist is to develop forms of knowledge work and approaches to research that take these sobering dynamics into account. This is the idea behind my articulation of the bricolage. Attempting to make use of a variety of philosophical, method-ological, cultural, political, and epistemological, and ontological discourses, the bricolage can be employed by criticalists con-cerned with the politics of knowledge to produce compelling insights that seek to challenge the neocolonial representations about others.

Utilizing these multiple perspectives from critics of Western research practices, peoples subjugated within Western societies, and individuals from non-Western societies, the bricolage offers alternate paths in regressive times. Such alternative paths open up new forms of knowledge production and researcher positionality that are grounded on more egalitarian relationships with individu-als being researched. Bricoleurs in their valuing of diverse forms of knowledge, especially those forms of knowledge that have been subjugated, come to value the abilities and the insights of those whom they research. It is in such egalitarian and interactive forms of researcher-researched relationships that new forms of researcher self-awareness is developed—a self-awareness necessary in the bricoleur's attempt to understand the way positionality shapes the nature of the knowledge produced in the research process. The following section of the chapter introduces the bri-colage and begins a conversation about what is conceptualized as elastic and tentative dimensions of the concept.

Introducing the Bricolage

The French word *bricoleur* describes a handyman or handywoman who makes use of the tools available to complete a task. Some connotations of the term involve trickery and cunning and reminds me of the chicanery of Hermes, in particular his ambiguity concerning the messages of the gods. If hermeneutics came to connote the ambiguity and slipperiness of textual meaning, then bricolage can also imply the imaginative elements of the presentation of all formal research. Indeed, as cultural studies of Western science have indicated, all scientific inquiry is jerry-rigged to a degree; science, as we all know by now, is not nearly as clean, simple, and procedural as scientists would have us believe. Maybe this is an admission many social science researchers would wish to keep in the closet.

In the first decade of the twenty-first century bricolage has typically been understood to involve the process of employing these methodological strategies, as they are needed in the unfolding context of the research situation. While this interdisciplinary feature is central to any notion of the bricolage, I propose that critical researchers go beyond this dynamic. Pushing to a new conceptual terrain, such an eclectic process raises numerous issues that researchers must deal with in order to maintain theoretical coherence and epistemological innovation. Such multidisciplinarity demands a new level of research self-consciousness and awareness of the numerous contexts in which any researcher is operating. As one labors to expose the various social, cultural, and political structures that covertly shape our own and other scholars' research narratives, the bricolage highlights the relationship between a researcher's ways of seeing and the social location of his or her personal history. Appreciating research as a power-driven act, the critical researcher-as-bricoleur abandons the quest for some naïve concept of realism, focusing instead on the clarification of his or her position in the web of reality and the social locations of other researchers and how they shape the production and interpretation of knowledge.

In this context, bricoleurs move into the domain of complexity. The bricolage exists out of respect for the complexity of the lived world. Indeed, it is grounded on an epistemology of critical complexity. One dimension of this complexity can be

illustrated by the relationship between research and the domain of social theory. All observations of the world are shaped either consciously or unconsciously by social theory—such theory provides the framework that highlights or erases what might be observed. Theory in a modernist empiricist mode is a way of understanding what operates without variation in every context. Since theory is a cultural and linguistic artifact, its interpretation of the object of its observation is inseparable from the historical dynamics that have shaped it. The task of the bricoleur is to attack this multicultural complexity, uncovering both the visible and invisible artifacts of multiple forms of power, and documenting the nature of its influence on not only their own but on scholarship and knowledge production in general. In this process, bricoleurs act upon the concept that theory is not an explanation of nature—it is more an explanation of our relation to nature. In the twenty-first century neocolonial era, this task becomes even more important as right-wing and neoliberal theories insidiously saturate so much of the knowledge produced about human beings and their world.

Cultivating Agency: An Active View of Research Methodology

In its hard labors in the domain of complexity, the bricolage views research methods actively rather than passively, meaning that we actively construct our research methods from the tools at hand rather than passively receiving the "correct," transcultural universally applicable methodologies. I ask, for example, all of my doctoral students to write extensively about the multiple theories and methodologies that inform their dissertations. I want them to construct their own bricolage of theory and method that helps them produce more rigorous, multidimensional knowledge. Avoiding modes of reasoning that come from certified processes of logical analysis, bricoleurs also steer clear of preexisting guidelines and checklists developed outside the specific demands of the inquiry at hand. In its embrace of complexity, the bricolage constructs a far more active role for humans both in shaping reality and in creating the research processes and narratives that represent it. Such an active agency rejects deterministic views of social reality that assume the effects of particular dominant social, political, economic, and educational processes. At the same time and in the same conceptual context, this belief in active human agency refuses standardized modes of knowledge production from particular power blocs (Dahlbom, 1998; McLeod, 2000; Selfe and Selfe, 1994; Young and Yarbrough, 1993).

In many ways, there is a form of instrumental reason, what critical theorists call a rational irrationality, in the use of passive, external, monological, monocultural research methods. In the active bricolage, we bring our understanding of the research context together with our previous experience with research methods. Using these forms of knowledge, we tinker in the Levi-Straussian sense with our research methods in field-based and interpretive contexts. This tinkering is a high-level cognitive process involving construction and reconstruction, contextual diagnosis, negotiation, and readjustment. Researchers' interaction with the objects of their inquiries, bricoleurs understand, are always complicated, mercurial, unpredictable and, of course, complex. Such conditions negate the practice of planning research strategies in advance. In lieu of such rationalization of the process, bricoleurs enter into the research act as methodological negotiators. Always respecting the demands of the task at hand, the bricolage, as conceptualized here, resists its placement in concrete as it promotes its elasticity. In light of Yvonna Lincoln's (2001) delineation of two types of bricoleurs, those who, first, are committed to research eclecticism allowing circumstance to shape methods employed; and, second, those who want to engage in the genealogy/archeology of the disciplines with some grander purpose in mind. In a critical pedagogical research context, my purpose entails both of Lincoln's articulations of the role of the bricoleur.

Research method in the bricolage is a concept that receives more respect than in more rationalistic articulations of the term. The rationalistic, colonialist articulation of method subverts the deconstruction of wide varieties of unanalyzed cultural assumptions embedded in passive methods. Bricoleurs in their appreciation of the complexity of the research process view research method as involving far more than procedure. In this mode of analysis bricoleurs come to understand research method as also a technology of justification, meaning a way of defending what we assert we know and the process by which we know it. Thus, the education of critical researchers demands that everyone take a step back from the process of learning research methods. Such a step back allows us

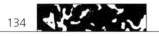

a conceptual distance that produces a critical consciousness. Such a consciousness refuses the passive acceptance of externally imposed research methods that tacitly certify modes justifying universal forms of knowledge that are decontextualized and reductionistic (Denzin and Lincoln, 2000; Foster, 1997; McLeod, 2000).

Bricolage and the Effort to Transcend Reductionism: The Zombies of Positivism

In the spirit of the critical multilogicality, an evolving critical pedagogy seeks to produce, we combine critical theory with indigenous and subjugated knowledge as well as other forms of knowledge from diverse cultures. Into this mix, we add a deep understanding of political economic forces, feminist theory, complexity and chaos theory, cultural studies, and phenomenological and hermeneutic understandings. I understand that this is asking much of critical scholars, but we must produce more rigorous forms of knowledge than the reductionistic protectors of the status quo. The pursuit of such complex understandings is a lifetime pursuit, not something that one can learn merely in a short span of time. So please understand that the first step is to gain an awareness of the need for such a bricolage of understandings followed by years of study and practice in applying them. Many will tell critical researchers that such work is not worth the effort, that the reductionism and hegemony critical bricoleurs are fighting do not exist, and that it is better to leave these theoretical and methodological questions alone. Don't believe them.

As we work to construct critical information that is useful in the struggle against oppression and human constructed human suffering, we also study ever-morphing forms of globalized power and new forms of colonialism. In this process, we take Paulo Freire's concept of radical love seriously, concurrently producing new modes of human connectedness and fresh ways of seeing the world that transport us to new dimensions of reality. Never underestimate the power of difference to help us develop new ways of seeing, new modes of consciousness, new forms of knowledge, and new ways of acting in the world. This critical power of difference or epistemological/ontological multilogicality helps us reap the benefits of the bricolage's diverse ways of perceiving and understanding a particular phenomenon. Ways of seeing and being that come from different geographical places in the natural world, different manifestations of Zeitgeist, diverse communities of practice, cultures from around the planet, and divergent **epistemes** provide critical researchers with unique insights into emancipatory work and knowledge production.

Bricolage-based research and social action in this context help to liberate us from the shackles of **reductionism.** The critical complexity of the bricolage upsets those researchers who are seeking simply differentiated boundaries separating humans from social context, power and knowledge, us and them. Learning more about epistemological and ideological frameworks and their effects on everyday life, we come to better understand why we see things as we do. We concurrently understand how subversive—and thus frightening—such insights can be to the dominant power. The forms that positivism takes in the contemporary era—even though mainstream researchers claim that positivism is long dead and buried—constructs the lived worlds of the marginalized in ways that are typically ignored or missed by hegemonized researchers. Positivism may be officially (and conveniently) proclaimed as dead but continues to shape knowledge production in an "undead" state. Thus, the zombies of positivism work their reductionistic black magic, proclaiming the correct ways to teach to raise test scores, and the scientific truth about students' intelligence.

In my teaching in the southern Appalachian Mountains of Tennessee and Virginia to the Sioux Reservation in South Dakota, I have listened to distressed mothers, fathers, guardians, and caregivers from poverty-stricken backgrounds tell of the pain caused by the school failure of their child. Possessed by the zombies of positivism, some of the principals and teachers who failed the child never understood how the assumptions of the educational establishment, modes of evaluation, and the structure of the curriculum contributed to the child's academic troubles. The zombies were invisible, stalking the sociopolitical, economic, and educational landscape free from confrontation and interrogation. I have sat in many middle school, high school, undergraduate, and graduate meetings about students where the unseen zombies sat at the table with us, imperceptibly whispering their reductionistic, decontextualized opinions to all participants in the room. The educational agents at many of these meetings had no idea where their ideas came from or what suffering their suppositions and deeds caused. The bricolage employed in a critical pedagogical context helps educators

not only appreciate the consequences of their actions but also recognize the influence of the hidden ideological and epistemological power structures that contributes to the failure of the marginalized students (Harding, 1998; Lapani, 1998; McClure, 2000).

The zombies of positivism have created a profoundly effective research tool to undermine the world's appreciation of the complexity of everyday life and the physical and social domains. Metaphorically, they have constructed a reductionistic tap that like a spigot regulates the mode of data allowed to claim standing as verified knowledge. Critical knowledge workers employing the bricolage focus on this reductionistic tap, tracing its actions, identifying tendencies in what is cut off and what is allowed to flow through, and pointing out the consequences of such an epistemological process. Data, critical bricoleurs understand, emerging from scientific induction usually finds its way into the flow through the reductionistic tap. In the language of research, scientific induction is based on the assumption that if a person engages in a particular action a specific outcome will consistently be the result. A teacher, according to the reductionists, who uses a particular pedagogical method can be rest assured that students will learn the, say, Periodic Chart in chemistry. Teachers understand that the educational process is just not that simple—too many intervening factors can change the dynamics of a classroom and the outcomes of a lesson.

The zombies of positivism call this the invariance principle: whenever teachers do X the result will be Y. Such a principle is not only intrinsically problematic but also ignores some of the most basic questions concerning the purposes of teaching and learning in general. In contemporary positivistic educational contexts does information about the murder of indigenous people, environmental racism, economic exploitation, ad infinitum characteristic of many transnational corporations make it through the reductionistic data tap? As I study schools in North America and Europe in the contemporary era, the answer is quite obvious—hell, no. Analyzing the reductionistic data tap even more deeply, critical bricoleurs raise issues around the complex interpretive dimensions of any knowledge contemporary positivism produces.

In this context, critical pedagogical knowledge producers deconstruct positivism's obsession with measurement and frequency, asking in the process questions of being and meaning—ontology and hermeneutics—about the phenomena in question. Such questions help increase the flow of the reductionistic data spigot, as critical analysis moves us to a new space in knowledge production. This new space claimed by the critical bricoleurs allows us to develop research strategies and pedagogies that appreciate the complexity of interpreting data and using such insights to act justly, intelligently, and creatively in the world. A scholar activist has to possess a well-informed and well-cultivated intellect to develop profound interpretations and formulate transformative actions around them.

Here we come back to the critical hermeneutics referenced in Chapter 2. The cultivation of such a critical interpretive facility helps challenge the invisible zombies of positivism who work their epistemological prestidigitation in both quantitative and qualitative research. Too often, it is assumed by many observers that the critique of positivism applies only to quantitative research, but it is important to note that qualitative research methods such as ethnography can embrace positivistic dimensions. In a positivistically influenced ethnography, the purpose of the research involves a mimetic motive. In other words, the purpose of the research involves producing a true reflection of what actually happened in a particular sociocultural/educational circumstance. The complex interpretive dimensions—including the critical analysis of the effects of unseen structures of power—are devalued and often excluded because they cannot be verified in a positivistic manner. We cannot triangulate such critical interpretations. Thus, like consciousness in traditional positivistic research, they don't exist!

As critical bricoleurs focus on these critical interpretive dimensions of the ethnographic act, we begin to increase the flow of knowledge from the reductionistic data tap. Indeed, the multiple methodologies of the bricolage and its use of critical hermeneutics demands that we rethink what the zombies of positivism have designated as "true reality." Once we engage in this truly radical act of reevaluating what we have been taught about the nature of reality, we realize that we can't stop the reevaluation process. In a critical ontological sense, we have to rethink who we are in relation to our changing and evolving view of the world around us. Alas, as we come to understand these knowledge related issues in the critical bricolage, we begin to understand that we may not be

who we think we are. Yikes, this observation raises some serious issues that deserve rigorous analysis and self-examination. We have crossed the event horizon of the black hole—there's no coming back to Pleasantville with its white, upper-middle class, English as first language, patriarchal, and heterosexist norms. Welcome to the critical planet, where we realize that the objects in the mirror may not be what they seem. There is a leak in the tap.

Thus, as critical knowledge producers and educators we cannot escape the reconceptualization of the data that the dominant power wielders and their positivistic coconspirators have bequeathed us. In this context, much of the research and pedagogy that comes from the critical bricolage involves a process of unlearning what has been transmitted to us as truth. Here we have to become sophisticated monitors of the data input spigot and its reductionistic guardians who often dismiss the most salient dimensions of political economic, social, cultural, psychological, and educational knowledge. Positivism with its naïve view of objectivity makes an effort to shield knowledge producers from an understanding of the way they and the knowledge they produce is inscribed by history, culture, and ideology.

An objective, rigorous science, the positivists argue, is free from such influences. Critical pedagogues who embrace the bricolage understand that such shielding is exactly the opposite of what a robust science should be doing. The bricolage helps us appreciate that researchers—as well as the phenomena they study—always interact with and are influenced by the historical, cultural, and ideological context of which they are a part. Rigorous and usable research insists that we understand how such forces shape our perspectives. The fact that we have not inspected this process of inscription is the very reason we have to reevaluate positivistic knowledge. The multidimensional matrix where cultural inscription, knowledge, meaning, consciousness, and the phenomena of the world intersect is central to any critical bricoleur's notion of research.

As critical researchers, our knowledge of this complex matrix positions us in a humble location, as we are confronted with new layers of complication in the analysis of what at first glance appeared to be a clear-cut issue. Scores and scores of Western researchers, for instance, have explored indigenous peoples around the world without considering the ways tacit formations of power shaped their assumptions about such individuals, the designs of their research projects, the questions they asked, the relation of their research to the colonial needs of their home countries, or the relevance of the knowledge produced to the subjects of their research. As critical bricoleurs consider these dimensions of positivist research, they come to understand at a deeper level the ways in which colonialism has shaped Western views of knowledge production and, obviously, the knowledge it has produced about "the other" and countless other topics (Coffee, Holbroook, and Atkinson, 1996; Grande, 2004; Harding, 1998; Mutra and Swadener, 2004; Semali and Kincheloe, 1999).

Knowledge production is complicated. There is no principle of what makes for high-quality research that can be employed outside of an understanding of diverse contexts and without numerous conscious or unconscious interpretive decisions being made about what such a principle might mean in a particular circumstance. There is nothing neat and tidy about such deliberations. Critical researchers drawing upon the bricolage appreciate how difficult it often is to trace the ways dominant ideology shapes decisions about knowledge production. The notion in the last years of the first decade of the twenty-first century that Eurocentrism permeates research and pedagogy in some overt prejudicial way is not sufficiently complex to understand the insidious nature of the process. Even scholars and activists, I regret to say, who express their revulsion against power-driven Eurocentric procedures may nevertheless promote such ethnocentric oppression in their knowledge work and pedagogical practices. Such men and women—myself included—must persist in seeking out the covert ways that dominant culture and ideology shape their consciousness, their identities/subjectivities, and their vocational practices (Steinberg, 2001; Thayer-Bacon, 2000, 2003).

Listening to the World: Diversity, Knowledge Production, and an Evolving Criticality

In Chapter I, I argued that critical pedagogy among other things is always vitally concerned with human suffering and the value of subjugated knowledge in helping us understand the causes of such ever-present anguish and pain. In this chapter about research and the multilogicality of the bricolage, these concerns are central to all dimensions of critical pedagogical

knowledge work. Any knowledge work—indeed, any critical work for that matter—begins with the recognition of the suffering of the oppressed in our local communities and around the planet. Such a recognition makes critical research and critical pedagogy possible, as it displaces the Western tendency for narcissism with an ethic of critical compassion. This recognition of and action in response to the suffering of the other changes the life of both the criticalist and the suffering individual—it gives existentially empty lives meaning in a sea of competitive, consumerist despair. As we turn our attention to human suffering and its human constructed causes, we move to the upper echelons of insight and inspiration. Critical pedagogy comes of age in this moment of radical love.

As we study subjugated, multicultural, and indigenous forms of knowledge, our goal is twofold: first, to help us serve as better allies to peoples under attack by the Western neoliberal, neo-colonial, and positivistic steamrollers of "progress"; and, second, to learn from the profound insights and perspectives such peoples have developed over the centuries in general and in dealing with Western oppression in particular. Thus, the listening and learning that take place with subjugated and indigenous peoples as well as individuals from diverse cultural backgrounds is in many ways merely a conversation—albeit a smart and informed one—among peers. It is certainly not a form of research where expert researchers engage ignorant individuals who are not actively engaged in the conceptualization and design of the research project. It is a dialogue where if we are prepared and a bit lucky, everyone benefits (Grande, 2004). The voices of individuals demeaned by their class positions, their gender, their sexuality, their physical ability, and their relationships to Western colonialism are viewed as treasures in the critical bricolage. Such treasures allow us a peek into new dimensions that reveal conceptual matrixes that can change our lives and the direction of history (Shoham, 1999; L. Smith, 1999; Reason and Bradbury, 2000).

Here we can make contact with Walter Benjamin's **Angel of History** and learn from the insights he has gained by his knowledge of people's lives in an earthly hell.

> This is how one pictures the angel of history. His face is turned towards the past. Where we perceive a chain of events, he sees one single catastrophe which keeps piling wreckage upon wreckage

and hurls it in front of his feet. The angel would like to stay, awaken the dead, and make whole what has been smashed. But a storm is blowing from Paradise; it has got caught in his wings with such violence that the angel can no longer close them. This storm irresistibly propels him into the future to which his back is turned, while the pile of debris before him grows skyward. This storm is what we call progress. (Benjamin, 1968, pp. 257–258)

The storm of Western progress has overwhelmed the Angel of History. Like us, he is blown into a future with his back turned away; he is engulfed in the whirlwind of the detritus of Western civilization. Critical researchers sense that there is much to be learned in their dialogue with the subjugated—insights that can connect them to Benjamin's angel.

Long suppressed by Western colonial and epistemological impulses subjugated forms of knowledge have slowly begun to reemerge in the contemporary era. Diverse non-Western forms of knowledge about everything from holistic health, cosmetics, medicine, to psychedelic drugs have exerted an increasingly powerful effect on North American, Australian, New Zealand, and European cultures over the last few decades. An evolving criticality seeks out such subjugated and indigenous forms of knowledge, working hard to employ them as diverse lenses through which to rethink the critical canon. In this epistemological context criticalists challenge dominant power and its power to "inflict" the "truth." Wherever dominant power is imposed, resistance emerges, whether in prisons, mental hospitals, religious institutions, or schools. Critical research grounded on the bricolage looks for the insights of these resistant forms of knowledge in multiple social and geographical locations. Many times over the last few decades when I have been giving a speech to a group of teachers, individuals have asked me: "where did you come up with those ideas about the way schools work? I've never heard them before."

My answer to such a question is very simple, as I tell the questioners that I listen carefully to those students who are failing or have failed in schools. Some of the most compelling insights I've ever heard about education have come from such "brilliant failures." Many indigenous peoples, viewed as ignorant by Westerners, contemplate the possible results of their actions sometimes for more than seven generations into the

future (Foucault, 1990; G. Jardine, 2005; Semali and Kincheloe, 1999). Contrast this to contemporary megacorporations who look no farther than the release of next September's quarterly profit announcement. Human and environmental concerns be damned, the only thing that matters is producing higher profits than the last report. Ah, the genius of the "superior civilization" of the West! The pathways to new definitions of humanness and ethical behavior may come by way of the Amazonian rainforests and the indigenous communities of the far north of Canada—if they're not destroyed—than through Los Angeles, New York, Toronto, London, or Sydney.

Avoiding Essentialism in Subjugated Knowledge, While Making Power-Saturated Conceptual Networks Visible: The Zone of Intersection

In societies stratified by the conceptual frameworks created by race, class, gender, sexuality, colonial relations, religion, physical ability work to structure meaning as well as sociocultural and political relationships. Of course, the aspect of these activities that makes it so hard for individuals to understand them is that such processes take place behind the curtain of power. This fact brings critical researchers back to the very basis of critical knowledge production—they study the invisible, the forces of power that try to operate under the radar to shape what is going on in the world, in media, in the political arena, and, of course, in schools. Thus, when many of us in critical pedagogy talk about educational research, we get such negative reactions. "What in the hell are you talking about?" mainstream hegemonic researchers will ask us. "You don't even know what you're looking for. Why, you're just chasing bogeymen under the bed." As they utter these words, they are frequently unconsciously acting as brokers for the dominant power, for the perpetuation of the status quo. Make no mistake, if you embrace critical pedagogy and its research activities, you will have to deal with the insults and the **ad hominem** attacks of the agents of power.

A central argument of this chapter is that our contentious struggle against the dominant power is facilitated by our use of subjugated and indigenous forms of knowledge. While this is central to critical research, education, and social action, we find that once we enter the zone of subjugated and indigenous forms of knowledge, there is nothing simple about the use of them in critical pedagogy. Critical researchers do not simply run into the domain and choose a universal **essentialized** model of subjugated and indigenous forms of knowledge. While we may ground our work on the perspectives of the oppressed, those perspectives may differ from place to place and from time to time. Thus, we always have to be aware of the multiplicities of such forms of knowledge. Such awareness demands that we become even more rigorous scholars who develop the ability to deal with such further complexity. In my work with indigenous peoples, for example, I have found that within one group of indigenous people there may be—like in any other community—a wide variety of perspectives in regard to a particular issue. Such diversity and complexity demand that I become a careful scholar of the indigenous community and understand the best I can the social construction of these diverse viewpoints. This is always a tricky enterprise.

Where we stand in the social web of reality influences but, thankfully, does not determine how we view ourselves and the world. If this was a deterministic relationship, we would have no room for cognitive and educational growth—we would simply reflect our experiences in the world. This is the case whether we are from the dominant culture or from an oppressed culture. Our location in the social web of reality given our multiple identities around race, class, gender, sexuality, relation to colonialism, religion, geographic place, physical ability, ad infinitum is a shifting and dynamic, not a static space. We may be concurrently in positions of privilege along one axis of power and marginalization along another axis.

An indigenous tribal member, for example, may have made much money on uranium found on his family's land, thus, making him a member of the upper-middle to upper-economic class. However, his indigeneity places him in a marginalized position in many circumstances. His class position, just as with any other individual from any sociocultural background may help shape—but not determine—his ideological perspective. In this context a feminist position is not the inborn perspective of a woman—men can be feminists. An anti-Eurocentric position is not inherent in a person from Gabon, as Europeans can be anti-Eurocentric as well as Africans. While humans can overcome the way in which

dominant power shapes them—men becoming feminists and Europeans becoming anti-Eurocentrists—it is not the common reaction. It often takes great courage and commitment for women to become feminists; obviously the same thing holds true for men who work to become feminists.

Often, knowledge of the suffering individuals and groups endures around these axes of power, thus facilitating these ideological moves to emancipatory ideological positions. I am a feminist because I have a sense of the pain of many women in a patriarchal society endure—I see how such androcentric power undermines the quality of women's lives, causes them to lose confidence in their ability to function in the world, to develop a negative self-image, and so on. While forms of emancipatory knowledge uncovered in the lives of oppressed peoples are necessary understandings in critical research, they are not sufficient to our liberatory goals. Such knowledge in a bricolage of critical knowledge production must be considered in relation to the epistemes, the commonsensical ways of seeing the sociocognitive structures of dominant power blocs in order to move to a rigorous, critical complex understanding of the oppressive practices that construct human suffering. It is in this context that we begin to understand not only the subjugated experience but also why colonialist oppression continues to take place.

In the critical bricolage, we find it necessary to examine numerous differing perspectives to develop a thick, rich, rigorous understanding of the hidden values and structures that shape everything from the logic of scientific projects to individual consciousness. Informed by these numerous perspectives, we gain the ability to expose helpful maps of dominant power matrixes and new methodologies (such as the bricolage) to transcend the impoverished dominant cultural accounts of how the sociopolitical world operates. In historical research (Villaverde, Kincheloe, and Helyar, 2006), it has become commonplace to argue that history is written by the victors, conceding the social construction and the role of power in historical knowledge production. It stands to reason that those who lost the historical battle may provide us with different and possibly quite valuable perspectives on the subject at hand. As losers of the conflict in question, these informants may have insights that come from having to deal on a daily basis with the disadvantages of their loss.

The same dynamics, it would seem obvious, are at work in the power relations in any disciplinary knowledge production. Thus, to a large degree all knowledge production is shaped by the victors in numerous struggles in the domains surrounding the information in question. This understanding is a central tenet of any aspect of critical theoretical/critical pedagogical perspectives on the politics of knowledge (Harding, 1998; G. Jardine, 2005; Kincheloe, 2001a). The space where diverse subjugated/indigenous forms of knowledge intersect with the mythologies of dominant power and the conceptual structures that shape dominant cultural perspectives and social relations is a sacred ground for critical researchers. It is in this convergent locale that rigorous insights into the way the world operates, the purposes to which education is put, can be explored in all their complexity. This hermeneutic dimension is a domain that critical researchers help construct when they are aware of the multilogical factors addressed here. Since critical pedagogy is always inexorably connected to the knowledge production of critical research, it is profoundly important that critical educators become as familiar as they can with this domain of multiple intersections in any pedagogy they promote.

There is a form of epistemological magic in this zone of intersection. Within the domain, new insights can be generated from the interaction of diverse perspectives. Bringing Maori insights about research into this fascinating domain, critical bricoleurs develop modes of inquiry that include Maori conceptions of decolonization, healing, transformation, and mobilization. According to the Maori, these research processes help bring together and illuminate the interactive dynamics shaping and reshaping the local, the regional, and the global. In this Maori context, critical bricoleurs gain a profound look into the way other cultures have conceptualized the complexity and interactive dimensions of research and knowledge production. With decolonization, for example, we gain new appreciations of the way dominant power inscribes our views of self and world and how we might identify and replace such perspectives. With healing, critical bricoleurs gain a deeper understanding of all that needs to be done to repair the damage of power's oppression.

With transformation, we better recognize that research is never simply a form of inert knowledge production but a process

that leads to action. Moreover, with mobilization, critical researchers come to an awareness that action always entails developing ways of bringing large groups of people together to work toward common emancipatory goals. The ways that the genius of Maori research intersects with the critical bricolage help us understand the value of multilogical notions of knowledge production. In the zone of intersection, we create new spaces and new tools as we examine one way of seeing in light of another. Always informed by a critical hermeneutics, we create a multilogical hermeneutic circle that brings diverse perspectives to the interpretive table. In the process, we gain new insights into the power networks that tacitly shape social and individual lives, while simultaneously developing new pragmatic strategies for resisting them (Harding, 1998; Kincheloe and Berry, 2004; Kincheloe and Steinberg, 1997; L. Smith, 1999).

Quechua (from the Native peoples of Peru) scholar-educator Sandy Grande (2004) is particularly helpful in this discussion of the critical zone of intersection. In the context of a much needed dialogue between indigenous peoples and criticalists, she asserts, that

> the predominantly white, middle class advocates of critical theory will need to examine how their language and epistemic frames act as homogenizing agents when interfaced with the conceptual and analytical categories persistent within American Indian educational theory and praxis. They will especially need to examine the degree to which critical pedagogies retain the deep structures of Western thought—that is, the belief in progress as change, in the universe as impersonal, in reason as the preferred mode of inquiry, and in human beings as separate from and superior to the rest of nature. (p. 3)

In Grande's vision of the dialogue, we see the hermeneutic circle of the zone of intersection at work. It is in the light of difference shed by indigenous conceptual structures that criticalists begin to view the ways that their transformative perspectives often unwittingly reflect the dominant cultural assumptions of Western societies. Here they can see that the knowledge they produce is insidiously inscribed by the dominant power matrixes of their cultural settings. I am reminded of myself as a 29-year-old scholar-teacher working as a professor at Sinte Gleska College on the Rosebud Sioux Reservation. In my naivete, I thought that as a critical pedagogue I had transcended the inscriptions of whiteness, Eurocentrism, and dominant power, as I assumed the chair of the teacher education department at the college.

I was quickly brought back to planet Earth as I realized in the face of indigenous difference how much I reflected the assumptions and inscriptions of the dominant culture. Almost thirty years later, I keep this insight close to my heart and mind as I interact and work with indigenous people. In the zone of interaction I still have much listening to do, much to learn, much to consider as I continue to analyze the ways my whiteness—and other dimensions of my location in the web of reality—inscribes my scholarship, pedagogy, and social action. I engage in my existential struggle in this zone of interaction and will continue for the rest of my life. It is my burden as a white male scholar in critical pedagogy. In an evolving criticality, I (as well as all of my white male colleagues engaged in the critical struggle) have no choice. This is not to say that individuals coming from other locales in the social web of reality don't have their own existential struggles—of course, they do, and they must deal with them in their own zones of interaction. Our late night dialogues with the Angel of History can often get quite personal.

Diversality, Research, and the Political Economic Dimensions of Western Monological Ways of Seeing

As critical pedagogues operate in the multilogical zone of interaction, they become more and more aware of the poverty of Western monological ways of seeing and their disastrous historical and contemporary effects. In a world that is as economically disparate and interacts as much as the globalized one of the twenty-first century, Western monological, neopositivistic, market-driven ways of seeing cannot continue to dictate the "correct" view of reality. Already around the globe, diverse groups—for differing reasons—are already rebelling against such epistemological colonialism. An evolving critical pedagogy seeks to decolonize research, knowledge production, and, of course, education in this imperial context. The future of knowledge production in this decolonized context will not constitute a new universalism of final truth, but it will be worldly in the sense that it will

multilogically draw on insights from divergent domains around the planet.

This diversity is central to an evolving criticality and the effort to produce ecologically sustainable economic growth around the world. In this context, research and knowledge production draws not only upon the particular forms of knowledge of diverse cultures but also their conceptual and cognitive frameworks, their epistemologies, ontologies, and cosmologies. Students engaged in a critical multilogical curriculum study African social theories, Indian scholarship, Islamic insights, Eastern philosophies, indigenous ways of seeing and being, and so on along with Western perspectives. Such diversalistic constructs are brought directly into the zone of interaction and rigorously studied in a border analysis. Such a border analysis not only denaturalizes the hegemony of Western constructs and decolonizes Western consciousness, but also helps produce new forms of knowledge for a new world. Such forms of knowledge demarcate the end of the old universal order and the birth a new diversity grounded on human dignity and synergistic cooperation.

The Western empire is not only economic and geopolitical, but it is also epistemological and educational. Indeed, the epistemological and educational dynamics are key "weapons" in justifying and making possible the spoils of the economic and geopolitical imperial domains. Thus, in addition to distorting our views of the world and ourselves, Eurocentric research and knowledge production have very specific material consequences—they help maintain the disparity of wealth and the environmental destruction perpetuated by the policies of the contemporary Western empire. Thus, critical pedagogy embraces a worldwide diversity initiative. This is exactly what Shirley Steinberg and I have done at McGill University in the Paulo and Nita Freire International Project for Critical Pedagogy.

The work of the project is grounded on the notion that critical pedagogy cannot survive as a North American appropriation of a South American concept (Kincheloe, 2007). The future of critical pedagogy and the work of the project involve seeking out new forms of criticality in diverse cultural and global geographical settings. In these contexts, critical pedagogy refuses to operate as the "great white savior" that bestows truth on the local residents. Instead, critical pedagogy—as referenced earlier—listens to and learns from the genius of diverse peoples in divergent locations. In the project, critical pedagogy also serves as an ally in the struggles against oppression in which subjugated peoples in North America and around the world are involved. Moreover, in the spirit of an evolving criticality, the project creates circumstances where critical pedagogues, subjugated peoples, colonized peoples, and indigenous peoples can create zones of interaction where new ways of seeing, researching, understanding, and acting in the world can be mutually developed.

Achieving the goals of the Paulo and Nita Freire International Project for Critical Pedagogy and of a critical diversity in general will not be easy in an era where so many Westerners—especially in the United States—are working in an opposite ideological direction: to reclaim the inherent superiority of the West, its imperial aspirations, and Eurocentric ways of producing knowledge (Steinberg and Kincheloe, 2006). In this context, it is important to note that by diversity I do not mean to imply a relativism that values diversity as a simple end in itself. To the contrary I am advocating a critically grounded diversity that is a transgressive option to a colonized, globalized, and corporatized world that fights for social justice, anticolonialism, and new ways of seeing and being. The critical diversity I am advocating here understands that being colonized and oppressed makes a huge difference in the way we perceive and make sense of the world and our relation to it.

Any notion of research, pedagogy, or social action that fails to account for this colonial/oppressive dynamic is simply naïve. In its Eurocentric parochialism, it will fail to construct a form of scholarship that is capable of producing dangerous and transformative knowledge, as it uses epistemological tools that tend to decontextualize and dismiss the very factors that open dominant power to critical examination. This is why diversality and multilogicality are so important to critical pedagogy—such concepts allow the experiences of seeing and being subjected to oppression into the coffers of legitimate knowledge. Concurrently, occluded semiotic dimensions and hidden structures of dominant power so often ignored in mainstream Western research are admitted as evidence in diverse and multilogical modes of critical knowledge work. In the context of diversity, the starting point of critical pedagogy shifts, becoming more attuned to times and places that fall outside the confines of Western cosmologies.

Indeed, the boundaries of Western dominant cultural forms of knowledge disintegrate at the point where subjugated, indigenous, and diverse global forms of knowledge rise up and demand an audience. In this context, the long buried histories of local places emerge as dramatic new insights into the nature of dominant power and subjugation. I remember as a young historical scholar how profoundly I was affected by studying U.S. President's Woodrow Wilson's orders to occupy the Mexican port of Veracruz in 1914. The order was given to the United States Navy because in an apology Mexico had made to the United States over a minor misunderstanding involving the Mexican occupation of an American boat in the port of Tampico, the nation had not complied with an order to raise the American flag over the port and fire a 21-gun salute to honor the United States. When this incident long relegated to the dustbins of American history was combined with scores of similar episodes in the history of Mexican-American relations, one could begin to gain a better sense of the anger of many Mexicans toward U.S. colonialism. I was quite excited when five years after I had written an essay on the affair, Warren Zevon included a song called "Veracruz" on his *Excitable Boy* (1978) album from the point of view of a Mexican resident of Veracruz whose life is disrupted by the U.S. invasion.

Diverse anticolonial perspectives come in unexpected places, and Zevon's musical phenomenology of U.S. colonialism is a compelling example of critical diversalist knowledge production (and performance). The difference oppression makes in our being, our ontological presence in the world can never be ignored—as it has consistently been in the mainstream hegemonic forms of knowledge produced in the West. Indeed, I would go as far to argue that in a critical pedagogy an awareness of the difference oppression makes induces us to develop a geopolitics of knowledge, a critical epistemology that removes itself ontologically, ideologically, and historically from a tradition that believes *civilization* began in ancient Greece and expanded into Europe and North America. By the definitions embedded in such a view of civilization, the perspectives and the forms of knowledge of the colonized and the indigenous are automatically excluded from human achievement.

The critical bricolage is always aware of these dynamics as it searches for multiple levels of diversity to bring to the knowledge

work of critical theory and critical pedagogy. Here the bricoleur seeks out ways of seeing and dangerous knowledge that will bring individuals from diverse cultural and geographical locations into the zone of interaction, into a praxiological dialogue (a conversation that leads to transformative action). One dimension of this transformative action involves creating a planet where diverse worlds can coexist in synergistic interaction, where differences between different cultures are viewed positively in the same way ecologists value diversity of species and life forms as contributing to the health of the Earth. Embedded in subjugated and indigenous forms of knowledge long dismissed by Western science and reason are grand secrets. Such life-changing secrets emerge in the work of critical bricoleurs as they value and respect the insights of peoples who fall outside the confines of European notions of civilization. Epistemological privilege (who has the authority to contribute to the conversation) is reconsidered in this critical context, as the definition of expertise is rethought in light of the demands of diversality (Mignolo, 2001, 2005; Thayer-Bacon, 2000, 2003).

Chaos, Complexity, and Criticality: The Positivist Rejection of Multiple Perspectives

Bricoleurs in critical pedagogy informed by chaos theory and complexity understand that difference—especially difference based on oppression—matters. Insights emerging from diverse perspectives can never be coopted by positivistic **reductionism.** Reductionism is a key dimension of a Eurocentric epistemology that produces ways of seeing that work to reduce the contextual dynamics that interfere with a positivistic notion of "pure" knowledge. Reductionism even reflects a positivist ontology, as it validates the superiority of the Western abstract individual and the knowledge *he* produces over the insights of diverse participants from different locales in the web of reality and their interactions (McClure, 2000). The zone of interaction so valued by critical bricoleurs is nothing more than a generator of cacophony. Western reductionism looks at diversality in the same way the Tennessee police viewed my teenage rock band in Kingsport, Tennessee—a law-breaking producer of unwanted knowledge.

Eurocentric reductionism does not allow for the interaction of local forms of knowledge with global needs. It does not

tolerate the fascinating movement of local forms of knowledge from the physical domain and the historical occasion of their production to other spaces and times. This, the positivists warn us, is not the way knowledge is properly constructed and validated. "We" as Europeans, the positivists tell us, possess a positional advantage over all other peoples, as we employ our superior methods of "discovering" the truth. There is no need for a zone of interaction or bricolage in such an advanced modus operandi—such concepts would simply dilute the superiority of the one best way. Diverse readings sparked by interaction with subjugated or indigenous perspectives do not add to our insights in the positivist universe—they merely detract from correct answers. The fact that we might gain new insights about particular cultural formations is frightening to a positivist mindset—such understanding might disrupt the status quo. They might reveal the discursive formations that legitimate oppressive practices commonly unquestioned by those who benefit from them. The less complexity and multilogicality positivistic studies bring to the interrogation of such practices, the better off those possessing privilege.

The bricolage uses a wide variety of interpretive strategies coming from hermeneutics, literacy criticism, cultural analysis, and historical inquiry to explore the sociocultural and political economic frameworks of dominant power. Such interpretive methods help critical pedagogues understand the power of positivism, for example, in the process revealing the impact of positivist truth claims, their social assumptions, the effects of the less than neutral metaphors they employ, and the influences of the cultural place and historical moment in which they are developed. All of this knowledge work in the positivistic frame takes place under the flag of neutrality, so gaining the ability to expose the misleading nature of such a claim is very important (Harding, 1998; Nowotny, 2000; L. Smith, 1999). It is especially important given the contemporary use of positivistic methods in all fields but in education in particular where the growing use of evidence-based research reestablishes decontextualized, instrumental rationality in the production of knowledge about schooling and its students. In the modes of educational research employed in the United States and other societies in the twenty-first century reductionism is back with a vengeance, assuming, for example, the

legitimacy of standardized tests and other forms of standardized evaluation (see Steinberg and Kincheloe, 2006, for an expansion of this topic).

In contemporary neopositivistic—not that positivism ever left the building—research concerns with the nature of the problem being explored or the use-value of the knowledge being produced are not relevant. The fact that a school has scored low on a state mandated standardized test is the only data that matters in such studies. The power-saturated notion that the school is populated by low-income, English as second language speakers who are new immigrants is not important in policies that sanction or close the school as a form of punishment for the low scores. In this case, we find not only a racist and class biased educational policy but also a mode of research that according to its protocols can't even raise such sociocultural and power-related questions in its research designs. How convenient for the dominant power. What a testimony to the foresight of early critical theorists about the ability of instrumental rationality and positivism to protect the interests of dominant power. No complexity needed here. Bill O'Reilly may have his "no spin zone"; dominant modes of educational research, employing a similar mindset, have their "no complexity zone."

The bricolage helps criticalists take their first step on the path to diverse forms of knowledge, to escaping reductionism and tapping into the power of complexity as a subversive force. In this context, oppressed peoples from Maori of New Zealand, the Torres Strait Islanders and aboriginal peoples of Australia, the people of African and Latin descent living in North America, indigenous individuals of North and South America to colonized people living in their original countries or as part of the diasporas of colonized peoples migrating throughout the world can begin to assert the validity of the forms of knowledge they produce. In this context, they no longer have to be the victims of positivistic ethnographies and other forms of research that deny their right to at least object to what colonial research says about them. It has been fascinating and profoundly disconcerting for me to read what mainstream research tells the world about a particular group of oppressed peoples and then to have an opportunity to personally engage with such people or to read the research they produce about themselves. The chasm between the divergent views is wide

enough to steer through a flotilla of U.S. battleships armed with Cruise Missiles and launching F-18 Hornets.

The complexity of the insights and knowledge produced by such oppressed peoples can change the way everyone—Europeans and North Americans from dominant cultural backgrounds included—sees the world. As critical bricoleurs work with oppressed peoples to gather and distribute these transformative forms of knowledge, the aforementioned epistemological magic reappears. In the context of such critical knowledge production long repressed modes of perception are recovered, the inhumane defects of the mechanistic worldview of positivism are laid bare, and Westerners are forced to rethink their comfortable notions of "the way things are." Thus, the power of these dangerous ways of seeing and the forms of knowledge they produce induces diverse individuals from mainstream cultures, classes, and power blocs to undergo a shift in the vantage point from which they view the world around them and their role in it. Their dominant power constructed consciousness in this context is open to reconstruction. In such forms of knowledge and the impact they exercise, hope lives; possibility is restored.

In the context of positivistic Western ways of seeing, there is an assumption that there is only one accurate worldview—that reality is what Western one-truth epistemology says it is. The idea that a group of individuals from the Micmac Nation living in Newfoundland 800 years ago viewed the world in the same way as I do is absurd. When one assumes such a similarity of worldview with historically and culturally different peoples, he or she is engaging in a form of intellectual provincialism that leads to serious problems when the "others" fail to reflect the dominant "truth." Of course, they don't just possess a different worldview—they are "ignorant" and "inferior." Here rests a central task of critical pedagogical knowledge work: the effort to serve as allies of oppressed peoples in their attempts to gain public voice, while concurrently employing and acting on their insights into and critiques of the institutions of dominant power blocs.

Once again, respect and a deep acquaintance with the subjugated forms of knowledge of such oppressed groups grant criticalists new ways of questioning the conceptual frameworks of power and the validated methods of producing "truth." Because of positivism's strict limitations on what humans are capable of experiencing, much of the knowledge that many indigenous and subjugated peoples bring to the zone of interaction is dismissed summarily. If we are to produce forms of knowledge and pedagogies that benefit oppressed peoples rather than the demands of the dominant power, we must develop a base of information that allows us to ask new questions of the world around us. Without such a grounding, educators often passively accept attacks on teacher professionalism and the right of teachers to have input into the purposes and content of education (Griffin, 1997; WEAC, 2004).

One of the key dimensions of many contemporary right-wing educational reforms is to subvert teaching as a profession. Once this insidious task is completed, teachers can be hired who have little background in the social, cultural, political, economic, psychological, and pedagogical issues referenced in critical pedagogy. If they can read at an eighth-grade level, follow the scripts their administrators give them, never comment on educational policy, they can become the Exxon "teacher of the month." Such winners will be placed in competition for the Disney "teacher of the year" award. Personally, I hope to win Blackwater Security Consulting's "assistant principal for discipline" award when deprofessionalization and privatization of schooling is established. I hope readers will help me live my dream to make sure that students learn the real truth in the Smith and Wesson High School for Patriotic Monitors. I kid, but such satirical imaginings are at the end of the first decade of the twenty-first century not too far from actuality.

The Resistant Power of Difference

As we observe the role of the school and the role of teachers mutate in the twenty-first century security state constructed by the perpetual "War of Terror," critical pedagogues realize that the need for resistance has never been greater. Never before have we so needed the allies of oppressed peoples within North American and European contexts and around the world to help us in the struggle against dominant colonial and other forms of power. As a criticalist, I stand in awe of the power of the narratives, histories, conceptual insights, interpretations, epistemologies, ontologies, and cosmologies diverse peoples bring to the struggle for social justice, ecological sustainability, sane economic

policies, and a critical pedagogy. Even so, still at this point in Western history such perspectives are viewed as epistemological trash. In critical research and critical pedagogy, the importance of subjugated history cannot be overstated.

Critical analysts understand that the history of business cannot be told without the insights of the laborers who struggled for livable wages and safe-working conditions. They know that a history of European expansion is not possible without the voices of those who lived in the areas into which the colonists moved. In contemporary society, it is fascinating to watch Western media cover the extension of economic globalization without the perspectives of those people in developing countries who have suffered under **structural adjustment** and other neocolonialist policies. The multilogicality of the critical bricoleur comes into clear focus in these concrete contexts. Using the cubist-like perspectives of Georges Braque or Juan Gris, bricoleurs understand the importance of viewing social, cultural, historical, political, or educational phenomena from diverse perspectives simultaneously. In the process, critical bricoleurs appreciate the profound value of seeing from the positionalities of discarded vantage points in particular.

Thus, a critical, complex, multilogical mode of research and knowledge work is dedicated to developing modes of resistance to dominant power blocs by encouraging multiple dialogues between Eastern and Western societies and Northern and Southern cultures. In contemporary critical studies Northern and Southern cultures have come to symbolize the great (and growing) disparity of wealth in the world: the Northern cultures are the haves; the Southern cultures are the have-nots. Critical resistance in the contemporary Zeitgeist involves engaging in the struggle against those who dismiss social justice as a central pillar of commerce, geopolitics, education, and other domains. In this spirit working-class peoples, theologians, scientists, social workers, doctors and nurses, educators and so forth begin to examine their work from the vantage point of their oppressed brothers and sisters in their own countries and around the world. Such cultural and cognitive cross-fertilization often reveals the hidden presuppositions that impede the development of innovative practices of resistance to the ways of seeing that undermine efforts for social justice.

In the new Western empire led by the **neoliberals** in the United States, some of these tacit assumptions often include the Western colonial tendency to view the "natives" of the developing countries being so exploited by globalization policies as entities of nature—not real human beings. The work such individuals do is seen in this colonial mindset not as real labor but as a primitive form of subsistence activity that does not lead to human progress or profits. The lands such peoples call home are perceived as undeveloped resources now lying fallow and empty. As belief in the unbridled free market has grown over the last couple of decades, the acceptance of such oppressive and dehumanizing ways of seeing peoples and their resources in "developing nations" has concurrently increased. With the migration of North American and European corporate manufacturing and farming to these poor nations, the human impact of such hidden belief structures can be more easily denied and covered up because of its geographical remoteness from the lived world of Westerners (Brooks, 2007; Harding, 1998). Again, criticalists believe that the need for political, social, economic, and educational resistance to such neocolonial practices is mandatory.

These are dire times for advocates of critical pedagogy. The predominance of neoliberal free market dogma in discussions and policy making in everything from economic globalization to education has changed both Western societies and the developing world. New modes of oppression, colonialism, and violence are being used to create "good business climates" for transnational corporations based in Western nations. Such organizations now control most of the information that reaches people in North America and Europe—and increasingly around the world. To the purveyors of this neocolonial power the arguments for multilogicality and diversity in knowledge production and research are viewed as dangerous but not yet sufficiently strong to be threatening enterprises. The more influence criticalists gain, the more draconian will be the response from the profiteers of the new order. We must draw on the impassioned spirit discussed in Chapter I to help us find the strength and the courage to resist the onslaught of the dominant power that we face. We must develop not only new forms of material resistance but new ways of thinking and new forms of consciousness in this struggle. This is the topic of the next chapter.

Glossary

Ad hominem—in argumentation the process of attacking the person making the argument rather than the topic in question.

Angel of History—critical theorist Walter Benjamin's ambiguous icon taken from his description of Swiss artist Paul Klee's 1920 drawing "Angelus Novus." Benjamin's angel is first and foremost a witness to the tragedy of history—a conception of history quite understandable from the vantage point of a depressed Benjamin overwhelmed by the horror of the Third Reich. From Benjamin's perspective Western "progress" is a great storm blowing the angel into an uncertain future. The angel has come to represent the tragic observer, the innocent victim of critical theory's description of the irrational rationality of Western reason and the advance of capitalism. The omnipresent question emerging as we ponder the image of the angel being blown backwards into the future involves whether or not criticality can resist the historical storm, calm the winds propelled by positivism and capitalism, and help the angel to regain control over his flight through time.

Cogito—reference to René Descartes' Cogito ergo sum meaning, I think, therefore I exist.

Critical multiculturalism—a concept defined by Kincheloe and Steinberg (1997) in their typology of the different uses of the term multiculturalism as what results when multiculturalism is viewed through the lens of critical theory and critical pedagogy. When discussing multiculturalism critically, scholars and activists focus on multiple forms of oppression involving race, class, gender, sexuality, ability, religion, geographic place, and colonialism. Appreciating the tacit ways in which these diverse forms of oppression take place in contemporary society, critical multiculturalism insists on the development of rigorous, multilogical forms of analysis that view oppressive practices in a number of ways and from different angles. Always focused on diverse power blocs, critical multiculturalism is particularly interested in the way the dominant power constructs sociocultural and political economic structures that perpetuate domination of peoples coming from the domains referenced above. Concurrently, it concentrates attention on the way dominant power constructs the consciousness of both oppressors and oppressed around these categories. In this transformational, power literate context, critical multiculturalism is not comfortable with the ways multiculturalism and multicultural education

have been used outside of this emancipatory context. Such uses of the concept have too often forms of mystification that tend to perpetuate oppression in the name of diversity and inclusiveness.

Epistemes—term used by French social theorist Michel Foucault to describe a "regime of truth." An episteme is the view of knowledge that dominates in a particular sociohistorical period, an epistemological era.

Essentialized—involving the philosophical view, essentialism, that maintains all elements of a specific grouping of phenomena possess fixed transhistorical, transcultural characteristics that differentiate them from other entities. A complex criticality is both antiessentialist and strategically essentialist as it avoids fixed, unchanging definitions of, say, a cultural group of individuals; concurrently, it is strategically essentialist as it understands that particular groups of people may be perceived in particular ways or suffer forms of oppression that are unique to the group in question.

Multilogicality—a critical complex concept that focuses on transcending reductionism by gaining access to a wide diversity of perspectives when involved with research, knowledge work, and pedagogy. Critical pedagogues who embrace multilogicality seek entry into a diverse community of people who know and inquirers—an inclusive group devoted to social justice and fighting oppression that comes from academia and beyond. Members of this multilogical community critique, support, and inform each other by drawing upon the diversity of their backgrounds and concerns. In this process, they expose and discuss one another's assumptions, the contexts that have shaped them, and their strengths and limitations in the exploration(s) at hand. The participants in this community come from a wide range of race, class, gender, sexual, ethnic, and religious groups and enter into their deliberations with humility and solidarity in the struggle against human suffering.

Neoliberals—the group that advocates neoliberalism. Neo-liberalism is both an orientation to economics and a philosophy that has driven finances and financial development policies in the United States and other Western societies over the last three decades. We can see neoliberal philosophical orientations in the way neoliberals view the market as a mode of social organization. Market imperatives, not ethical or humane considerations, drive social, political, economic, and educational policy in neoliberalism. Advocates of the position tend to see the world in relation

to market metaphors, imposing "market solutions" on national economies around the world via the International Monetary Fund, the World Bank, and the World Trade Organization. From a critical perspective, the result of these actions is to make the rich richer and the poor poorer. The "neo" in neo-liberalism comes from proponents' efforts to reintroduce the "discipline" of the market on global economies. Literally, "neo" means "new."

Reductionism—an epistemological position that asserts that a researcher can best appreciate phenomena by reducing them to their constituent parts and then piecing the elements back together according to causal laws. There is no need in reductionism for multiple perspectives and a variety of research methods. Reductionists believe that such multilogical activity would just add noise and confusion to a simple process.

Structural adjustment—course of action often imposed by neo-liberal, market driven international policy makers based on privatization and free trade strategies. Such structural adjustment policies are touted by promoters as paths to increasing wealth and eliminating poverty, but typically, they have resulted in fiscal deterioration and more economic oppression for the poorest people in the poorest nations. In many cases much of any wealth that is generated goes to the local elites and transnational corporations based in Western societies. It reflects a policy of increasing privatization and trade liberalization intended to help countries generate greater wealth and reduce poverty. It has been criticized for inducing economic decline and endangering the welfare of the economically vulnerable.

Critical Pedagogy and Cognition

Instead of promoting mind as memory chips, advocates of a critical pedagogy embrace a psychology of complexity that views learning as an untidy process of constructing new *relationships* in the interaction of cultural understandings, the influences of the information environment, familiar stories, idiosyncratic ways of making meaning, and schooling. Critical teachers work to help construct for themselves and their students insights and inter- pretations of concepts emerging in the interplay of these various knowledge forms. In the linear, straight-ahead world of positivist schooling, one must not venture into the land of untidiness, the domain where learning matters for something other than meeting the standards and scoring high on the tests. When teachers and students venture into untidiness in these pious domains, they have "gotten off the subject." Top-down technical standards and the form of testing for retention of bits of data they necessitate actually undermine the struggle for a rigorous, high-quality, equi- table, and democratic education. As they promote a conception of mind that is archaic in light of what scholars from numerous fields have asserted over the last few decades, technical standards promote intellectual poverty in the guise of excellence.

thing-in-itself
the Cartesian modernist ontological orientation that sees the primary unit of being in the world as the individual entity—**not** a relationship or a process.

constructivist analysis
an epistemological position that maintains that the knower personally participates in all acts of knowing and understanding. Knowledge does not exist "out there" in isolation from the knower.

In the early psychologist Edwin Thorndike's persisting psychometric model an entity—a **thing-in-itself**—called intelligence existed within each individual. The quantity of this intelligence each person possessed would shape how well he or she performed both in school and in life. Such a view has been challenged from numerous quarters, including Howard Gardner and his multiple intelligences, minority scholars in their analysis of African American and Latino performance in schools, gender analysts and their examination of the patriarchal inscriptions on cognitive theories, and **constructivist analysis** and their studies of concept building and meaning-making. Drawing on all of these analyses, a critical psychology of complexity is emerging that accounts for the interaction of self and context, the intricacies of memory and concept building, and the value of cross-cultural cognitive insights. It is this critical psychology of complexity that can provide one of the supports for standards that move educators to pursue new levels of human possibility.

This complex notion of human possibility is generative in the Freirean sense as it seeks deeper understanding. Moving beyond the traditional model of educational and cognitive psychology, a psychology of complexity addresses modes of criticism, creativity, theorizing, imagination, and meaning-making. Shirley Steinberg and I have worked to develop a new view of educational psychology in our version of postformalism (Kincheloe and Steinberg, 1993, 1999). This postformal psychology of complexity attempts to blur boundaries separating cognition, culture, epistemology, history, psychoanalysis, economics, and politics. Without this boundary crossing and contextualization, the psychology that supports positivist education promotes a form of mass learning disability. Such a truncated form of learning manifests itself in an inability to keep up with changes in the world of commerce, ideas, scholarship, information, social, and technological needs. The types of thinking that were conceptualized and taught in the past are insufficient for the present electronic culture and the hyperchanges that will occur in the coming decades.

Such dramatic changes in information and human interaction demand a critical psychology of complexity and a new rigor in the education it grounds. This critical psychology is characterized by a deep concern with cognitive processes and analytical abilities. Contrary to the way process-oriented cognitive and pedagogical theories are often represented by positivist critiques, this does not imply a lack of concern with knowledge and curricular content. Indeed, any effort to build cognitive processes must be undertaken in relation to a body of content. Human beings simply cannot think outside the boundaries of something to "think about"—what constitutes this object of cognition is always important. Thus, critical pedagogy and the critical psychology of complexity—its companion cognitive theory—create an interacting dialectic between content and cognitive processes. As analysts trace this connection, they blur the boundaries that covertly induce educators to fragment thinking processes, content/curriculum, student background, and sociocultural context. Operating in this "connected" domain, the discipline of educational psychology enters into a stage of metamorphosis. Emerging from its disciplinary cocoon, the field begins to grasp the critical issues with power and culture as well as the broader complexity its narrow vision had eclipsed.

Thus, a critical psychology of complexity makes such a dramatic entrance into the conversation about educational reform that it cannot be ignored. Understanding the impact of sociocultural, political, and economic context, a psychology of complexity exposes the way a more traditional cognitivism has tended to construct ability or aptitude as a quality found only among the privileged few. Viewing intelligence as a biological thing-in-itself (substance), a positivist psychology creates a pedagogy of hopelessness that assigns students—especially marginalized ones—to lifelong categories. When a critical psychology of complexity begins to examine the ways cultural, economic, political, and social forces inscribe both this psychology and the education it promotes, those students we consider capable of learning begin to change. The cognitive sophistication of these students who fall outside the domain of the cultural mainstream—nonwhite, lower socioeconomic class, English as a second language, and with nonformally educated parents—in this fresh psychological context begins to materialize before newly focused eyes.

In addition, a critical psychology of complexity changes the debate about educational reform and the quest for a high-quality education with its understanding that not only is cognitive ability expressed in diverse ways but that it is *learnable*. Individuals of various ages, backgrounds, and IQ scores can learn conceptual systems

that help them make meaning, that facilitate their understanding of and ability to negotiate the world around them. Given this realization, there is no reason for educators to equate a high failure rate with a high-quality education. Of course, in a critical pedagogy a key goal involves making sure that a far greater number of students perform better in school. A critical psychology of complexity is central to the achievement of this critical pedagogical goal.

Teachers operating in a context shaped by a critical pedagogy and a psychology of complexity are empowered to help students gain the disposition to learn usable analytical skills in school. Teachers can guide such students in their attempt to focus their impassioned spirits and direct their energies toward certain academic, social, and individual goals. Although such goals may not seem especially difficult to achieve—and they aren't—they are not even considered in positivist psychology and the schooling it supports. Great hope is generated by a critical psychology of complexity, as it rejects the cognitive hopelessness of a rigid hereditarian psychology. Not only is intelligence learnable, I contend, but it can be taught in numerous places: the schools, workplaces, civic organizations, union halls, and in any other place where people interact. This critical psychology induces educators to make use of these places and to enter into collaborative educational relationships with people involved with them. Such understandings can revolutionize the concept and practice of education in this society.

Postformalism

I have written about postformalism, another name for the critical psychology of complexity referenced here. In this context, it is important to explain briefly what postformalism entails. Postformalism transcends much of the cognitive theory typically associated with Piagetian and many other theories of cognitive development. While more positivist cognitive science has associated disinterestedness, objectivity, adult cognition, and problem solving with higher-order thinking, postformalism challenges such concepts. Postformalism is

- not disinterested, as it is committed to critical pedagogy and the notion of social justice it assumes
- not objective; it is unabashedly subjective with its celebration of intimacy between the knower and the known

- not simply an adult stage of cognition, as it recognizes expressions of postformal cognition in children and adolescents
- not attempting to solve only defined and structured problems but ill-defined and ill-structured ones as well
- curious about where puzzles and problems come from and who recognized them as being in need of a solution
- able to resituate cognitive theory as a critical discourse
- cognizant of the social and linguistic construction of the methods we employ to transmit and interpret experience
- aware that reason is socially mediated.

Postformalism is closely linked to the concept of alternative rationalities. Contrary to the claims of positivist psychologists, postformalism does not seek to embrace irrationalism or to reject the entire enterprise of empirical research. We borrow the phrase "alternative rationality" from Stanley Aronowitz (1988), whose critique of mainstream science helps shape our vision of postformalism. In this schema, new rationalities employ forms of analysis sensitive to signs and symbols, the power of context in relation to thinking, the role of emotion and feeling in cognitive activity, and the value of the psychoanalytical process as it taps into the recesses of (un)consciousness. In the spirit of critical theory and critical pedagogy, postformalism attempts to democratize intelligence. In this activity, postformal cognitivists study issues of purpose, meaning, and value. Do certain forms of cognition and cognitive theory undermine the quest for justice? Do certain forms of psychological research cause observers to view problematic ways of seeing as if they involved no issues of power and privilege?

Positivist educational psychology has simply never encouraged a serious conversation about the reason humans engage in certain behavior, about the purposes of higher-order thinking, or about the social role of schooling in a democratic society. For the most part, the discipline has never considered the implications that Paulo Freire's notion of conscientization holds for the work of practitioners. What happens in the realm of cognition when individuals begin to gain a new consciousness via the process of:

- transforming themselves through changing their reality?
- grasping an awareness of the mechanisms of oppression?
- reclaiming their historical memory in order to gain an awareness of their social identity?

Understanding the implications of this process, Philip Wexler (1996a) describes an alternative rationality that involves the effort to move beyond the limitations imposed by the discipline of psychology. In recent scholarship on the ethnography of being, alternative rationalities emerge as analysts study altered states of consciousness. In such moments of transcendence, individuals gain insight into the constructed nature of what is labeled normal Western consciousness—an insight that allows for a reframing of experience in exciting new ways. Postformalism and critical pedagogy have much to learn from Wexler's work, as it brings questions of knowledge (epistemology) and questions of being (ontology) into the cognitive domain. Such questions move scholars to consider critical analyses of power's role in shaping consciousness vis-à-vis the effort to live more fully. In the fusion of these compelling considerations, postformalism opens new paths of human development and insight to students of critical theory and critical pedagogy.

Connecting Cognition to Critical Pedagogy

Many analysts begin their description of Frankfurt School critical theory by maintaining that Adorno, Horkheimer, and Marcuse based their notion of critical pedagogy on the theoretical fusion of Marx and Freud. Such an approach helped them in the attempt to understand the relationship between the mind and socioeconomic and political forces. In this articulation of critical pedagogy and critical psychology, we are attempting to carry this project forward, delving deeply into the concept of mind vis-à-vis sociocultural and political structures in light of new insights developed since the inception of critical theory in the 1920s.

The scholars of the Frankfurt School were fascinated by the ways this mind-society relationship operated to impede popular support for political movements dedicated to freedom, democracy, and justice. No emancipatory politics, they argued, is complete without a political psychology that traces the effects of particular political arrangements on human consciousness and vice versa. In the course of their analysis, the critical theorists came to the conclusion that the growth of the traditional disciplines of academic forms of knowledge has not led to a profound understanding of consciousness, moral growth, or human happiness. Indeed, the influence of this "irrational rationality" of disciplinary expertise has often served the interests of dominant power blocs by repressing human self-direction and undermining the development of a critical consciousness. Of course, the Frankfurt School did not achieve final success in their efforts to reveal the connections between the mind and the political. They did, however, establish a line of inquiry and mode of theorizing that remain extremely valuable to the development of critical pedagogy and the concept of a critical psychology of complexity.

As advocates of critical pedagogy follow the paths blazed by the Frankfurt School, they come to the stark realization that educational psychology is isolated from the critical theorists' concern with both the political realm and the process of critical consciousness formation. The study of the complexity that characterizes the production of identity seems to be lost in mainstream educational psychology to the point that such issues cannot even be discussed at the discipline's conferences and in its mainstream literature. Whereas the Frankfurt School was concerned primarily with the insights of psychoanalysis in its marriage of the political and the psychological, our critical complex psychology works to reintroduce the psychological into both the critical domain and into the contemporary conversation about schooling. Critical theorists realize in this psychological context that power helps shape the choices that determine the types of aptitudes and cognitive abilities individuals develop. Not only do humans become the sort of beings they are as a consequence of their location in the web of power relations, but also such political dynamics even define the characteristics educational psychologists designate as higher-order thinking. Intelligence itself is not simply socially influenced; it is politically inscribed and constructed in part by the nature of one's relationship to power. The closer a student operates in relation to dominant power, the more likely she is to be labeled intelligent.

As discussed earlier, though grounded on the work of the Frankfurt School, critical theory and critical pedagogy, have continually evolved—our notion of an evolving criticality. Buoyed by the rediscovery of Gramsci and his hegemony theory, the critical tradition has profited from its encounter with feminism and poststructuralism over the last quarter of the twentieth century. In this psychological and cognitive context, it is important to

understand the impact of these discourses on critical theory and critical pedagogy. Social theory in the mid-1970s embraced new understandings of ideology and the formation of subjectivity (identity). No longer was power/ideology viewed as producing a distortion of "true reality" as seen by an "authentic undistorted consciousness." This meant that no theorists, critical ones included, could ever gain a God-like picture of true reality. This reconceptualized social theory challenged the possibility of critical scholars ever telling the "whole truth." Thus, this evolving notion of critical pedagogy sought a new humility. In this spirit, I do not contend that what I write is the truth; it is simply my effort at these points in time and space to provide a fair and compelling view of the topic at hand.

Advocates of critical pedagogy and other scholars in the new paradigm would have to be content with providing partial explanations of phenomena from their particular vantage points in the web of reality. Thus, postformalist psychologists operating in the zone of critical complexity critique the authoritative pronouncements of positivistic educational psychology about higher-order thinking. In its stead, they offer no objective, final revelation about the eternal nature of such a mode of thinking. Their call to democratize the beast is open ended, motivated by an effort to diversify its meaning and admit more marginalized people into the community of the intelligent. In part, the call is an admission that we don't exactly know what cognition involves and never will; our only alternative is to simply keep looking for and collecting manifestations of it that met the standards of our historically constructed critical judgments. Such uncertainty is preferable to the antidemocratic, ethnocentric tyranny of positivistic certainty. A critical complex psychology in this context works to get beyond such reductionism.

A central dimension of critical theoretically informed cognition involves, of course, its concern with power and oppression. Such a dimension of thinking involves an understanding of the insidious work of hegemony. Richard Cary (2003) is very helpful in understanding this dimension as he discusses hegemony as the oppression of particular groups who unconsciously perpetuate their own regulation via various forms of cooperation with dominant power. In this context, Cary references the ways individuals will give consent to power by accepting the official knowledge that experts produce. To avoid being ensnared in hegemony, critical psychologists always see knowledge as contestable. Such questioning involves asking whether the knowledge provided is hegemonic. Does it attempt to win our consent to a dominating power? How does it seek to accomplish this task? Modes of critical psychology and critical pedagogy that do not possess and promote this critical understanding will fail to promote a just, equitable, and rigorous education. In hegemonically directed situations, our notion of a critical psychology will be shot down because it fails to operate under the ideological flag of neutrality, objectivity, and rationality. Critical psychologists and pedagogues are always aware of the ways ideology turns ideas that support the status quo into common sense. We need an objective psychology, they contend, even though such a psychology employs culturally specific ways of viewing the mind as universal norms. Understanding the ideological dimensions of such arguments is central in the attempt to develop a critical psychology.

Contrasting a Critical Complex Cognition to Reductionistic Ways of Thinking

Our notion of a critical complex cognition that takes into account a wide variety of social, cultural, political, cognitive, and pedagogical discourses will not play well in some quarters of the educational psychology cosmos. In reductionistic forms of educational psychology, higher-order thinking is viewed as a puzzle-solving process. Advocates of such a cognition cut through the purple haze of complexity to find set solutions to neatly outlined problems. The higher-order thinker enters a virtual world without rough edges in which the nature of all relationships is in place and easily discerned. The assumptions behind such a virtual world are beyond questioning, and inquiries into the disjunction between the virtual world and complex lived experience are ignored. In this uncritical model of thinking, a macho element prevails, as "doubters" assume combative positions to insure clarity and to hone argumentation. Such psychologists tie their vision of higher-order thinking to the rugged cross of rationality—the traditional cognitive/pedagogical dimension of the white man's burden. As they view rationality as a monocultural, monolithic domain, these defenders of the faith fight off those who would defile the sanctity of Western reason.

regimes of truth
the French social theorist/historian Michel Foucault's notion that what is deemed true depends on particular configurations of power (regimes of truth) and what it deems to be the validated process for producing validated knowledge.

normal science of a paradigm
the philosopher of science Thomas Kuhn's concept of the work that takes place in the dominant paradigm—the accepted model of producing validated knowledge—using certified methodologies and asking questions emerging from this particular way of seeing.

In this corner of the cognitive world, rationalists can't imagine why anyone would want to call the sanctity of Western science and reason into question. They speak with outrage about the uses of phrases such as **"regimes of truth,"** "conceptual frames," "the power dimensions of rationality," and "the **normal science of a paradigm**." Science and rationality are universal concepts, they argue, that do not need historicization or cultural contextualization—they are above all that. Cognition based on these notions, they assert, occupies a transcendent location as well (Hatcher, 1995). What more could Western peoples want? We have a mode of understanding the world that is objective, value free, efficient, and to the point. But *all* views of rationality and cognition make assumptions about the world, human beings, the nature of knowledge, and values—in the language of philosophy, they hold cosmological, ontological, epistemological, and axiological presuppositions. Indeed, all teaching, all definitions of educational purpose and intelligence make these assumptions. Those who engage in a critical complex cognition use these insights to recognize what assumptions are being made in their own and other analysts' versions of higher-order thinking.

Thus, in a positivistic psychology, there is no need to seek out and analyze such assumptions because such students and teachers are comfortable with the *final truth* of their conceptions about what does and does not constitute rational behavior. Forget, they entreat, all this critical theoretical blather about emancipatory social change and modes of postformal thinking that point out the fingerprints of power and dominant ideology's support of an unjust status quo. True social change will occur, they insist, only when the world is Westernized/rationalized, only when sufficient numbers of individuals attain a Cartesian form of rational cognition. This will lead to higher-order thinking at the social level and, thus, human progress. Such a positivistic mode of cognition emerges from the physical sciences and focuses on developing rationality and consistent modes of logic.

Critical pedagogy and postformal thinking value these abilities and contend that all students and teachers should understand their historical and cultural development, their contributions to the world, and their contemporary benefits. But postformalists also believe that teachers and students should understand their limitations and exclusions as well as the tacit social interests they often serve. A central debate in the discourse of cognition that reflects a larger conflict in contemporary academic life involves the value of exposing the limitations, blindness, and political implications of traditional modes of Western Cartesian rationalistic thinking. This is the reductionism that plagues the discipline of educational psychology and cognitive theory, which undermines the quest for a critical vision, Freirean critical consciousness, and critical emancipation.

Our critical psychology of complexity and postformalism's questioning of the benefits of reductionism and rationalism is often characterized as a "postmodern" rejection of positivist reason. Shaped by rationalistic philosophers and supported by mainstream articulations of psychology, what we are calling reductionism buys into a Western Enlightenment (the period characterized by the Scientific Revolution occurring between circa 1650 and circa 1800) search for meaning in a postmedieval, post-theocentric age. As traditional religious views of truth as divine revelation fell like bamboo huts in the wake of the intellectual tsunami produced by scholars such as Rene Descartes, Isaac Newton, and Francis Bacon, modern disciplines of knowledge began to emerge in order to reestablish modes of certainty and stability. The modernist social and behavioral sciences offered the hope that humans could escape religious dogmatism and oppressive authority by pursuing rational, neutral, and objective science. Of course, such ways of thinking produced successes, but flaws in the structure began to appear as the decades passed:

- efficiency at the expense of human well-being
- environmental destruction
- male-centeredness
- a tendency to view humans just like any other variable in an equation
- the devaluation of feeling and emotion
- an overemphasis on dynamics that lend themselves to mathematical measurement and a deemphasis on those profound human qualities that do not.

All of these features and many others gradually began to reveal themselves as the decades of the nineteenth and twentieth centuries passed.

The social 'scientific' and psychological disciplines that arose in the nineteenth century employed an epistemology that assumed the world was perceived similarly by everyone. Complex critical thinkers see this epistemological dynamic as one of the fatal flaws of the rationalistic tradition that finds one of its contemporary expressions in the top-down standards movement and the standardization of education it supports. Critical teachers understand that what we know is always tied to the context that shapes us as humans. Indeed, different people will hold diverse perceptions and find profoundly different meanings in the "same event." The recognition of this knowledge-related phenomenon holds dramatic implications for regressive efforts at educational reform and the professional lives of teachers working in elementary and secondary classrooms.

Diverse students with divergent frames of reference will understand not only particular lessons in varying ways but will conceptualize the entire school process differently. In childhood education and developmental psychology, for example, this feature takes on special importance in light of the language and material effects of psychological theories of developmentalism and developmental appropriateness. Assuming that everyone perceives schooling in a similar manner and that all students are operating on a level playing field, developmental appropriateness is riddled with monocultural, gender, and class-based presuppositions about behavioral norms, cognitive styles, and educational goals. When students operating outside of white, middle-/upper-middle-class boundaries do not match these culturally inscribed expectations, they are deemed incompetent and provided with "remediation" to make them more "orderly" and "structured." They are deemed incapable of higher-order thinking. It is this type of analysis of hidden assumptions that makes the insights of critical pedagogy and postformalism so important to teachers of all levels and subjects.

Critical Cognition: On to a New Terrain of Possibility

Using critical theory, critical pedagogy, complexity theory, and other diverse ways of seeing and making meaning, postformalists begin to discern interconnections between ideas, ideologies, ways of thinking, modes of evaluation, and everyday life in schools. A critical psychology of complexity is aware of many different perspectives, the vantage points of diverse disciplines of knowledge (e.g., history, philosophy, sociology) and transdisciplinary ways of seeing such as cultural studies. Critical teachers informed by these multiple perspectives understand relations between values and different interpretations of the world (Weinstein, 1998). They understand the way one's location in the world or position in the web of reality helps shape how one sees self and world. With these concepts in mind, critical teachers gain the ability to help students understand multiple perspectives and the influence of their own location in the web of reality on how they see the world.

These are basic skills of the critical students we would like to graduate from our schools. Indeed, we want them to recognize and understand the benefits of diverse ways of thinking and understanding the world. In an interesting way, such students and teachers become students of differing forms of intelligence to be found and constructed around the globe. They explore the world looking for and constructing new forms of insight and intelligence. Critical pedagogical theorists Herman Garcia and Teresa Valenzuela (2003) highlight this point when they contend that critical thinkers have to operate to find diverse ways of seeing in an educational system that has deleted the experience of marginalized students.

Although advocates of critical pedagogy and postformalists respect those who have come before us and have helped us get where we are, we are ambitious—we want to go farther. Whereas benefits have come from teaching logic, past practice in cognitive studies is not sufficient. Although a critical pedagogy that teaches traditional Western logic is inadequate, a critical pedagogy that teaches only how to discern the political inscriptions of texts and academic practices is also not enough. There is more to learn, more to be addressed, more to do. Critical teachers need to question more deeply what is the nature of critical pedagogy: What does it mean to be critical in a variety of uses of the term? Such a deep critical pedagogy moves us to question ourselves, our assumptions, our notion of self, our comfortable views of everyday life (Burbules and Beck, 1999). We view ourselves and our ways of seeing in the light of new horizons, new contexts, in the process recognizing previously unnoticed connections. Such

connections alert us to new dimensions of what we are capable of engaging. We break through the cognitive confines of Western ways of thinking into a new domain of cognitive theory and practice.

Although postformalists escape on extreme modes of hyper-rationality that limit our questions to "how to" rather than "why should," we do not simply discard reason. As this hyperrationality reminds us of the meticulous Nazi medical researchers obsessed with recording and analyzing the "cephalic index" (the shape of one's head) of those entering Hitler's death camps while ignoring the moral implications of genocide, we do not throw out the baby of reason with the bathwater. Indeed, to resist such rationalism postformal criticalists need not tie our horse to the hitching post of irrationality characterized by a nihilism and relativism that offer no hope for cognitive improvement or moral action. In this context, we avoid these untenable extremes and search for alternate modes of rationality—in other words, new and higher forms of thinking that allow us to understand more so that we an engage in empowered action for our individual and social good.

Critical cognitivists believe that such alternative cognitive practices are often grounded in cooperative interaction between and among diverse peoples. In this cooperative domain, individuals are privy to the various forms of interrelatedness. Attending to the characteristics of such connections, individuals come to see order instead of chaos. The concept of interconnection provides us with a good opportunity to bring Humberto Maturana and Francisco Varela's cognitive theory of enactivism into our critical theoretical melange. In such interconnections, and the patterns and process enfolded within them, we begin to discern one of the most amazing phenomena uncovered in recent times. Francisco Varela (1999) writes that, as unlikely as it may seem,

> Lots of simple agents having simple properties may be brought together, even in a haphazard way, to give rise to what appears to be a purposeful and integrated whole, without the need for central supervision. (p. 52)

In this simple statement, we begin to uncover a whole new dimension of not only higher-order cognition but also of the character of "the self." In this domain, we blaze new trails into the epistemological and ontological domains. In the epistemological domain, we begin to realize that knowledge is stripped of its meaning when it stands alone. This holds profound implications in education and knowledge production because European science has studied the world in a way that isolates the object of study, abstracts it from the contexts and interrelationships that give it meaning. Thus, to be a critical pedagogue in a manner that takes Varela's enactivist notion into account, we have to study the world "in context." Critical thinkers have to search for the interrelationships and contexts that give knowledge meaning while avoiding reliance on decontextualized study.

In the ontological realm, critical teachers informed by post-formalism begin to understand that to be in the world is to operate in context, in relation to other entities. Western Cartesian (coming from the tradition of the scientific method delineated by Rene Descartes in the 1600s) science traditionally has seen the basic building blocks of the universe as things-in-themselves. What much recent research in physics, biology, social science, the humanities, and cognitive science has posited involves the idea that relationships—not things-in-themselves—are the most basic properties of things in the world. In the ontological realm, this would include human beings themselves (Kincheloe, 2003b). To *be* in the world is to be in relationship. People are not abstract individuals who live as fragments, in isolation from one another. Humans come to be who they are and change who they are as a result of their interrelationships, their connections to the social sphere. They learn to think and talk via the socially constructed languages, deport themselves via cultural norms in their communities, and take care of themselves by imitating significant others in their immediate environment. Race, class, gender, sexual, religious, geographical place affiliations exert powerful influences on how they see themselves and their relation to the world. To be human is to be in relation to. And, importantly, for this book on critical pedagogy, is that to be human is to possess the power to change, to be better, to be smarter, to become a transformative agent.

Enactivism and Critical Pedagogy

A central and often neglected aspect of the theoretical base on which a critical and complex cognitive theory involves Humberto Maturana and Francisco Varela's Santiago school of

enactivism

a theory of mind that begins with an understanding of the relationship between mind and its contextual surroundings. Such an understanding demands that we ask why we see mind or any other phenomena as separate from its surroundings. Enactivism places great emphasis on how an entity interacts with its environment. In such interaction, enactivism argues, entities actually crete themselves.

enactivism. Enactivism picks up where our understanding of the social construction of knowledge and human selfhood ends. Humberto Maturana and Francisco Varela argue in a constructivist vein that the world we know is not pregiven but enacted. Thus, the act of cognition in this context does not involve the Cartesian effort to commit to memory *"mental* reflections" of the real world. Cognition is more complex than this—an insight educational reformers and standards devisors should try to grasp. Instead of attempting to reconstruct "true" mental reflections of the "real world," learners should focus on how our actions *in relation* to the world create it.

This notion of cognition and learning as acts of reflecting or representing reality is a key dimension of the history of Western cognitive psychology. In this Cartesian cognitivism, sensory imputs are reconstituted by the brain in a manner that renders them internal representations of the world "out there." Such a view of cognition produces fixed perspectives and particular viewpoints as reality itself. Conversation retreats as canons are created and minds are closed. Scholars in this positivist cognitive theoretical domain can announce that they have deduced the truth, that they have represented reality correctly. The curriculum can thus be constructed around such truth, and everyone else can go home and "just learn it." Enactivism throws a monkey wrench into such cognitive arrogance, forcing us in the process to account for the profoundly different constructions of reality that emerge when the world is encountered in different times and places. Teaching that does not take such cognitive complexity into account is short changed.

The problems of the physical, social, psychological, and educational domains rarely present themselves in a well-structured, puzzle-like way. Rationalistic technical thinking does not work very well when it confronts lived world problems that are complex and ill structured. Such situations demand more than procedural, technical reasoning. Analysts have to understand a range of tacit forms of knowledge, the multiple contexts in which the problem is situated, and thinking processes that may or may not be of value. Critical teachers make an important breakthrough in this context. They understand that the step-by-step procedures laid down by rationalists and the rules of rigorous research specified by positivists can hinder rather than help in the complications of the

lived world. Enactivists maintain that such rules must melt away in the specificity and improvisation of immediate experience.

Looking at the concept of mind from biological and psychological perspectives, enactivists begin the reparation process necessitated by the Western rationalistic reduction and fragmentation of the world. When enactivism is added to our theoretical bricolage of an evolving critical pedagogy, we emerge with a powerful grounding for a reconceptualized way of thinking about the educational process. As Jean Lave, Valerie Walkerdine, James Wertsch, Etienne Wenger, Roy Pea, and numerous other cognitive theorists have argued in the spirit of Lev Vygotsky over the last two decades, cognition and the knowledge it produces are socially situated activities that take place in concrete historical situations. Varela adds to this description, arguing that it is in the particular historical circumstance that we realize who we are and what we can become—a notion that resonates with critical pedagogy. Indeed, we realize our cognitive capabilities in the specific concrete circumstance while concurrently gaining the power to imagine what capabilities we can develop.

It is important to ask what does this cognitive theorizing say to advocates of critical pedagogy. A few ideas here may be helpful. With the help of the social, pedagogical, political, and cognitive theories we have explored, we can begin to understand that the world in general and the educational realm in particular may be more complex than we have been taught. In this informed context, we begin to understand that simple workshop procedures for implementing critical pedagogy don't work. The key here is that teachers must become scholars who understand the multiple dimensions of the cognitive act, the reasons that it has been conceptualized so differently by different analysts at different times. Teacher scholars begin to realize that the development of critical pedagogy has to be both theoretically understood and enacted in particular circumstances. Indeed, the proof is in the concrete pudding, as teachers and students take multiple understandings into account as they improvise critical pedagogy in specific lived situations. They learn to ask these questions as reflectors-in-action:

- What are the consequences of my actions from interpersonal, political, moral, and ethical perspectives?
- Where did the definitions of what I am calling critical pedagogy emanate?

- How might I have operated in this situation if I had employed different definitions of good teaching and higher-order thinking?
- Can critical teachers disagree on what might be considered the informed actions of a critical agent in these specific circumstances?
- Do I personally buy into the definitions of critical pedagogy that are being theorized and taught in this situation?

In the enactivist frame, we crawl outside the conceptual window and move into our postpositivist world of possibility. In a biological context, we come to understand that throughout the world of animals all beings possess knowledge that is constituted in the concrete situation. I have often marveled at how my dogs, Celtic, Ozzy, and Ali, will negotiate a difficult physical maneuver in a way that is cognitively sophisticated and totally improvised within a split-second time frame. In this context, we grasp Varela's point: "what we call general and abstract are aggregates of readiness-for-action" (1999, p. 18). This means that complex critical agents don't manifest their intelligence simply by developing efficient mental file cabinets for storing data; it tells us that various forms of knowledge are important as we discern their meanings and relationships and become empowered to use them in the improvisation demanded by particular circumstances. In an academic setting, the particular circumstance might involve making an argument, defending a position, figuring out how to use knowledge of oppression to help an individual who is suffering, or a teacher knowing how to deal with a student who is having difficulty in a math class.

With this in mind, we are ready for another critical cognitive theoretical step forward. Understanding these enactivist concepts concerning the realization of our cognitive abilities in concrete circumstances, we return to the complex dynamics of self-production. In critical pedagogy, the understanding of how the self is produced and how this process shapes, how we construct the world becomes profoundly important. In modes of critical teaching where this feature is omitted, nothing can be done to make up for the exclusion. Enactivism refuses to ignore the disjunction between what cognitive psychology has traditionally confirmed vis-à-vis our immediate experience, consciousness, or awareness of selfhood. At times in the recent history of

cognitive psychology—for example, in behaviorism—scientists insisted that consciousness did not exist because it did not lend itself to empirical measurement. Other cognitive perspectives simply ignored it. Obviously, such approaches to consciousness, immediate experience, and awareness of selfhood left an unfillable theoretical hole in its wake. Why, Varela asks, do humans experience the self so profoundly? Just ignoring the hole will not make it go away.

Critical cognitivists and postformalists ask what is the nature of the disjunction between scientifically validated cognitive theory and our experience of consciousness. Operating on the grounding of our political understanding of consciousness construction, we follow Varela's description of the emergent and self-organizing dimensions of selfhood, his notion of the virtual self. The emergent, virtual self arises out of a maze of relationships. It has no definable central processing mechanism, no "brain command" where control is coordinated. Consider this cognitive dynamic in light of our critical theoretical understanding of the cultural politics of self-production. Such a process operates to create new social, cultural, political, and economic relationships to produce new and more market-compliant selves. In this context, we begin to understand the pedagogical implications of the emergent self. The self is infinitely more malleable, more open to change than we had previously imagined. Given one's motivation, of course, this dimension of selfhood can be mobilized for great benefit or manipulated for great harm.

Critical pedagogues enter the arena with a new insight into what can be. They know that despite the power of generations of cognitive determinists operating under the flag of IQ, human beings can learn to become more intelligent. And, in this context, they understand that selfhood is even more of a miraculous phenomenon than many had imagined. We gain a perspective; indeed, to live is to have a point of view. Varela writes of a moment-to-moment monitoring of the nature of our selfhood. Such monitoring involves gaining metaawareness of the various connections we make to diverse dimensions of the sociophysical world around us. It involves isolating and letting go of an egocentrism that blinds us to the virtual and relational nature of our selfhood. In a critical pedagogy it means avoiding those definitions of critical work that position it as an egocentric manifestation of

the combative proponent of rationality. In the process, we also elude the cultural and gender inscriptions such perspectives drag along with them.

Digging deeper in the enactivist mine, we encounter a new vein of insight into the nature of abstract thought that holds profound implications for critical pedagogy. Obviously, the symbolic and abstract dimensions of human thought are very important, but enactivists maintain that this constitutes only one dimension of cognition. In everyday decision-making, abstract and symbolic thinking are joined by emotional consideration, gut feelings (sensations from the body), and other more tacit dimensions of thinking. Of course, cognitive science and pedagogy have typically ignored the "nonrational" aspects of the thinking process. Varela's moment-by-moment monitoring obviously includes all of these dynamics. The traditional Cartesian emphasis of rationality dismisses such considerations from the domain of learning. Such a narrowing of focus limits what is seen and constricts the horizon on which cognition is conceptualized.

This is exactly what has happened in the study of artificial intelligence. It was not long until scholars in artificial intelligence (AI) began to realize that their computer programs could not duplicate these nonrational dimensions of human thinking. Some of them understood that one of the central features of human intelligence and the teaching and learning process involves negotiating a problem that is ill-defined with solutions that are not obvious. Moreover, there may be multiple solutions contingent on the values an individual brings to the situation. In this case, rationality actually works to blind computers and AI researchers to "what could be" in the cognitive realm. The same rational blindness afflicted Jean Piaget, as he focused on the domain of human thought most prized by Western science and rationalistic traditions. The notion that learning may involve a panoply of human capabilities outside the rational domain has been lost in the positivist snowdrift. Cognitive science has been asleep at the wheel, focusing on types of thinking that operate in isolation from everyday life.

Now, to be sure, advocates of critical pedagogy are careful not to draw the wrong lessons from these insights. The point is not that we abandon rationality in favor of trivial "getting in touch with our feelings" workshops. The moral of the story is that we keep searching for alternative rationalities—read more rigorous, smarter rationalities—that are unafraid to take into account the unique capacities of the body, the emotions, the intuition that humans bring to the thinking process. As postformalists, we immerse ourselves in the specifics of how these rigorous rationalities operate in the specific domain of immediate action, in the improvisation of living in concrete circumstances. Such circumstances demand we understand:

- as Gadamer and other researchers using hermeneutic have contended, previously constructed cultural meanings
- as Foucault and many poststructuralists have argued, epistemes, meaning the ways truth is produced and knowledge is constructed
- as Horkheimer and Adorno argued, the deployment of rationality for irrational and oppressive goals
- as Judith Butler and critical feminist theorists have maintained, how larger political issues show up in concrete personal interactions
- as James Paul Gee and discourse analysts in pedagogy have posited, the ways language practices set tacit rules that regulate what can and cannot be said, who can speak and who must listen, and whose pronouncements are valid and learned and whose are ignorant in everyday conversation
- as Vygotsky, Lave, and the sociocognitivists have pointed out, the socially embedded dimensions of all forms of cognitive activity
- as Paulo Freire posited, the ways that all acts of teaching and learning are shaped by one's relationship with modes of power and domination.

All of these understandings help us deal with the enactivist concern with sophisticated cognition in the concrete situations of everyday life. In the interaction of this concern and these diverse theoretical insights emerges a powerful form of critical cognition.

Postformal thinking as intelligent awareness shaped by a knowledge of the intersection of abstract with concrete modes of thinking is an important step forward in the discourse of critical cognition and critical pedagogy. When moral and ethical concerns are injected into this intersection, new modes of

being human and new concepts of thoughtful living begin to emerge. The goal of such an orientation of living and thinking is to achieve a nonegocentric, interconnected, *intentionless* state of virtual selfhood. Explained another way, these modes of thinking and being become second nature to us, a central aspect of who we are. Drawing upon Buddhist insights, Varela implores us to develop a self devoid of self-nature. Such a position opens us to a wide range of new self-understandings that bring about ever-expanding forms of intelligent awareness. If this process results in simply a reinforcement of the unfortunately all-too-common egocentrism of the critical scholar, then our cognitive theorizing has failed. Unless such a position induces a mode of letting go that moves us to new forms of interconnection and compassion, then critical pedagogy is a sham, and we are no more than inside traders of intellectual commodities.

Glossary

Constructivist analysis—an epistemological position that maintains that the knower personally participates in all acts of knowing and understanding. Knowledge does not exist "out there" in isolation from the knower.

Enactivism—a theory of mind that begins with an understanding of the relationship between the mind and its contextual surroundings. Such an understanding demands that we ask why we see mind or any other phenomena as separate from its surroundings. Enactivism places great emphasis on how an entity interacts with its environment. In such interaction, according to the Principle of enactivism, entities actually create themselves.

Normal science of a paradigm—the philosopher of science Thomas Kuhn's concept of the work that takes place in the dominant paradigm—the accepted model of producing validated knowledge—using certified methodologies and asking questions emerging from this particular way of seeing.

Regimes of truth—the French social theorist/historian Michel Foucault's notion that what is deemed true depends on particular configurations of power (regimes of truth) and what it deems to be the validated process for producing validated knowledge.

Thing-in-itself—the Cartesian modernist ontological orientation that sees the primary unit of being in the world as the individual entity—not a relationship or a process.

References
and Resources

BOOKS, ARTICLES, WEB SITES AND CHAPTERS—
INCLUDES BIBLIOGRAPHY FOR THIS VOLUME

Agger, B. (1992). *The Discourse of Domination: From the Frankfurt School to Postmodernism.* Evanston, IL: Northwestern University Press.

Allison, C. (1995). *Present and Past: Essays for Teachers in the History of Education.* New York: Peter Lang.

Apple, M. (1979). *Ideology and Curriculum.* Boston: Routledge.

Apple, M. (1982). *Education and Power.* Boston: Routledge.

Apple, M. (1988). *Teachers and Texts: A Political Economy of Class and Gender Relations in Education.* New York: Routledge.

Apple, M. (1996). *Cultural Politics and Education.* New York: Teachers College Press.

Apple, M. (1999). *Power, Meaning, and Identity: Essays in Critical Educational Studies.* New York: Peter Lang.

Apple, M., and Weis, L. (Eds.). (1983). *Ideology and Practice in Schooling.* Philadelphia: Temple University Press.

Armstrong, M. (1981). The Case of Louise and the Painting of Landscapes. In J. Nixon (Ed.), *A Teachers' Guide to Action Research.* London: Grant McIntyre.

Aronowitz, S. (1973). *False Promises: The Shaping of American Working Class Consciousness.* New York: McGraw-Hill.

Aronowitz, S. (1981). *The Crisis in Historical Materialism: Class, Politics, and Culture in Marxist Theory.* New York: Praeger.

Aronowitz, S. (1988). *Science as Power: Discourse and Ideology in Modern Society.* Minneapolis: University of Minnesota Press.

Aronowitz, S. (1992). *The Politics of Identity: Class, Culture, and Social Movements.* New York: Routledge.

Aronowitz, S. (1993). *Dead Artists, Live Theories and Other Cultural Problems.* New York: Routledge.

Aronowitz, S. (2001). *The Knowledge Factory: Dismantling the Corporate University and Creating True Higher Learning.* Boston: Beacon.

Aronowitz, S. (2003). *How Class Works: Power and Social Movement.* New Haven, CT: Yale University Press.

Aronowitz, S., and DiFazio, W. (1994). *The Jobless Future: Sci-Tech and the Dogma of Work.* Minneapolis: University of Minnesota Press.

Aronowitz, S., and Giroux, H. (1991). *Post-Modern Education: Politics, Culture, and Social Criticism.* Minneapolis: University of Minnesota Press.

Bamburg, J. (1994). Raising Expectations to Improve Student Learning. Available from http://www.ncrel.org/sdrs/areas/issues/educatrs/leadrshp/ie0bam.htm.

Barone, T. (2000). *Aesthetics, Politics and Educational Inquiry: Essays and Examples.* New York: Peter Lang.

Bartolomé, L. (1996). Beyond the Methods Fetish: Towards a Humanizing Pedagogy. In P. Leistyna, A. Woodrum, and S. Sherblom (Eds.), *Breaking Free: The Transformative Power of Critical Pedagogy.* Cambridge, MA: Harvard Educational Review Press. pp. 173–194.

Bartolomé, L. (1998). *The Misteaching of Academic Discourses: The Politics of Language in the Classroom.* Boulder, CO: Westview.

Bauman, Z. (1995). *Life in Fragments: Essays in Postmodern Morality.* Cambridge, MA: Blackwell.

Beck, R. (1991). *General Education: Vocational and Academic Collaboration.* Berkeley: NCRVE.

Beck-Gernsheim, E., Butler, J., and Puigvert, L. (2003). *Women and Social Transformation.* New York: Peter Lang.

Bello, W. (2003). The Crisis of the Globalist Project and the New Economics of George W. Bush. *New Labor Forum.* Available from http://www.nudir.org/nadir/initiativ/agp/free/bello/crisis-globalist.htm.

Berry, K. (1998). Nurturing the Imagination of Resistance: Young Adults as Creators of Knowledge. In J. Kincheloe and S. Steinberg

(Eds.), *Unauthorized Methods: Strategies for Critical Teaching*. New York: Routledge.

Berry, K. (2000). *The Dramatic Arts and Cultural Studies: Acting Against the Grain*. New York: Falmer.

Bingham, C. (2003). Knowledge Acquisition. In D. Weil and J. Kincheloe (Eds.), *Critical Thinking and Learning: An Encyclopedia*. Westport, CT: Greenwood.

Blackler, F. (1995). Knowledge, Knowledge Work, and Organizations: An Overview and Interpretation. *Organization Studies*, 16, 6, pp. 1021–1046.

Blades, D. (1997). *Procedures of Power and Curriculum Change: Foucault and the Quest for Possibilities in Science Education*. New York: Peter Lang.

Block, A. (1995). *Occupied Reading: Critical Foundations for an Ecological Theory*. New York: Garland.

Bohm, D., and Edwards, M. (1991). *Changing Consciousness*. San Francisco: Harper.

Bottomore, T. (1984). *The Frankfurt School*. London: Tavistock.

Britzman, D. (1986). Cultural Myths in the Making of a Teacher: Biography and Social Structure in Teacher Education. *Harvard Educational Review*, 56, 4, pp. 442–455.

Britzman, D. (1991). *Practice Makes Practice: A Critical Study of Learning to Teach*. Albany: State University of New York Press.

Britzman, D. (2003). *After-Education: Anna Freud, Melanie Klein, and Psychoanalytical Histories of Learning*. Albany: State University of New York Press.

Britzman, D., and Pitt, A. (1996). On Refusing One's Place: The Ditchdigger's Dream. In J. Kincheloe, S. Steinberg, and A. Gresson (Eds.), *Measured Lies: "The Bell Curve" Examined*. New York: St. Martin's.

Brooks, E. (2007). *Unraveling the Garment Industry: Transnational Organizing and Women's Work*. Minneapolis: University of Minnestora Press.

Brosio, R. (1994). *The Radical Democratic Critique of Capitalist Education*. New York: Peter Lang.

Brosio, R. (2000). *Philosophical Scaffolding for the Construction of Critical Democratic Education*. New York: Peter Lang.

Browning, M. (2002). Antonio Gramsci and Hegemony in the United States. *The Review of Communication*, 2, 4, pp. 383–386.

Burbules, N., and Beck, R. (1999). Critical Thinking and Critical Pedagogy: Relations, Differences, and Limits. In T. Popkewitz and L. Fendler (Eds.), *Critical Theories in Education*. New York: Routledge.

Cannella, G. (1997). *Deconstructing Early Childhood Education: Social Justice and Revolution*. New York: Peter Lang.

Cannella, G., and Kincheloe, J. (2002). *Kidworld: Childhood Studies, Global Perspectives, and Education.* New York: Peter Lang.

Capra, F. (1996). *The Web of Life: A New Scientific Understanding of Living Systems.* New York: Anchor.

Carlson, D. (1997). *Making Progress: Education and Culture in New Times.* New York: Teachers College Press.

Carlson, D., and Apple, M. (Eds.) (1998). *Power/Knowledge/Pedagogy: The Meaning of Democratic Education in Unsettling Times.* Boulder, CO: Westview.

Carson, T., and Sumara, D. (1997). *Action Research as a Living Practice.* New York: Peter Lang.

Carter, R. (2003a). Art Education and Critical Thinking. In D. Weil and J. Kincheloe (Eds.), *Critical Thinking and Learning: An Encyclopedia.* Westport, CT: Greenwood.

Carter, R. (2003b). Visual Literacy: Critical Thinking with the Visual Image. In D. Weil and J. Kincheloe (Eds.), *Critical Thinking and Learning: An Encyclopedia.* Westport, CT: Greenwood.

Carter, V. (1998). Computer-Assisted Racism: Toward an Understanding of Cyber-whiteness. In J. Kincheloe, S. Steinberg, N. Rodriguez, and R. Chennault (Eds.), *White Reign: Deploying Whiteness in America.* New York: St. Martin's.

Cary, R. (1998). *Critical Art Pedagogy: Foundations for Postmodern Art Education.* New York: Garland.

Cary, R. (2003). Art and Aesthetics. In D. Weil and J. Kincheloe (Eds.), *Critical Thinking and Learning: An Encyclopedia.* Westport, CT: Greenwood.

Center for Policy Research (CPRE). (1995). Dimensions of Capacity. Available from http://www.ed.gov/pubs/CPRE/rb18/rb18b.html.

Clark, L. (2002). Critical Theory and Constructivism: Theory and Methods for the Teens and the New Media @ Home Project. Available from http://www.colorado.edu/journalism/mcm/qmr-crit-theory.htm.

Coben, D. (1998). *Radical Heroes: Gramsci, Freire and the Politics of Adult Education.* New York: Garland.

Cochran-Smith, M. (2000, April). The Outcomes Question in Teacher Education. Paper Presented at AERA, New Orleans.

Coffee, A., Holbroook, B., and Atkinson, P. (1996). Qualitative Data Analysis: Technologies and Representations. *Sociological Research Online,* 1, 1. http://www.socresonlonve.org.uk/socresonline/1/1/4/html.

Cole, M., and Scribner, S. (1978). Introduction. In L. Vygotsky (Ed.) *Mind in Society: The Development of Higher Psychological Processes.* Cambridge, MA: Harvard University Press.

Cole, M., and Wertsch, J. (2003). Beyond the Individual—Social Antimony in Discussions of Piaget and Vygotsky. Available from http://www.massey.ac.nz/~alock/virtual.colevyg.htm.

Collins, J. (1995). *Architectures of Excess: Cultural Life in the Information Age.* New York: Routledge.

Covaleskie, J. (2003). Philosophical Instruction. In D. Weil and J. Kincheloe (Eds.), *Critical Thinking and Learning: An Encyclopedia.* Westport, CT: Greenwood.

Crebbin, W. (2001). The Critically Reflective Practitioner. Available from http://www.ballarat.edu.au/~wcrebbin/TB780/Critreflect.html.

Cruz, A. (1997a). *An Examination of How One Deaf Person Constructs Meaning in Music: A Phenomenological Perspective.* Unpublished doctoral dissertation, University of Tennessee, Knoxville.

Cruz, A. (1997b). Critical Thinking in Music: Insights from Teaching Music to a Deaf Teenager. *Canadian Music Educator,* 38, 2, pp. 35–38.

Dahlbom, B. (1998). Going to the Future. Available from http://www.viktoria.infomatik.gu.se/~max/bo/papers.html.

Darder, A. (1991). *Culture and Power in the Classroom.* Westport, CT: Bergin and Garvey.

Darder, A. (2002). *Reinventing Paulo Freire: A Pedagogy of Love.* Boulder, CO: Westview.

Darder, A., Baltodano, M., and Torres, R. (2002.). *The Critical Pedagogy Reader.* New York: Routledge.

Darder, A., and Torres, R. (2003). *After Race: Racism after Multiculturalism.* New York: New York University Press.

Degener, S. (2002). Making sense of critical pedagogy in adult literacy. *The Annual Review of Adult Learning and Literacy.* Available from http://www.gse.harvard.edu/~ncsall/ann_rev/vol2_2.html.

Dei, G., Karumanchery, L., and Karumanchery-Luik, N. (2004). *Playing the Race Card: Exposing White Power and Privilege.* New York: Peter Lang.

Denzin, N. (1994). The Art and Politics of Interpretation. In N. Denzin and Y. Lincoln (Eds.), *Handbook of Qualitative Research.* Thousand Oaks, CA: Sage.

Denzin, N., and Lincoln Y. (2000). Introduction: The Discipline and Practice of Qualitative Research. In N. Denzin and Y. Lincoln (Eds.), *Handbook of Qualitative Research* (2nd ed.). Thousand Oaks, CA: Sage.

Dewey, J. (1916). *Democracy and Education.* New York: The Free Press.

Drummond, L. (1996). *American Dreamtime: A Cultural Analysis of Popular Movies and Their Implications for a Science of Humanity.* Lanham, MD: Littlefield Adams.

Du Bois, W. (1973). *The Education of Black People: Ten Critiques, 1906–1960.* New York: Monthly Review Press.

Edwards, A. (2000). Researching Pedagogy: A Sociocultural Agenda. Inaugural Lecture, University of Birmingham. Available from http://www.edu.bham.ac.uk/SAT/Edwards1.html.

Ellis, J. (1998). Interpretive Inquiry as Student Research. In S. Steinberg and J. Kincheloe (Eds.), *Students as Researchers: Creating Classrooms That Matter.* London: Falmer.

Fehr, D. (1993). *Dogs Playing Cards: Powerbrokers of Prejudice in Education, Art, and Culture.* New York: Peter Lang.

Fernandez-Balboa, J. (2003). Emancipatory Critical Thinking. In D. Weil and J. Kincheloe (Eds.), *Critical Thinking and Learning: An Encyclopedia.* Westport, CT: Greenwood.

Ferreira, M., and Alexandre, F. (2000). Education for Citizenship: The Challenge of Teacher Education in Postmodernity. Available from http://www.ioe.ac.uk./ccs/conference2000/papers/epsd/ferreiraandalexandre.html.

First Annual Urban Schools Symposium Report (FAUSSR) (1998). Relationship, Community, and Positive Reframing: Addressing the Needs. Available from http://www.inclusiveschools.org/procsho.htm.

Fischer, F. (1998). Beyond Empiricism: Policy Inquiry in Postpositivist Perspective. *Policy Studies Journal,* 26, 1, pp. 129–146.

Fiske, J. (1993). *Power Plays, Power Works.* New York: Verso.

Flecha, R., Gomez, J., and Puigvert, L. (2003). *Contemporary Sociological Theory.* New York: Peter Lang.

Flossner, G., and Otto, H. (Eds.). (1998). *Towards More Democracy in Social Services: Models of Culture and Welfare.* New York: de Gruyter.

Foote, M., and Goodson, I. (2001). Regulating Teachers—A Sword over Their Heads: The Standards Movement as a Disciplinary Device. In J. Kincheloe and D. Weil (Eds.), *Standards and Schooling in the United States: An Encyclopedia.* 3 vols. Santa Barbara, CA: ABC-CLIO.

Forgacs, D. (1988). *An Antonio Gramsci Reader.* New York: Schocken Books.

Foster, R. (1997). Addressing Epistemologic and Practical Issues in Multimethod Research: A Procedure for Conceptual Triangulation. *Advances in Nursing Education,* 202, 2.

Foucault, M. (1990). *Politics, Philosophy, Culture: Interviews and Other Writings, 1977–1984.* New York: Routledge.

Freire, A. (2001). *Chronicles of Love: My Life with Paulo Freire.* New York: Peter Lang.

Freire, P. (1970). *Pedagogy of the Oppressed.* New York: Herder and Herder.

Freire, P. (1972). Research Methods. Paper Presented to a Seminar, Studies in Adult Education, Dar-es-Salaam, Tanzania.

Freire, P. (1978). *Education for Critical Consciousness.* New York: Seabury.

Freire, P. (1985). *The Politics of Education: Culture, Power, and Liberation.* South Hadley, MA: Bergin and Garvey.

Freire, P. (1998). *Pedagogy of the Heart.* New York: Continuum.

Freire, P., and Faundez, A. (1989). *Learning to Question: A Pedagogy of Liberation.* New York: Continuum.

Freire, P., and Macedo, D. (1987). *Literacy: Reading the Word and the World.* South Hadley, MA: Bergin and Garvey.

Gabbard, D. (1995). NAFTA, GATT, and Goals 2000: Reading the Political Culture of Post-industrial America. *Taboo: The Journal of Culture and Education,* 2, pp. 184–199.

Gadamer, H. (1989). *Truth and Method.* New York: Continuum Books.

Gall, J., Gall, M., and Borg, W. (1999). *Applying Educational Research: A Practical Guide.* New York: Longman.

Gallagher, S. (1992). *Hermeneutics and Education.* Albany: State University of New York Press.

García, H., and Valenzuela, T. (2003). Bilingual Education: Toward a Critical Comprehension of Engaging an Emancipatory Paradigm. In D. Weil and J. Kincheloe (Eds.), *Critical Thinking and Learning: An Encyclopedia.* Westport, CT: Greenwood.

Gee, J. (1996). *Social Linguistics and Literacies: Ideology in Discourses* (2nd ed.). London: Taylor and Francis.

Gee, J., Hull, G., and Lankshear, C. (1996). *The New Work Order: Behind the Language of the New Capitalism.* Boulder, CO: Westview.

Geeland, D., and Taylor, P. (2000). Writing Our Lived Experience: Beyond the (Pale) Hermeneutic. *Electronic Journal of Science Education,* 5. Available from http://unr.edu/homepage/crowther/ejse/geelanetal.html.

Gergen, M., and Gergen, K. (2000). Qualitative Inquiry: Tensions and Transformations. In N. Denzin and Y. Lincoln (Eds.), *Handbook of Qualitative Research* (2nd ed.). Thousand Oaks, CA: Sage.

Gibson, R. (1986). *Critical Theory and Education.* London: Hodder and Stoughton.

Giroux, H. (1981). *Ideology, Culture, and the Process of Schooling.* Philadelphia: Temple University Press.

Giroux, H. (1983). *Theory and Resistance in Education.* South Hadley, MA: Bergin and Garvey.

Giroux, H. (1988). *Schooling and the Struggle for Public Life.* Minneapolis: University of Minnesota Press.

Giroux, H. (1992). *Border Crossings: Cultural Workers and the Politics of Education.* New York: Routledge.

Giroux, H. (1997). *Pedagogy and the Politics of Hope: Theory, Culture, and Schooling.* Boulder, CO: Westview.

Giroux, H., Lankshear, C., McLaren, P., and Peters, M. (1997). *Counternarratives: Cultural Studies and Critical Pedagogies in Postmodern Spaces.* New York: Routledge.

Giroux, H., and McLaren, P. (Eds.). (1989). *Critical Pedagogy, The State, and Cultural Struggles.* Albany: State University of New York Press.

Giroux, H., and Simon, R. (Eds.). (1989). *Popular Culture: Schooling and Everyday Life.* Granby, MA: Bergin and Garvey.

Gomez, J. (2004). *El Amor en la Sociedad del Riesgo.* Barcelona: El Roure.

Goodlad, J. (1994). *Educational Renewal: Better Teachers, Better Schools.* San Francisco: Jossey-Bass.

Goodson, I. (1997). *The Changing Curriculum: Studies in Social Construction.* New York: Peter Lang.

Gramsci, A. (1988). *A Gramsci Reader.* Ed. D. Forgacs. London: Lawrence and Wishart.

Gramsci Archives. (2003). Why read Gramsci? Available from http://www. charm.net/~vacirca.

Grande, S. (2004). *Red Pedagogy: Native American Social and Political Thought.* Boulder, CO: Rowman and Littlefield.

Grange, L. (2003). Educational Research as Democratic Praxis. Available from http://www.kas.org.za/publications/seminarreports/ democratictransformationofeducation/le%20grange.pdf.

Gresson, A. (1995). *The Recovery of Race in America.* Minneapolis, MN: University of Minnesota Press.

Gresson, A. (2004). *America's Atonement: Racial Pain, Recovery Rhetoric, and the Pedagogy of Healing.* New York: Peter Lang.

Grimmett, P. (1999). Teacher Educators as Mettlesome Mermaids. *International Electronic Journal for Leadership in Learning.* 3, 12. Available from http:// www.ucalgary.ca/~iejll.

Grondin, J. (1994). *Introduction to Philosophical Hermeneutics.* New Haven, CT: Yale University Press.

Gross, A., and Keith, W. (Eds.). (1997). *Rhetorical Hermeneutics: Invention and Interpretation in the Age of Science,* Albany: State University of New York Press.

Grossberg, L. (1997). *Bringing It All Back Home: Essays on Cultural Studies.* Durham, NC: Duke University Press.

Grubb, N., Davis, G., Lum, J., Plihal, J., and Marjaine, C. (1991). *The Cunning Hand, the Cultured Mind: Models for Integrating Vocational and Academic Education.* Berkeley, CA: NCRVE.

Harding, S. (1998). *Is Science Multicultural? Postcolonialisms, Feminisms, and Epistemologies.* Bloomington, IN: Indiana University Press.

Hatcher, D. (1995). Critical Thinking and the Postmodern View of Reality Available from http://www.bakera.edu/html/crit/literature/ dlhctpostmodern.htm.

Held, D. (1980). *Introduction to Critical Theory: Horkheimer to Habermas.* Berkeley: University of California Press.

Hicks, E. (1999). *Ninety-Five Languages and Seven Forms of Intelligence.* New York: Peter Lang.

Hinchey, P. (1998). *Finding Freedom in the Classroom: A Practical Introduction to Critical Theory.* New York: Peter Lang.

Hoban, G., and Erickson, G. (1998). Frameworks for Sustaining Professional Learning. Paper Presented at the Australasian Science Education Research Association. Darwin, Australia.

hooks, b. (1981). *Ain't I a Woman?: Black Women and Feminism.* Boston: South End.

hooks, b. (1984). *Feminist Theory: From Margin to Center.* Boston: South End.

hooks, b. (1989). *Talking Back: Thinking Feminist, Thinking Black.* Boston: South End.

hooks, b. (1991). *Yearning: Race, Gender, and Cultural Politics.* Boston: South End.

hooks, b. (1994). *Teaching to Transgress: Education as the Practice of Freedom.* Boston: South End.

Horn, R. (2000) *Teacher Talk: A Postformal Inquiry into Educational Change.* New York: Peter Lang.

Horn, R. (2003). Scholar-Practitioner Leaders: The Empowerment of Teachers and Students. In D. Weil and J. Kincheloe (Eds.), *Critical Thinking and Learning: An Encyclopedia.* Westport, CT: Greenwood.

Horton, M., and Freire, P. (1990). *We Make the Road by Walking: Conversations on Education and Social Change.* Ed. B. Bell, J. Gaventa, and J. Peters. Philadelphia: Temple University Press.

Howell, S. (1998). The Learning Organization: Reproduction of Whiteness. In J. Kincheloe, S. Steinberg, N. Rodriguez, and R. Chennault (Eds.), *White Reign: Deploying Whiteness in America.* New York: St. Martin's.

The Human Sciences (1999). What Is It To Be Human? Available from http://www.barnaed.ua.edu/~stomlins/607/607w3ahs1.html.

Humphries, B. (1997). From Critical Thought to Emancipatory Action: Contradicting Research Goals? *Sociological Research Online,* 2, 1. Available from http://www.socresonline.org.uk/socresonlin/2/1/3.html.

Jardine, D. (1998). *To Dwell with a Boundless Heart: Essays in Curriculum Theory, Hermeneutics, and the Ecological Imagination.* New York: Peter Lang.

Jay, M. (1973). *The Dialectical Imagination: A History of the Frankfurt School and the Institute of Social Research 1923–1950.* Boston: Little, Brown.

John-Steiner, V., and Souberman, E. (1978). Afterword. In L. Vygotsky (Ed.), *Mind in Society: The Development of Higher Psychological Processes.* Cambridge, MA: Harvard University Press.

Joshua, J. (1998). The Philosophical and Sociological Foundations of Educational Research. Paper Presented to the Australian Association of Research in Education, Adelaide.

Keesing-Styles, L. (2003). The Relationship between Critical Pedagogy and Assessment in Teacher Education. *Radical Pedagogy.* Available from http://radicalpedagogy.icaap.org/content/issue5_1/03_keesing-stules.html.

Kellner, D. (1989). *Critical Theory, Marxism, and Modernity.* Baltimore, MD: Johns Hopkins University Press.

Kellner, D. (1995). *Media Culture: Cultural Studies, Identity, and Politics between the Modern and Postmodern.* New York: Routledge.

Kilduff, M., and Mehra, A. (1997). Postmodernism and Organizational Research. *Academy of Management Review,* 22, 2, pp. 453–481.

Kincheloe, J. (1993). *Toward a Critical Politics of Teacher Thinking: Mapping the Postmodern.* Westport, CT: Bergin and Garvey.

Kincheloe, J. (1995). *Toil and Trouble: Good Work, Smart Workers, and the Integration of Academic and Vocational Education.* New York: Peter Lang.

Kincheloe, J. (1998). Critical Research in Science Education. In B. Fraser and K. Tobin (Eds.), *International Handbook of Science Education* (part 2). Boston: Kluwer.

Kincheloe, J. (1999). *How Do We Tell the Workers? The Socio-Economic Foundations of Work and Vocational Education.* Boulder, CO: Westview.

Kincheloe, J. (2001a). *Getting Beyond the Facts: Teaching Social Studies/Social Sciences in the Twenty-First Century.* New York: Peter Lang.

Kincheloe, J. (2001b). Describing the Bricolage: Conceptualizing a New Rigor in Qualitative Research. *Qualitative Inquiry,* 7, 6, pp. 679–692.

Kincheloe, J. (2002). *The Sign of the Burger: McDonald's and the Culture of Power.* Philadelphia: Temple University Press

Kincheloe, J. (2003a). Into the Great Wide Open: Introducing Critical Thinking. In D. Weil and J. Kincheloe (Eds.) *Critical Thinking and Learning: An Encyclopedia.* Westport, CT: Greenwood.

Kincheloe, J. (2003b). Critical Ontology: Visions of Selfhood and Curriculum. *JCT: Journal of Curriculum Theorizing,* 19, 1, pp. 47–64.

Kincheloe, J. (2004). Iran and American Miseducation: Cover-ups, Distortions, and Omissions. In J. Kincheloe and S. Steinberg (Eds.), *The Miseducation of the West: Constructing Islam.* Westport, CT: Greenwood.

Kincheloe, J., Berry, K. (2004). *Rigor and Complexity in Qualitative Research: Constructing the Bricolage.* London: Open University Press.

Kincheloe, J., and Bursztyn, A., and Steinberg, S. (2004). *Teaching Teachers: Building a Quality School of Urban Education.* New York: Peter Lang.

Kincheloe, J., and McLaren, P. (2004). Rethinking Critical Theory and Qualitative Research. In N. Denzin and Y. Lincoln (Eds.), *Handbook of Qualitative Research* (3rd ed.) Thousand Oaks, CA: Sage.

Kincheloe, J., and Pinar, W. (1991). *Curriculum as Social Psychoanalysis: Essays on the Significance of Place*. Albany: State University of New York Press.

Kincheloe, J., and Steinberg, S. (1993). A Tentative Description of Post-Formal Thinking: The Critical Confrontation with Cognitive Theory. *Harvard Educational Review*, 63, 3, pp. 296–320.

Kincheloe, J., and Steinberg, S. (1997). *Changing Multiculturalism*. London: Open University Press.

Kincheloe, J., and Steinberg, S. (1998). *Unauthorized Methods: Strategies for Critical Teaching*. New York: Routledge.

Kincheloe, J., and Steinberg, S. (1999). Politics, Intelligence, and the Classroom: Postformal Teaching. In J. Kincheloe, S. Steinberg, and L. Villaverde (Eds.), *Rethinking Intelligence: Confronting Psychological Assumptions About Teaching and Learning*. New York: Routledge.

Kincheloe, J., and Steinberg, S. (2004). *The Miseducation of the West: Constructing Islam*. New York: Greenwood.

Kincheloe, J., Steinberg, S., and Gresson, A. (Eds.). (1996). *Measured Lies: The "Bell Curve" Examined*. New York: St. Martin's.

Kincheloe, J., Steinberg, S., Rodriguez, N., and Chennault, R. (1998). *White Reign: Deploying Whiteness in America*. New York: St. Martin's Press.

Kincheloe, J., Steinberg, S., and Slattery, P. (2000). *Contextualizing Teaching*. New York: Longman.

Kincheloe, J., Steinberg, S., and Tippins, D. (1999). *The Stigma of Genius: Einstein, Consciousness, and Education*. New York: Peter Lang.

Kincheloe, J., Steinberg, S., and Villaverde, L. (Eds.). (1999). *Rethinking Intelligence: Confronting Psychological Assumptions about Teaching and Learning*. New York: Routledge.

Kincheloe, J., and Weil, D. (Eds.). (2001). *Standards and Schooling in the United States: An Encyclopedia*. Santa Barbara, CA: ABC-CLIO.

Knobel, M. (1999). *Everyday Literacies: Students, Discourse, and Social Practice*. New York: Peter Lang.

Kogler, H. (1996). *The Power of Dialogue: Critical Hermeneutics after Gadamer and Foucault*. Cambridge, MA: MIT Press.

Kozulin, A. (1997). Vygotsky in Context. In L. Vygotsky (Ed.) *Thought and Language*. Cambridge, MA: Massachusetts Institute of Technology Press.

Kraft, N. (2001). Certification of Teachers—A Critical Analysis of Standards in Teacher Education Programs. In J. Kincheloe and D. Weil (Eds.), *Standards and Schooling in the United States: An Encyclopedia*, 3 vols. Santa Barbara, CA: ABC-CLIO.

Lankshear, C., and Knobel, M. (2003). *New Literacies and Changing Knowledge in the Classroom*. London: Open University Press.

Lankshear, C., and McLaren, P. (1993). *Critical Literacy: Politics, Praxis, and the Postmodern*. Albany: State University of New York Press.

Lapani, B. (1998). Information Literacy: The Challenge of the Digital Age. Available from http://www.acal.edu.au/lepani.htm.

Lather, P. (1991). *Getting Smart: Feminist Research and Pedagogy within the Postmodern.* New York: Routledge.

Lather, P., and Smithies, C. (1997). *Troubling the Angels: Women Living with HIV/AIDS.* Boulder: Westview/ HarperCollins.

Lave, J., and Wenger, E. (1991). *Situated Learning: Legitimate Peripheral Participation.* New York: Cambridge University Press.

Leistyna, P., Woodrum, P., and Sherblom, S. (1996). *Breaking Free: The Transformative Power of Critical Pedagogy.* Cambridge, MA: Harvard Educational Review.

Lemke, J. (1995). *Textual Politics: Discourse and Social Dynamics.* London: Taylor and Francis.

Lemke, J. (1998). Analyzing Verbal Data: Principles, Methods, and Problems. In B. Fraser and K. Tobin (Eds.), *International Handbook of Science Education* (part 2). Boston: Kluwer.

Lincoln, Y. (2001). An Emerging New *Bricoleur*: Promises and Possibilities— A Reaction to Joe Kincheloe's 'Describing the Bricoleur'. *Qualitative Inquiry,* 7, 6, pp. 693–696.

Lull, J. (1995). *Media, Communication, Culture: A Global Approach.* New York: Columbia University Press.

Macedo, D. (1994). *Literacies of Power: What Americans Are Not Allowed to Know.* Boulder, CO: Westview.

Macedo, D. (2006). *Literacies of Power: What Americans Are Not Allowed to Know* (2nd ed.). Boulder, CO: Westview.

Macedo, D., and Bartolomé, L. (2001). *Dancing with Bigotry: Beyond the Politics of Tolerance.* New York: Palgrave.

Macedo, D., and Steinberg, S. (Eds.). (2007). *Media Literacy: A Reader.* New York: Peter Lang.

Madison, G. (1988). *The Hermeneutics of Postmodernity: Figures and Themes.* Bloomington: Indiana University Press.

Marijuan, P. (1994). Information Revisited. Paper Presented to the First Conference on the Foundations of Information Science. Madrid, Spain.

Mayers, M. (2001). Interpretation—Hermeneutics Invitation to Meaning Making: The Ecology of a Complexity of Standards, Educational Research, Policy, and Praxis. In J. Kincheloe and D. Weil (Eds.), *Standards and Schooling in the United States: An Encyclopedia.* 3 vols. Santa Barbara, CA: ABC-CLIO.

Mayers, M., and Field, J. (2003). Critical Hermeneutics in the Classroom. In D. Weil and J. Kincheloe (Eds.), *Critical Thinking and Learning: An Encyclopedia.* Westport, CT: Greenwood.

Mayo, P. (2000). Synthesizing Gramsci and Freire: Possibilities for a Theory of Transformative Adult Education. In S. Steiner, H. Krank, P. McLaren, and R. Bahruth (Eds.) *Freirean Pedagogy, Praxis, and Possibilities: Projects for the New Millennium.* New York: Falmer.

McClure, M. (2000). Chaos and Feminism—A Complex Dynamic: Parallels Between Feminist Philosophy of Science and Chaos Theory. Available from http://www.pamij.com/feminism.html.

McLaren, P. (1980). *Cries from the Corridor: The New SuburbanGhettoes.* New York: Methuen.

McLaren, P. (1986). *Schooling as a Ritual Performance: Toward a Political Economy of Educational Symbols and Gestures.* London: Kejan Paul.

McLaren, P. (1989). *Life in Schools: An Introduction to Critical Pedagogy in the Foundations of Education.* New York: Longman.

McLaren, P. (1995). *Critical Pedagogy and Predatory Culture: Oppositional Politics in a Postmodern Era.* New York: Routledge.

McLaren, P. (1997). *Revolutionary Multiculturalism: Pedagogies of Dissent for the New Millennium.* Boulder, CO: Westview.

McLaren, P. (1998). Revolutionary Pedagogy in Post-Revolutionary Times: Rethinking the Political Economy of Critical Education. *Educational Theory,* 48, pp. 431–462.

McLaren, P. (2000). *Che Guevara, Paulo Freire, and the Pedagogy of Revolution.* Lanham, MD: Rowman and Littlefield.

McLaren, P., Hammer, R., Reilly, S., and Sholle, D. (1995). *Rethinking Media Literacy: A Critical Pedagogy of Representation.* New York: Peter Lang.

McLaren, P., and Kincheloe, J. (Eds.). (2007). *Critical Pedagogy: Where Are We Now?* New York: Peter Lang.

McLaren, P., and Lankshear, C. (1994). *Politics of Liberation: Paths from Freire.* New York: Routledge.

McLeod, J. (2000). Qualitative research as bricolage. Paper presented at the Society for Psychotherapy Research Annual Conference, Chicago.

McSwine, B. (1998). The Educational Philosophy of W.E.B. Du Bois. *Philosophy of Education Yearbook.* Available from http://www.ed.uicu.edu/eps/pes-yearbook/1998/kmcswine.htm.

McWilliam, E., and Taylor, P. (Eds.). (1996). *Pedagogy, Technology, and the Body.* New York: Peter Lang.

MDRC for the Council of the Great City Schools. (2002). Foundations for Success: Case Studies of How Urban School Systems Improve Student Achievement. Available from http://www.cgcs.rg/reports/foundations.html.

Mignolo, W. (2001). The Geopolitics of Knowledge and Colonial Difference. Available from http://multitudes.samizdat.net/article194.html.

Mignolo, W. (2005). Prophets Facing Sidewise: The Geopolitics of Knowledge and the Colonial Difference. *Social Epistemology*, 19, 1, pp. 111–127.

Molnar, A. (1996). *Giving Kids the Business: The Commercialization of America's Schools.* Boulder, CO: Westview.

Monteiro, T. (1995). W. E. B. Du Bois: Scholar, Scientist, and Activist. Available from http://members.tripod.com/~Du Bois/mont.html.

Morgan, W. (1996). Personal Training: Discourses of (Self) Fashioning. In E. McWilliam and P. Taylor (Eds.), *Pedagogy, Technology, and the Body.* New York: Peter Lang.

Mullen, C. (1999). Whiteness, Cracks and Ink-Stains: Making Cultural Identity with Euroamerican Preservice Teachers. In P. Diamond and C. Mullen (Eds.), *The Postmodern Educator: Arts-Based Inquiries and Teacher Development.* New York: Peter Lang.

Mutua, L., and Swadener, B. (2004). Introduction. In K. Mutua and B. Swadener (Eds.), *Decolonizing Research in Cross-Cultural Contexts: Critical Personal Narratives.* Albany: State University of New York Press.

Nicholl, T. (1998). Vygotsky. Available from http://www.massey.ac.nz/ ~alock//virtual/trishvyg.gtm.

Nicholson, L., and Seidman, S. (Eds.). (1995). *Social Postmodernism: Beyond Identity Politics.* New York: Cambridge University Press.

Noone, L., and Cartwright, P. (1996). Doing a Critical Literacy Pedagogy: Trans/forming Teachers in a Teacher Education Course. Available from http://www.atea.schools.net.au/ATEA/96conf/noone.html.

Norris, N. (1998). Curriculum Evaluation Revisited. *Cambridge Journal of Education*, 28, 2, pp. 207–219.

Novick, R. (1996). Actual Schools, Possible Practices: New Directions in Professional Development. *Education Policy Analysis Archives*, 4, 14.

Nowotny, H. (2000). Re-thinking Science: From Reliable Knowledge to Socially Robust Knowledge. Available from http://www.wiss.ethz.ch/pub/helga/re-thnking.pdf.

Oakes, J. (1985). *Keeping Track: How Schools Structure Inequality.* New Haven: Yale University Press.

Oldroyd, D. (1985). Indigenous Action Research for Individual and System Development. *Educational Management and Administration*, 13, pp. 113–118.

O'Riley, P. (2003). *Technology, Culture, and Socioeconomics: A Rhizoanalysis of Educational Discourses.* New York: Peter Lang.

Pailliotet, A. (1998). Deep Viewing: A Critical Look at Visual Texts. In J. Kincheloe and S. Steinberg (Eds.), *Unauthorized Methods: Strategies for Critical Teaching.* New York: Routledge.

Parenti, M. (2002). *The Terrorism Trap: September and Beyond.* San Francisco: City Lights.

Peters, M., and Lankshear, C. (1994). Education and Hermeneutics: A Freirean Interpretation. In P. McLaren and C. Lankshear (Eds.), *Politics of Liberation: Paths from Freire.* New York: Routledge.

Peters, M., Lankshear, C., and Olssen, M. (2003). *Critical Theory and the Human Condition: Founders and Praxis.* New York: Peter Lang.

Pfeil, F. (1995). *White Guys: Studies in Postmodern Domination and Difference.* New York: Verso.

Pickering, J. (2000). Methods Are a Message. In M. Velmans (Ed.), *Investigating Phenomenal Consciousness: Methodologies and Maps.* Amsterdam: John Benjamins.

Pinar, W. (Ed.). (1998) *Curriculum: Toward New Identities.* New York: Garland.

Pinar, W., and M. Grumet (1988). Socratic *Caesura* and the Theory-Practice Relationship. In W. Pinar (Ed.), *Contemporary Curriculum Discourses.* Scottsdale, AZ: Gorsuch Scarisbrick.

Pinar, W., Reynolds, W., Slattery, P., and Taubman, P. (1995). *Understanding Curriculum.* New York: Peter Lang.

Powell, R. (2001). *Straight Talk: Growing as Multicultural Educators.* New York: Peter Lang.

Prigogine, I. (1997). End of certainty. New York: The Free press.

Pruyn, M. (1994). Becoming Subjects through Critical Practice: How Students in an Elementary Classroom Critically Read and Wrote Their World. *International Journal of Educational Reform,* 3, 1, pp. 37–50.

Pruyn, M. (1999). *Discourse Wars in Gotham-West: A Latino Immigrant Urban Tale of Resistance and Agency.* Boulder, CO: Westview.

Purpel, D. (1999). *Moral Outrage in Education.* New York: Peter Lang.

Rapko, J. (1998). Review of The Power of Dialogue: Critical Hermeneutics after Gadamer and Foucault. Criticism, 40, 1, pp. 133–138.

Reason, P., and Bradbury, H. (2000). Introduction: Inquiry and Participation in Search of a World Worthy of Human Aspiration. In P. Reason and H. Bradbury (Eds.), *Handbook of Action Research: Participative Inquiry and Practice.* Thousand Oaks, CA: Sage.

Reason, P., and Torbert, W. (2001). Toward a transformational science: A further look at the scientific merits of action research. *Concepts and Transformations,* 6, 1, pp. 1–37.

Ritzer, G. (1993). *The McDonaldization of Society.* Thousand Oaks, CA: Pine Forge.

Roberts, P. (2003). Knowledge, Dialogue, and Humanization: Exploring Freire's Philosophy. In M. Peters, C. Lankshear, and M. Olssen (Eds.), *Critical Theory and the Human Condition: Founders and Praxis.* New York: Peter Lang.

Rodriguez, N., and Villaverde, L. (2000). *Dismantling White Privilege.* New York: Peter Lang.

Roediger, D. (1991). *The Wages of Whiteness: Race and the Making of the American Working Class.* New York: Verso.

Roman, L., and Eyre, L. (Eds.). (1997). *Dangerous Territories: Struggles for Difference and Equality in Education.* New York: Routledge.

Rose, K., and Kincheloe, J. (2003). *Art, Culture, and Education: Artful Teaching in a Fractured Landscape.* New York: Peter Lang.

Rosen, S. (1987). *Hermeneutics as Politics.* New York: Oxford University Press.

Samaras, A. (2002). *Self-Study for Teacher Educators: Crafting a Pedagogy for Educational Change.* New York: Peter Lang.

Sanders-Bustle, L. (2003). *Image, Inquiry, and Transformative Practice: Engaging Learners in Creative and Critical Inquiry through Visual Representation.* New York: Peter Lang.

Scering, G. (1997). Themes of a Critical/Feminist Pedagogy: Teacher Education for Democracy. *Journal of Teacher Education.* 48, 1, pp. 62–69.

Schon, D. (1995). The New Scholarship Requires a New Epistemology. *Change,* 27, 6.

Schubert, W. (1998). Toward Constructivist Teacher Education for Elementary Schools in the Twenty-first Century: A Framework for Decision-Making. Available from my.netian.com/~yhhknue/ coned19.htm.

Selfe, C., and Selfe, R. (1994). The Politics of the Interface: Power and Its Exercise in Electronic Contact Zones. Available from http://www.hu.mtu.edu/~cyselfe/texts/politics.html.

Semali, L., and Kincheloe, J. (1999). *What Is Indigenous Knowledge? Voices from the Academy.* New York: Falmer.

Shaker, P., and Kridel, C. (1989). The Return to Experience: A Reconceptualist Call. *Journal of Teacher Education,* 40, 1, pp. 2–8.

Shoham, S. (1999). *God as the Shadow of Man.* New York: Peter Lang.

Shor, I. (1980). *Critical Teaching and Everyday Life.* Chicago: University of Chicago Press.

Shor, I. (1986). *Culture Wars: School and Society in the Conservative Restoration, 1969–1991.* Chicago: University of Chicago Press.

Shor, I. (1987). *Freire for the Classroom: A Sourcebook for Liberatory Teaching.* Portsmouth, NH: Heinemann.

Shor, I. (1992). *Empowering Education: Critical Teaching for Social Change.* Portsmouth, NH: Heinemann.

Shor, I., and Freire, P. (1987). *A Pedagogy for Liberation: Dialogues on Transforming Education.* Westport, CT: Bergin and Garvey.

Shor, I., and Pari, C. (1999a). *Education Is Politics: Critical Teaching Across Differences, K-12—A Tribute to the Life and Work of Paulo Freire.* Portsmouth, NH: Heinemann.

Shor, I., and Pari, C. (1999b). *Critical Literacy in Action: Writing Words, Changing Worlds—A Tribute to the Teachings of Paulo Freire.* Portsmouth, NH: Heinemann.

Simpson, D., and Jackson, M. (2001). John Dewey and Educational Evaluation. In J. Kincheloe and D. Weil (Eds.), *Standards and Schooling in the United States: An Encyclopedia.* Santa Barbara, CA: ABC-CLIO.

Slater, J., Fain, S., and Rossatto, C. (2002). *The Freirean Legacy: Educating for Social Justice.* New York: Peter Lang.

Sleeter, C. (1993). How White Teachers Construct Race. In C. McCarthy and W. Crichlow (Eds.), *Race, Identity, and Reproduction in Education.* New York: Routledge.

Smith, D. (1999). *Pedagon: Interdisciplinary Essays in the Human Sciences, Pedagogy, and Culture.* New York: Peter Lang.

Smith, D. (2006). *Trying To Teach in a Season of Great Untruth: Globalization, Empire, and the Crises of Pedagogy.* Rotterdam: Sense Publishers.

Smith, D. (2003). On Enfraudening the Public Sphere, the Futility of Empire and the Future of Knowledge after America. *Policy Futures in Education,* 1, 3, pp. 498-504.

Smith, L. (1999). *Decolonizing Methodologies: Research and Indigenous Peoples.* New York: Zed.

Smith, R., and Wexler, P. (Eds.). (1995). *After Post-Modernism: Education, Politics, and Identity.* London: Falmer.

Snook, I. (1999). Teacher Education: Preparation for a Learned Profession. Available from http: www.aare.edu.au/99pap/sno99148.htm.

Soto, L. (1998). Bilingual Education in America: In Search of Equity and Justice. In J. Kincheloe and S. Steinberg (Eds.), *Unauthorized Methods: Strategies for Critical teaching.* New York: Routledge.

Spencer, L. (2003). Antonio Gramsci, 1891–1937. Available from http://www.tasc.ac.uk/depart/media/staff/is/modules/theory/gramsci/htm.

Stallabrass, J. (1996). *Gargantua: Manufactured Mass Culture.* London: Verso.

Steinberg, S. (1996). Students under Suspicion: Is It True that Teachers Are Not as Good as They Used to Be? In J. Kincheloe and S. Steinberg (Eds.), *Thirteen Questions: Reframing Education's Conversation* (2nd ed.). New York: Peter Lang.

Steinberg, S. (1997). The Bitch That Has Everything. In S. Steinberg and J. Kincheloe (Eds.), *Kinderculture: The Corporate Construction of Childhood.* Boulder, CO: Westview.

Steinberg, S. (1998). Appropriating Queerness: Hollywood Sanitation. In W. Pinar (Ed.), *Queer Theory in Education.* Mahwah, NJ: Lawrence Erlbaum.

Steinberg, S. (2000). The New Civics: Teaching for Critical Empowerment. In D. Hursh and E. Ross (Eds.), *Democratic Social Education: Social Studies for Social Change.* New York: Falmer.

Steinberg, S. (2002a). From the Closet to the Corral: Neo-Stereotyping in *In and Out.* In S. Talburt and S. Steinberg (Eds.), *Thinking Queer: Sexuality, Culture, and Education.* New York: Peter Lang.

Steinberg, S. (2002b). French Fries, Fezzes, and Minstrels: The Hollywoodization of Islam. *Cultural Studies—Critical Methodologies.* 2, 2, pp. 205–210.

Steinberg, S. (Ed.). (2001). *Multi/Intercultural Conversations: A Reader.* New York: Peter Lang.

Steinberg, S. R. (2004). Desert Minstrels: Hollywood's Curriculum of Arabs and Muslims. In J. L. Kincheloe and S. R. Steinberg (Eds.), *The Miseducation of the West: Constructing Islam.* Westport, CT: Greenwood.

Steinberg, S., and Kincheloe, J. (1997). *Kinderculture: Corporate Constructions of Childhood.* Boulder, CO: Westview.

Steinberg, S., and Kincheloe, J. (1998). *Students as Researchers: Creating Classrooms That Matter.* London: Falmer.

Steinberg, S., and Kincheloe, J. (Eds.). (2006). *What You Don't Know About Schools.* New York: Palgrave.

Steiner, S., Krank, H., McLaren, P., and Bahruth, R. (Eds.). (2000). *Freirean Pedagogy, Praxis, and Possibilities: Projects for the New Millennium.* New York: Falmer.

Subbotsky, E. (2003). Vygotsky's Distinction Between Lower and Higher Mental Functions and Recent Studies on Infant Cognitive Development. Available from http://psych.hanover.edu/vygotsky/subbot.html.

Sumara, D. (1996). *Private Readings in Public: Schooling the Literary Imagination.* New York: Peter Lang.

Sünker, H. (1998). Welfare, Democracy, and Social Work. In G. Flosser and H. Otto (Eds.), *Towards More Democracy in Social Services: Models of Culture and Welfare.* New York: de Gruyter.

Surber, J. (1998). *Culture and Critique: An Introduction to the Critical Discourses of Cultural Studies.* Boulder, CO: Westview.

Thayer-Bacon, B. (2000). *Transforming Critical Thinking: Thinking Constructively.* New York: Teachers College Press.

Thayer-Bacon, B. (2003). *Relational "(E)pistemologies."* New York: Peter Lang.

Thomas, S. (1997). Dominance and Ideology in Cultural Studies. In M. Ferguson and P. Golding (Eds.), *Cultural Studies in Question.* London: Sage.

Thomson, C. (2001). Massification, Distance Learning and Quality in INSET Teacher Education: A Challenging Relationship. Available from http:www.ru.ac.za/academic/adc/papers/Thomson.htm.

21st Century Schools. (2003). Philosophical Foundations of Critical Theory and Critical Pedagogy. Available from http://www.21stcenturyschools.com/philosophical_foundation.htm.

Van Manen, M. (1999). The Practice of Practice. In M. Lange, J. Olson, H. Hanson, and W. Bunder (Eds.), *Changing Schools / Changing Practices: Perspectives on Educational Reform and Teacher Professionalism.* Luvain, Belgium: Garaut.

Varela, F. (1999). *Ethical Know-How: Action, Wisdom, and Cognition.* Stanford, CA: Stanford University Press.

Vattimo, G. (1994). *Beyond Interpretation: The Meaning of Hermeneutics for Philosophy.* Stanford, CA: Stanford University Press.

Vavrus, M., and Archibald, O. (1998). Teacher Education Practices Supporting Social Justice: Approaching an Individual Self-Study Inquiry into Institutional Self-Study Process. Paper Presented to the Second International Conference on Self-Study of Teacher Education Practice, Herstmonceux Castle, UK.

Villaverde, L. (2003). Developing Curriculum and Critical Pedagogy. In D. Weil and J. Kincheloe (Eds.), *Critical Thinking and Learning: An Encyclopedia.* Westport, CT: Greenwood.

Villaverde, L., Kincheloe, J., and Helyar, F. (2006). Historical Research in Education. In K. Tobin and J. Kincheloe (Eds.), *Doing Educational Research: A Handbook.* Rotterdam: Sense Publishers.

Vygotsky, L. (1978). *Mind in Society: The Development of Higher Psychological Processes.* Cambridge, MA: Harvard University Press.

Vygotsky, L. (1997). *Educational Psychology.* (R. Silverman, Trans.). Boca Raton, FL: St. Lucie Press.

Wang, M., and Kovach, J. (1996). Bridging the Achievement Gap in Urban Schools: Reducing Educational Segregation and Advancing Resilience-Promoting Strategies. In B. Williams (Ed.), *Closing the Achievement Gap: A Vision for Changing Beliefs and Practices.* Alexandria, VA: ASCD.

WEAC (Wisconsin Education Association Council). (2004). The American Board and Fast Track Certification: An Attack on the Teaching Profession. Available from http://ww.weac.org/pdfs/2003–2004/certification_research.pdf

Weil, D., and Kincheloe, J. (Eds.). (2003). *Critical Thinking and Learning: An Encyclopedia.* Westport, CT: Greenwood.

Weinstein, M. (1998). *Robot World: Education, Popular Culture, and Science.* New York: Peter Lang.

Wertsch, J. (1991). *Voices of the Mind: A Sociocultural Approach to Mediated Action.* Cambridge, MA: Harvard University Press.

Wesson, L., and Weaver, J. (2001). Administration—Educational Standards: Using the Lens of Postmodern Thinking to Examine the Role of the School Administrator. In J. Kincheloe and D. Weil (Eds.), *Standards and Schooling in the United States: An Encyclopedia,* 3 vols. Santa Barbara, CA: ABC-CLIO.

West, C. (1993). *Race Matters.* Boston: Beacon.

Wexler, P. (1992). *Becoming Somebody: Toward a Social Psychology of School*. London: Falmer Press.

Wexler, P. (1996). *Critical Social Psychology*. New York: Peter Lang.

Wexler, P. (1996b). *Holy Sparks: Social Theory, Education, and Religion*. New York: St. Martin's.

Wexler, P. (2000). *The Mystical Society: Revitalization in Culture, Theory, and Education*. Boulder, CO: Westview.

Wexler, P. (Ed.). (1991). *Critical Theory Now*. New York: Falmer.

Willinsky, J. (1991). *The Triumph of Literature / The Fate of Literacy: Teaching English in the High School*. New York: Teachers College Press.

Willinsky, J. (1994). *Empire of Words: The Reign of the OED*. Princeton, NJ: Princeton University Press.

Willinsky, J. (1998). *Learning to Divide the World: Education at Empire's End*. Minneapolis: Minnesota University Press.

Willinsky, J. (2006a). High School Postcolonial, and the Students Ran Ahead. In Y. Kanu (Ed.) *Curriculum as Cultural Practice: Postcolonial Imaginations*. Toronto: University of Toronto Press.

Willinsky, J. (2006b). *The Access Principle: The Case for Open Access to Research and Scholarship*. Cambridge, MA: MIT Press.

Willinsky, J., and Bedard, J. (1989). *The Fearful Passage: Romeo and Juliet in the High School: A Feminist Perspective*. Ottawa, ON: Canadian Council of Teachers of English.

Wood, P. (1988). Action Research: A Field Perspective. *Journal of Education for Teaching*, 2, pp. 135–150.

Yale-New Haven Teachers Institute. (1993). The minority artist in America. Available from http://www.yale.edu/ynhti/curriculum/units/1993/4/93.04.intro.x.html.

Young, T., and Yarbrough, J. (1993). Reinventing Sociology: Mission and Methods for Postmodern Sociologists. Red Feather Institute. Transforming Sociology Series, 154.

Yudice, G. (1995). Neither Impugning Nor Disavowing Whiteness Does a Viable Politics Make: The Limits of Identity Politics. In C. Newfield and R. Strickland (Eds.), *After Political Correctness*. Boulder, CO: Westview Press.

Zuss, M. (1999). *Subject Present: Life-Writings and Strategies of Representation*. New York: Peter Lang.

Peter Lang
PRIMERS
in Education

Peter Lang Primers are designed to provide a brief and concise introduction or supplement to specific topics in education. Although sophisticated in content, these primers are written in an accessible style, making them perfect for undergraduate and graduate classroom use. Each volume includes a glossary of key terms and a References and Resources section.

Other published and forthcoming volumes cover such topics as:

- Standards
- Popular Culture
- Critical Pedagogy
- Literacy
- Higher Education
- John Dewey
- Feminist Theory and Education

- Studying Urban Youth Culture
- Multiculturalism through Postformalism
- Creative Problem Solving
- Teaching the Holocaust
- Piaget and Education
- Deleuze and Education
- Foucault and Education

Look for more Peter Lang Primers to be published soon. To order other volumes, please contact our Customer Service Department:

800-770-LANG (within the US)
212-647-7706 (outside the US)
212-647-7707 (fax)

To find out more about this and other Peter Lang book series, or to browse a full list of education titles, please visit our website:

www.peterlang.com